STUDENTS OF THE COVENANT

SOCIETY OF BIBLICAL LITERATURE

CONFESSIONAL PERSPECTIVES SERIES

Editorial Board
Adela Yarbro Collins
Kent Harold Richards
Gene M. Tucker

Editor of this Volume
Gene M. Tucker

STUDENTS OF THE COVENANT

written and edited by
S. David Sperling

STUDENTS OF THE COVENANT

A History of Jewish Biblical Scholarship
in North America

written and edited by
S. David Sperling

with contributions by
Baruch A. Levine
B. Barry Levy

Scholars Press
Atlanta, Georgia

STUDENTS OF THE COVENANT

A History of Jewish Biblical Scholarship
in North America

written and edited by
S. David Sperling

© 1992
Society of Biblical Literature

Library of Congress Cataloging-in-Publication Data

Students of the covenant : a history of Jewish biblical scholarship in
   North America / written and edited by S. David Sperling ; with contributions by
   Baruch A. Levine, B. Barry Levy.
      p. cm. — (Confessional perspectives series)
   ISBN 1-55540-655-6. — ISBN 1-55540-656-4 (pbk.)
   1. Bible. O.T. — Criticism, interpretation, etc.—North America—
History. 2. Bible. O.T.—Criticism, interpretation, etc., Jewish—
History. 3. Jewish learning and scholarship—North America—
History. 4. Old Testament scholars—North America. 5. Scholars,
Jewish—North America. I. Sperling, S. David. II. Levine, Baruch A.
III. Levy, B. Barry. IV. Series.
BS1160.S78 1992
221.6'089924073—dc20   91-37639
                                                          CIP

Printed in the United States of America
on acid-free paper

Contents

ABBREVIATIONS	vii
FOREWORD TO THE CONFESSIONAL PERSPECTIVES SERIES	ix
ACKNOWLEDGMENTS	xi
INTRODUCTION S. David Sperling	1
CHAPTER ONE: THE EUROPEAN BACKGROUND Baruch A. Levine	15
CHAPTER TWO: AMERICAN BEGINNINGS S. David Sperling	33
CHAPTER THREE: BETWEEN THE WARS S. David Sperling	69
CHAPTER FOUR: THE SECOND WAVE Baruch A. Levine	89
CHAPTER FIVE: THE CURRENT SCENE S. David Sperling	115
CHAPTER SIX: TRANSLATIONS, COLLABORATIONS AND COMPENDIA S. David Sperling	149
CHAPTER SEVEN: ON THE PERIPHERY: NORTH AMERICAN ORTHODOX JUDAISM AND CONTEMPORARY BIBLICAL SCHOLARSHIP B. Barry Levy	159
CONCLUDING EXTREMELY UNSCIENTIFIC POSTSCRIPT S. David Sperling	205

ABBREVIATIONS

ACIEB *Actes du Congrès International des Études Balkaniques*

AJS Newsletter Newsletter of the Association for Jewish Studies

AJSL *American Journal of Semitic Languages and Literatures*

AV Authorized Version

BAR *Biblical Archaeologist Reader*

BASOR *Bulletin of the American Schools of Oriental Research*

CBQ *Catholic Biblical Quarterly*

EncJud *Encyclopaedia Judaica*

HUC Hebrew Union College

HUCA *Hebrew Union College Annual*

IDB G. A. Buttrick (ed.), *Interpreter's Dictionary of the Bible*

IDBSup Supplementary Volume to *IDB*

JANES *Journal of the Ancient Near Eastern Society*

JAOS *Journal of the American Oriental Society*

Jastrow, *Dictionary* M. Jastrow, *A Dictionary of the Targumin, the Talmud Babli and Yerushalmi and the Midrashic Literature*

JBA *Jewish Book Annual*

JBL *Journal of Biblical Literature*

JIR Jewish Institute of Religion

JNES   Journal of Near Eastern Studies

JPS   Jewish Publication Society of America

JQR   Jewish Quarterly Review

JSS   Journal of Semitic Studies

JTS   Jewish Theological Seminary of America

OT   Old Testament

NJV   New Jewish Version

NT   New Testament

PAAJR   Proceedings of the American Academy for Jewish Research

RIETS   Rabbi Isaac Elhanan Theological Seminary

RRC   Reconstructionist Rabbinical College

RSV   Revised Standard Version

VTSup   Vetus Testamentum, Supplements

YU   Yeshiva University

ZAW   Zeitschrift für die alttestamentliche Wissenschaft

N.B. "Orthodox" is capitalized in the text when reference is to the modern Jewish religious denomination of that name as distinguished from "Conservative," "Reform," and "Reconstructionist." When contrast with "heterodox" is intended, "orthodox" is not capitalized.

Foreword to the
Confessional Perspective Series

The study of the Bible is shaped by divergent forces. On the one hand, Judaism and Christianity, the communities that understand the Bible as Holy Writ, find warrants within the Bible for study and reflection. The oft-cited instruction from Moses to Joshua recalls this tradition. "This book of the law shall not depart out of your mouth, but you shall meditate on it day and night, that you may be careful to do according to all that is written in it; for then you shall make your way prosperous, and then you shall have good success" (Joshua 1:8, RSV).

On the other hand, these communities that hold the Bible as authoritative were challenged from outside. The Bible records earlier challenges from foreigners and "pagans" confronting those inside the faith. Questions raised for the communities of faith, whether as recorded in the Bible or as presented later, have led them to search out their traditions and the scriptures. Outsiders not only questioned the bearers of "the book" but began to create their own relationship with the Bible. Individuals during the Enlightenment used the Bible to illustrate what *not* to do and believe. Critical biblical scholarship from the early nineteenth century to the present day has been understood as both friend and foe of the communities of faith.

The Society of Biblical Literature (SBL) commissioned this *Confessional Perspectives* series in order to examine the Bible within diverse religious communities. This particular volume examines Jewish biblical scholarship. The SBL takes pride in bringing this volume to readers. This book symbolizes the cooperation found among scholarly organizations, who find the interpretation of the Bible central to their mission. This series gives careful attention to the benefits and tensions between confessional perspectives and the outsiders' views. The studies highlight the perplexing dilemmas encountered when an object, the Bible, common to diverse groups, yields such an array of responses.

The religious and intellectual life of North America forms the background for these volumes. This social-geographical focus stems from the SBL's interest in coming to terms with the Bible in the region where the society began in 1880. The interest is not grounded in chauvinism or imperialism but in a spirit of discovery. Although it might seem surprising, very few studies on American biblical scholarship or the role of the Bible in the North America setting have emerged. The centenary celebrations of the society are yielding diverse publication series on every aspect of the Bible in North America: *Biblical Scholarship in North America, The Bible in American Culture, The Bible and Its Modern Interpreters* (all published by the Society of Biblical Literature and available through Scholars Press) and this series on *Confessional Perspectives.*

Although the Bible emerged from a world distant in time and ethos, it has no rival as a founding document that shapes life in North America. The religious communities that brought it to this shore could not have known the enormous impact it would have on them or their institutions, thought, customs, and practices. The confluence of old and new, familiar and strange, sparked creative ideas in the New World.

These books on "the book" in confessional perspective come at an important time. North American biblical scholarship plays an increasingly influential role in the intellectual communities of the world. Not only have the religious communities of the Bible journeyed over the globe, but critical biblical scholarship extends into Japan and other Eastern countries. Religion is discussed in the media and in the private conversations of many. The knowledge that Judaism and Christianity are not the only religions with books saved texts become increasingly familiar even in the West. Buddhism and Hinduism, just to mention two religious traditions, have key texts. Contributions to the understanding of the confessional perspective surrounding one book helps us to understand other religions, our own confessional perspectives, and the impact of a book on a people.

Kent Harold Richards

Acknowledgments

It is our pleasant duty to thank various individuals for their guidance and assistance. First and foremost, we express our deepest gratitude to Professor Harry M. Orlinsky, Effie Wise Ochs Professor of Bible at the New York School of the Hebrew Union College-Jewish Institute of Religion. Dr. Orlinsky gave unstintingly of his time and energy to supply us with data and personal recollections of many of the personalities and institutions described in the following pages. We are extremely grateful as well to Professor Abraham J. Karp, Philip Bernstein Professor of American Jewish History at the University of Rochester who provided us with an invaluable introduction to the sources of American Jewish historiography as well as with personal recollections of some key figures. Thanks as well to Professor Lance Sussman of the Department of History at State University of New York at Binghamton for his guidance into the life and times of Isaac Leeser. To Professor Benjamin Ravid of Brandeis University, we owe extremely helpful information about the early history of that institution. We are likewise grateful for biographical information about her father E. A. Speiser, supplied us by Mrs. Jean Speiser Polen of Merion Station, Pennsylvania. In similar fashion, we gratefully acknowledge the assistance of Rabbi Ezra M. Finkelstein of the Midway Jewish Center of Syosset, New York for details about his uncle Israel Friedlaender. Our dear friend Professor Richard Rand of the University of Alabama receives our thanks for guidance in matters of English style, but is absolved of responsibility for any remaining barbarisms. My best friend, colleague and wife, Rabbi Judith Lewis, was a constant source not only of encouragement but of intellectual stimulation, prodding me to engage issues of theory and forcing me always to say what I meant. Thanks are due as well for the support given by the staff of the library of the New York School of Hebrew Union College-Jewish Institute of Religion, directed by Dr. Philip E. Miller. Mr. Henry Resnick, assistant to the Librarian saved us considerable time by patiently double-checking references, allowing us to use the phone rather than the Long Island Expressway. Finally, to our many colleagues who took time from their labors in biblical scholarship to address our requests for information about their work, their methods and the influences which motivated them, we humbly express our gratitude.

INTRODUCTION

Our present volume renders a historical account of Jewish biblical scholarship in North America. The first chapter, which deals with the European background of American Jewish scholarship, explains why the pioneering academic movement of the nineteenth century called "Science of Judaism" or *Wissenschaft des Judentums,* did little to advance the serious study of the Bible. The second chapter sketches social and religious trends in American Jewish life, providing a backdrop for the scholarly activity that began with the Bible translations by Isaac Leeser and continued through the writings of scholars who flourished before World War I. With the third, fourth and fifth chapters, we turn, respectively, to the accomplishments of the scholars who came to prominence between the wars, to the biblicists earning their doctorates before 1965, and to the generation completing their graduate training between 1965–1980. Our sixth chapter surveys compendia, those under Jewish sponsorship and those in which Jewish participation has been significant. Our seventh chapter addresses the question of why the North American Orthodox Jewish community continues to relegate the serious study of Bible to the periphery of its academic interests. The postscript presents our conclusions and projections concerning the future of Jewish biblical scholarship in North America.

We have included, along with researchers who have written exclusively on the Hebrew Bible, those whose concentration was elsewhere but who chose regularly to bring their focus to bear on the Bible itself. Regrettably, this criterion has compelled us to omit the survey of scholarship in such fields as Versions, Dead Sea Scrolls, Middle Eastern Archaeology, Assyriology, Northwest Semitic, Classical Rabbinics, Medieval Commentaries and the like. At the same time we have attended occasionally to non-professional biblicists whose interest in Bible has impelled them to make useful observations and significant contributions. Thus, to cite just one example, the reader will find an account of the scholarship of the Assyriologist E. A. Speiser of the University of Pennsylvania, who published on biblical subjects.

By "scholarship in North America" we mean the activity of scholars both native and foreign born whose work has been done to a great extent in the United States or Canada.[1] In some cases this includes biblicists who moved to Israel after establishing their reputations in the United States but who have perpetuated their North American connection by publishing extensively in English and teaching rather frequently on the North American continent.

In recent years, scholars Jewish and Gentile have often asked whether there is such an entity as "Jewish Bible scholarship"[2] or a "Jewish School" of biblical studies. For the purposes of this book, "Jewish Bible scholarship" is the scholarship done by Jews. On this criterion Arnold Ehrlich is included because he did not remain a convert to Christianity. Similarly, Anson Rainey is included because he converted from Christianity to Judaism.[3]

The present introduction provides an opportunity to proceed beyond the labels of religious affiliation in order to identify specific traits that, in our opinion, characterize Jewish scholarship within the larger pluralistic world of biblical studies. First, however, let us review some previously proposed criteria.

In the past, one could make a case that, among the subfields of biblical studies, Jews predominated in some, and Gentiles in others. As observed by the Israeli scholar Moshe Goshen-Gottstein, in the nineteenth century "Jews could not become Bible scholars in the full academic sense" because "Bible" included New Testament and Christian theology.[4] Accordingly, early Jewish scholars such as the Europeans Luzzatto, Geiger, Graetz, and Barth and the Americans Szold, Ehrlich, Eitan and Margolis concentrated on the study of language, text and versions rather than on source criticism, political history or history of Israelite religion. This division of labor between Christians and Jews[5] has blurred in recent times.

Two decades ago, Moshe Greenberg, predicting the trends of the field, distinguished Jewish from Gentile biblical scholarship in terms of a literary approach that emphasized the "books" of the Bible. Greenberg defined a "book" as:

"an organization of literary units meant to convey a complex ideational message . . . By ideational message we . . . mean . . . only what is found in the components of the book and implied by the manner of their disposition . . . The primary object of understanding is the book's own message, and that must be gathered . . . from the book itself."[6]

Greenberg lamented the fact that ever since the recognition of the composite nature of the Pentateuch:

"attention has been diverted from the textual entity transmitted by tradition to its newly analyzed **hypothetically attested** (emphasis added) datum."[7]

Greenberg thought this state of affairs especially regrettable because only the "textual entity" (the "book") is available for examination and "it alone is the undoubted product of Israelite creativity."[8]

Although outstanding Christian scholars such as von Rad and Muilenberg and some non-mainstream Jewish biblicists such as Umberto Cassuto and Benno Jacob had anticipated Greenberg's holistic approach,[9] most had continued to emphasize source-analysis. Greenberg's remarks could be seen as a program for a Jewish approach to Bible scholarship, seconding the view of traditional rabbinic exegesis that Scripture constitutes a unity. By concentrating on a particular "book," a scholar affirmed the integrity of material to which tradition had ascribed a single author. At the same time, no scholar need jettison critical method, which sought to recover the prehistory of particular "books." Especially attractive to Jewish scholars was Greenberg's reference to "Israelite creativity," which as we have observed elsewhere, was doubtless written as a deliberate rejoinder to those trends in Christian scholarship which regarded the redactional process as the work of second-rate Jewish minds.[10] In Greenberg's inversion of Wellhausenian thinking, the Bible was, in a positive sense, more "Jewish" than "Israelite." If so, then Jews especially had sound scholarly reasons to read the "Bible as literature," an activity which had previously been viewed with disdain outside of departments of English Literature, and Jews might be expected quickly to claim this new subfield as their own. Indeed, as will be seen in the chapter on "The Current Scene," a number of Jewish scholars in the last two decades have enthusiastically followed Greenberg's lead. Yet, a significant cultural development has kept Jewish scholars from claiming the literary approach to the Bible as their own field of specialization. Simply stated, the past two decades have witnessed the expansion of literary theory into areas where it had previously played a minor role, notably in the study of the Bible. In consequence, the study of "the Bible as literature" has become a pursuit shared equally by Jewish and Gentile scholars.

Indeed, it has been the narrowing of differences between Jewish and non-Jewish Bible scholarship which has stimulated Jewish Bible scholars to attempt to delineate the specifically Jewish character of their enterprise. In no small degree that impetus has not come from Christianity but from within Judaism itself. First, for some "secular"[11] Jewish biblicists, study of the Bible has provided an alternative means of fulfilling religious or quasi-religious commitments. While, *mutatis mutandis*, the same might be said for a similarly oriented student of Talmud, or of the history of Zionism or of the demographics of Jewish labor movements, the specifically Jewish character of these latter pursuits is self-evident in a manner that the "Judeo-Christian" Bible is not. As such, the search for "Jewish Bible scholarship" is, for more than one Jewish biblicist, a matter of personal and religious concern. A second impetus is provided by the internal dynamics of the larger Jewish community. As will be seen repeatedly in the body of this book, critical biblical study has from its inception been regarded with suspicion in many orthodox Jewish circles. Interdenominational Jewish collaborative efforts such as the translations and commentaries sponsored by the Jewish Publication Society, and standard references such as *The Jewish Encyclopedia*, and *Encyclopaedia Judaica* have attempted to mitigate orthodox criticism by professing adherence to the "Masoretic text"[12] and avoiding emendations (the JPS translations); by printing articles with the "critical view at the end" so that potentially offensive views might be avoided by readers *(The Jewish Encyclopedia);* or by allotting space both to orthodox and critical views *(Encyclopaedia Judaica).* But none of these approaches confronts one of the most censorious twentieth-century Orthodox objections, namely, that critical biblical scholarship, by approaching Scripture diachronically and placing the individual units of Bible in their historical contexts has "dejudaized" the Bible. For the Orthodox analyst, the critical Bible scholar has followed Wellhausen in destroying the continuity between Israelite religion and Judaism. Especially objectionable to Orthodoxy has been the historical analysis of the legal sections of the Pentateuch, which provide the theoretical basis for all subsequent Jewish law. As Sidney Hoenig, an Orthodox scholar of hellenistic Judaism, prescribed in a review in *Tradition,* one of the more moderate Orthodox journals: "The Bible must be interpreted according to rabbinic standards,"[13] for, as he pointedly observed:

"One of the major concerns to the traditional Jew is the rendition of the Bible in accordance with the the Halakhah [traditional law] and rabbinic tradition. Otherwise its spirit is Saducean or Karaitic."[14]

It is noteworthy that Hoenig's "traditional Jew" of the twentieth century is more rigid in this matter than some of the best known medieval Jewish scholars such as Rashi and Rashbam who frequently remarked that the plain sense of a particular text differed from its rabbinic interpretation,[15] and comfortably cited both. In theory, the pluriform approach presented no theological difficulty because it was a given of medieval Jewish and Christian exegesis that plain sense interpretation and self- conscious misreading could exist side by side.[16] At least as significant was the fact that the medieval commentators were, for the most part, undeviating adherents of the legal and doctrinal principles of their Jewish communities.[17] Thus, despite the greatest variation among the commentaries, even when a commentator departed from the rabbinic interpretation of a particular verse, he continued to operate within the self-validating limits of rabbinic tradition. In contrast, the most serious modern Jewish study of the Bible has been done by non-orthodox[18] Jews, some of them not religious in any traditional sense. Accordingly, Orthodox opposition to critical Bible scholarship cannot be separated from opposition to heterodoxy, or to deviation from what Hoenig terms "rabbinic standards."[19] Another significant reason for the relatively greater inflexibility of twentieth century "rabbinic standards," is that the medieval Jewish commentaries have themselves become a secondary scripture for the orthodox. No small part in this development has been played by the material changes in the experience of reading the Bible over the past four centuries. Printing and photomechanical reproduction have disseminated the *Miqra'ot Gedolot*, or rabbinic Bibles in which small sections of biblical text are surrounded or footnoted by authoritative, virtually canonical, medieval and post-medieval commentaries.[20] Where a non-orthodox Jewish biblicist regards such commentaries as supplementary, an Orthodox Jew regards them as complementary, so much so that a Bible which lacks them is held to be defective. Hoenig's "rabbinic standards" support this Orthodox view; they therefore serve in the view of the non-orthodox scholar, as an apology for "standards" narrowly defined and unacceptably so. Much as they might wish to practice a specifically Jewish Bible scholarship, non-orthodox biblicists cannot follow Hoenig's dictum, for precisely at the point that they invoke the authority of "rabbinic standards" they have ceased to be biblicists and become apologists.

A recent, historicizing view of Jewish biblical scholarship was advanced by James Kugel. Kugel argues that:

"Modern biblical criticism's encounter with the text is in its very essence, Protestant. How so? Just as the very stance of Protestant belief was the flush encounter between men and God, unmediated by Church hierarchy and functionaries, by saints and human interveners, so was the encounter between man and text to be similarly unmediated. Nothing was to intervene between the open page of the Bible and its interpreter, no tradition of what the text has meant or how it had been interpreted in the past—nothing save the inspiring spirit shared by book and reader."[21]

From this original, personal, spiritual encounter between the Christian and the Bible derives, says Kugel:

"the modern-day exclusive focus on the 'original' meaning of a text . . . and along with it the devaluation of all that is subsequent to the earliest capturable moment [including] the whole long body of speculations and commentaries upon the significance of a particular received text, stretching through late antiquity and the Middle Ages to modern times."[22]

Jewish Bible scholarship, argues Kugel, should depart from the Protestant model and instead present a paradigm of coexistence with the past:

"Central here is the existence of that great corpus of rabbinic writings which in effect constitute an **authoritative** (emphasis added) interpretation of the Bible. With such a legacy subsequent generations of Jewish biblicists have been obliged constantly to refer not only to the text but to its interpreters, and even radical revisions of the tradition have had to live alongside of it through a variety of strategies."[23]

There is no question that Kugel is correct with regard to some extreme positions in biblical studies,[24] which have devalued everything but the "original" meaning of a text.[25] We take issue however, with two of Kugel's points. First, we must challenge the claim that tolerance of pluriform senses is especially Jewish.[26] It would be more accurate to characterize such tolerance as "medieval."[27] True, classical rabbinism claimed that Scripture contained multiple senses[28] but this claim was not unique. Origen (ca. 185–253), contemporary with the framers of Mishnah and early Midrash likewise acknowledged multiplicity of meaning when he spoke of Scripture's three-fold literal, moral and spiritual senses. By the fifth century, John Cassian had evolved the scriptural hermeneutic that assigned every verse in the Bible a four-fold sense; literal, allegorical, tropological and anagogical. Thanks to Gregory the Great, pope from 590–604, the quest after the four-fold sense became standard in

Christian biblical exegesis until the Reformation.[29] As to Kugel's second point, the need to refer to the "interpreters" along with the "text" served the earlier Jewish communities by enabling them to innovate while at the same time maintaining roots in Scripture. But the need of Jewish communities today to combine continuity with innovation is not necessarily the need of Bible scholarship, and the two should be distinguished. In addition, Kugel overstates the negative attitude of biblical criticism towards the history of exegesis. Scholars of the late nineteenth and earlier twentieth century often resorted to exaggerated rhetoric in criticizing their predecessors.[30] In contrast, only the rarest contemporary Bible scholar will go so far as to claim that "what the text has meant" is irrelevant. If anything, the past two decades have witnessed an increased recognition of the importance of earlier scholarship. For most contemporary biblicists however, respect for earlier exegesis coexists with the recognition that "what the text has meant," it has often meant by default. It remains the case that whether we speak of "Old Testament," "Hebrew Bible," or "TaNaKh," our knowledge of the corpus is still rudimentary. Almost every newly-unearthed Northwest-Semitic inscription from Syria-Palestine of the first pre-Christian millennium reveals a previously unattested lexeme, thus demonstrating the limitation of our knowledge of ancient Israelite vocabulary. Our ignorance is compounded by a lack of important secondary tools, such as an adequate biblical lexicon,[31] and a serious critical text-edition of the Bible.[32] Indeed, students of Assyrian annals, of Mishnah and of Midrash have more reliable texts at their disposal than do biblicists.

Accordingly, modern scholars who turn, for example, to comparative Semitics to solve biblical cruxes are not turning their backs on previous scholarship. Jewish comparative Semiticists in particular are emulating their medieval predecessors who employed Mishnaic Hebrew, Aramaic and Arabic in their lexical researches. It must also be emphasized that when contemporary biblicists examine data drawn from archaeology to uncover realia of the first millennium B.C. or employ explanatory models drawn from the social sciences, they are not ignoring or devaluing the scholarship of earlier generations. The are, instead, following the leads of Martin Luther[33] and his Jewish predecessor of the second century, the sage Rabbi Nehemiah,[34] both of whom insisted that proper interpretation of texts requires broad contexts.

What then may be said about the specific characteristics of Jewish biblical scholarship? First, on several levels the biographical fact of Jewishness proves academically relevant. One does not find Jewish biblicists denigrating the spiritual teachings of the Old Testament in comparison to the New, a tendency which, unfortunately, can still be found in some contemporary Christian Bible scholarship.[35] For that matter, Jewish scholars do not consider the Old Testament (which term fewer and fewer use,[36] preferring instead the acronym "TaNaKh"[37]) to be half of the Bible. We are not speaking here simply of the impossibility for practicing Jews to accept traditional Christian teaching that the New Testament is the literal fulfillment and completion of the Old.[38] Jewish scholarly reluctance to acknowledge the continuity of OT and NT extends to modern formulations of "Biblical theology"[39] as well as to more secularized notions that view "the Bible" as a unified work embracing both Testaments in an interlocking literary and mythic unity.[40] It is probably also fair to say that Jewish biblicists will readily affirm that rabbinic Judaism, although continuous with the Bible in many ways, is not a plain sense interpretation of Scripture.[41] Christian scholars seem less likely to make the homologous declaration regarding the relation of the New Testament to the Old.[42]

As of this writing, Jewish biblicists can be expected more than their Gentile counterparts to be fluent in Modern Hebrew, to have spent considerable time in Israel and accordingly to be more conversant with Israeli Bible scholarship. This factor, however, may be expected to decrease in significance as more Christian scholars spend time in Israel. In addition, because of the enthusiasm of Israeli Bible scholars for participation in the international academic community, most of their work appears rapidly, if not simultaneously, in Western languages. Another salient characteristic of Jewish Bible scholarship is that Jews, especially those with some seminary experience, are more likely than Gentiles[43] to employ the later dialects of Hebrew in their philological research, more likely to pursue insights found in classical midrash in the service of plain-sense exegesis, and more likely to consult the medieval Jewish exegetes.[44] For similar reasons Christian OT scholars would be expected to be more prone to bring insights from NT and Christian tradition.[45]

If these differences between Jewish and non-Jewish biblical scholarship appear minimal, this may be all to the good. Perhaps the combined efforts of the different confessional groupings will enable the coming generations better to understand the ancient writings they share in the form of the Bible.

The ancient rabbis claimed that if the Jews were not prophets they were at least descendents of the prophets.[46] Despite this testimonial to their prophetic lineage, the contributors to the present volume have resisted the temptation to offer more than a sketch of the future directions of biblical scholarship and of its specifically Jewish component in North America. We hope, however, to have provided a fair and accurate account of where we have been and where we now are.

Notes to Introduction

1. The Jewish community of Mexico, which numbered about 35,000 in 1984 has not yet produced any biblicists. For population figures see *American Jewish Year Book* 86 (1986), 357.

2. For recent discussions see J. Neusner's preface to J. Neusner, B. Levine and E. Frerichs (eds.), *Judaic Perspectives on Ancient Israel* (Philadelphia: Fortress, 1987), ix–xiii; Cf. E. Frerichs, ibid, 1–6; See further the report on the symposium "Biblical Studies and Jewish Studies in the University," held at the 1985 meeting of Association for Jewish Studies. The papers were published in *Association for Jewish Studies Newsletter,* 36, Fall, 1986.

3. We were somewhat tempted to claim Georg Fohrer as a Jewish Bible scholar, but his conversion to Judaism came after retiring from academic life. In addition, some of his earlier writing is in that tradition of nineteenth century Bible Scholarship which portrayed the post-exilic Jewish community as poor custodians of the prophetic message. See C. Klein, *Anti-Judaism in Christian Theology* (Philadelphia: Fortress, 1978), 16–18. As we shall see in our second chapter, that ideology was a factor in the absence of Jews from Bible scholarship.

4. See M. H. Goshen-Gottstein, "Christianity, Judaism and Modern Bible Study," *VTSup* 28 (1975), 68–88.

5. As noted by Goshen-Gottstein (ibid, 83), although "there are Christian and Jewish scholars of Islam, Buddhism and so on there are no Muslim or Buddhist scholars of the Old Testament . . . However we try to ignore it—practically all of us are in it because we are either Christians or Jews."

6. M. Greenberg, *Understanding Exodus* (New York: Melton Research Center JTS, 1969), 1.

7. ibid, 4–5.

8. ibid.

9. See our chapter on "The Current Scene," below.

10. Cf. S. D. Sperling, "Judaism and Modern Biblical Research," in L. Boadt and L. Klenicki (eds.), *Biblical Studies: Meeting Ground of Jews and Christians* (New York: Stimulus, 1980), 40–41.

11. Our definition of "secular" includes more than one observant Jewish scholar. Primarily, "secular" is employed here to characterize an academic approach in which, for example, Ugaritic poetry and biblical psalms are studied in much the same way without asserting the privileged character of the biblical corpus and then allowing that character to determine interpretation.

12. On the inadequacy of this term see H. M. Orlinsky, "The New Jewish Version of the Torah: Toward a New Philosophy of Bible Translation," in idem, *Essays in Biblical Culture and Bible Translation* (New York, Ktav: 1974), 412.

13. S. Hoenig, "Notes on the New Translation of the Torah—A Preliminary Inquiry," *Tradition A Journal of Orthodox Jewish Thought* Vol. 5, No. 2 (Spring, 1963), 204.

14. ibid, 193.

15. "With the exception of emending the text—which is categorically prohibited in respect to the Bible, . . . [Jewish law dictates no] single authoritative mode of interpreting the Bible, providing it is . . . not overtly heretical and . . . you do not behave accordingly." So, D. Halivni, apud J. Petuchowski, *New Perspectives on Abraham Geiger An HUC-JIR Symposium* (New York: Hebrew Union College and Ktav: 1975), 33.

16. See below.

17. Membership in the Jewish community was not voluntary. (See below.) Medieval Jews who found the Jewish community intolerable could leave only by converting to another religion.

18. A promising new direction in serious Bible study has been taken by Israeli Orthodox Jews. The Kook Institute has published several volumes of a Hebrew multi-volume Bible commentary known as *Da'at Miqrâ (Scriptural Knowledge)*. The commentaries make extensive use of maps, realia and background archeological data. There is a minimal amount of lower criticism, based solely on Hebrew manuscripts, but no reference is made to higher criticism. See e.g. Y. Kil, *Sefer Melakim* (Kings) I, II (Jerusalem: Mossad Harav Kook, 1989).

19. Hoenig's reference to "Karaitic" is particularly apt. One of the most important medieval interpreters, Saadia (882–942), was very careful to interpret the Bible according to "rabbinic standards" in order to refute the "Karaites," or "Scripturalists," who, in some ways anticipated the *sola scriptura* ideology of the Christian Reformation.

20. For a good basic introduction with bibliography see E. Greenstein, "Medieval Bible Commentaries," in B. Holtz (ed.), *Back to the Sources* (New York: Summit, 1984), 212–259. On P. 212 ibid there is a photograph of a page in a standard rabbinic Bible.

21. J. Kugel, *AJS Newsletter,* 36, 22. This is somewhat of an overstatement. Many of the Reformers believed that the Church Fathers were reliable and needed to be consulted and that decline had set in only after the patristic age. Luther regularly read such medieval authorities as the Glossa Ordinaria, Aquinas and Nicholas of Lyre. See G. R. Evans, *The Road to Reformation* (Cambridge: Cambrdige University, 1963), 21–23.

22. *AJS Newsletter* 36, 23.

23. ibid.
24. Kugel (ibid, 24) cites C. A. Briggs who referred to the "debris of the traditional interpretations," and who described the task of historical criticism as "searching . . . to recover the real Bible . . . sifting out all that rubbish." Note however, that Briggs made these statements in 1901. See idem, *General Introduction to the Study of Holy Scripture* (New York, 1901), 531.
25. Theorists such as Hirsch have made a strong case that meaning is assigned by an author. If so, then the pursuit of "original meaning" is not misguided. Other theorists, from Eliot to Derrida, have argued with equal vigor against an author's control over meaning, in which case "original meaning" is a red herring.
26. Indeed, the need for pluriform interpretation may have been more pronounced in Christianity. The discrepancies among the canonical Gospels should have troubled literate Christians more than the similar divergences between Kings and Chronicles troubled their Jewish counterparts. Nonetheless, it was Tatian's harmony of the Gospels, the Diatessaron, which was destroyed by the zealots, while the conflicting Gospels survived.
27. In general see B. Smalley, *The Study of the Bible in the Middle Ages* (Notre Dame, Indiana: Notre Dame University, 1964).
28. e.g. Palestinian Talmud Sanhedrin 4:2.
29. See K. Froehlich, *Biblical Interpretation in the Early Church* (Philadelphia: Fortress, 1984), 17–28; For the Jewish borrowing of the four-fold sense from the Christians see E. Rosenthal apud P. Lampe (ed.), *The Cambridge History of the Bible Volume 2 The West from the Fathers until the Reformation* (Cambridge: Cambridge University, 1969), 278.
30. This had surely been the case with Briggs and Arnold Ehrlich to name just two. See Chapter two of the present work.
31. The completion of our book coincided with the publication of the long-awaited final volume of the revision of Koehler-Baumgartner. Because this new work, *Hebräisches und Aramäisches Lexikon zum Alten Testament* (Leiden: Brill, 1967–1990), unlike its predecessor, has no English accompanying its German translations and is very expensive, it is likely that all but the most advanced OT students will continue to rely on BDB.
32. See H. M. Orlinsky, "The Textual Criticism of the Old Testament," in G. E. Wright (ed.), *The Bible and the Ancient Near East* (Garden City: Doubleday, 1965), 140–169; Cf. M. Smith, "The Present State of Old Testament Studies," *JBL* 88 (1969), 22–23. In respect to text criticism, the old International Critical Commentary was often much stronger than such widely-utilized contemporary series as Anchor Bible, Hermenia and even Kommentar zum Alten Testament.
33. See J. Dillenberger, *Martin Luther Selections from his Writings* (Garden City: Doubleday, 1961), 173.
34. Palestinian Talmud Rosh Hashanah 3:5.
35. See Klein, *Anti-Judaism*, 1–66.
36. Jewish scholars of an earlier generation were not so sensitive. H. L. Ginsberg showed no hesitation in referring to "Old Testament." See e.g. idem, *Jewish Quarterly Review* 33 (1942–43), 481; JBL 62 (1943) 109; Nei-

ther did Sheldon Blank. See e.g. *HUCA* 7 (1930). Nor did Harry Orlinsky. See e.g., idem, *Essays in Biblical Culture and Bible Translation* (New York: Ktav, 1974), 387, 392, 394, 395; idem *JBL* 78 (1959), 26; or Matitiahu Tsevat. See e.g. *VTSup* 28 (1975), 217. Obviously, these writers considered "Old Testament" a convenient literary term, more precise than "Hebrew Scriptures" (which excludes the Aramaic portions) and "Jewish Scriptures," (which denies the historical reality that these writings are also Scripture for Christians) to distinguish the shared part of the canon from its specifically Christian section, the New Testament. Incidentally, it is difficult to find Jewish scholars (or laics) who studiously avoid reference to "New Testament," which, in theory, should be as theologically objectionable as "Old Testament."

37. The popularity of the term TaNaKh, formed from the initials of the threefold Jewish division Torah, (Pentateuch), Nevi'im (Prophets) and Kethubim (Hagiographa) is a relatively recent development. Mishnah refers to Scripture collectively as *kithbê haqqodesh* (lit.: "God's writings;" see Shabbat 16:1; Erubin 10:3; Baba Batra 1:6; Sanhedrin 10:6; Yadayim 3:5; Parah 10:3) and as *miqrâ* (lit.: "that which is [publicly] read." See Hagigah 1:8; Qiddushin 1:10; Nedarim 4:3; Abot 5:21). Among Yiddish speaking Eastern European Jews it was customary to refer to the divisions of the Bible separately. Thus Pentateuch was either *toyra* or *ḥumesh* (lit: "five-fold division," derived from Hebrew *ḥomesh*); and the Prophets were *novi*. The books of the Hagiographa were usually referred to individually by name.

38. To be sure, the Christian claim that the OT is fulfilled in the NT is somewhat parallel to the claims of rabbinic Judaism that its "oral Torah" is one with the "written Torah." (On the rabbinic notion see E. Urbach, *The Sages—Their Concepts and Beliefs* [Jerusalem: Magnes at Hebrew University, 1971], 266-267.) We say "somewhat," in agreement with Levenson that classical rabbinic attitudes toward the Hebrew Bible are more relaxed and more pluriform than NT "fulfillment exegesis." See J. Levenson, "Why Jews are Not Interested in Biblical Theology," in Neusner, Frerichs, et al (eds.), *Judaic Perspectives*, 286-287. The difference between the classical rabbinic approach to the Hebrew Bible and that of the NT to the OT continues to influence the respective Christian and Jewish outlooks.

39. See J. Blenkinsopp, "Old Testament Theology and the Jewish-Christian Connection," *Journal for the Study of the Old Testament*, 28 (1984), 3-15.

40. A notable exponent of this view is N. Frye, *The Great Code: The Bible and Literature*. (New York: Harcourt, Brace, Jovanovich, 1982).

41. Cf. Levenson, "Biblical Theology," apud Neusner et al (eds.), *Judaic Perspectives*, 286.

42. The difference is largely due to external variables. Dogmatic theology has always played a very minor role in Jewish rabbinic training. Accordingly, even those Jewish biblicists with a seminary education have rarely evinced the kind of theological interests found among Christian biblicists. In addition, as a group Jewish biblicists are probably more religiously liberal than their Christian counterparts.

43. This significant difference in the background resources of Gentiles

and Jews is likely to decline. One may note the increased use of rabbinics and Jewish medieval exegesis in the work of Yale scholars Brevard Childs and Marvin Pope. As a harbinger of the growing competence of Gentile biblicists in rabbinics, modern Hebrew and Israeli scholarship see D. Wright, *The Disposal of Impurity* (Atlanta: Scholars, 1987) and the review by S. D. Sperling in *Jewish Quarterly Review* 80 (1989), 194–98.

44. For recent fine examples of these traits see M. Greenberg, "MSRT HBRYT, 'The obligation of the covenant,' in Ezekiel 30:27," in C. Meyers and M. O'Connor (eds.), *The Word of the Lord Shall Go Forth Essays in Honor of David Noel Freedman in Celebration of His Sixtieth Birthday* (Winona Lake: Eisenbrauns, 1983), 37–46.

45. To cite just one example, see M. Noth, "For All who Rely on Works of the Law are under a Curse," in idem, *The Laws in the Pentateuch* (Philadelphia: Fortress, 1967), 118–131. The study is directed to Deut 27:26 and to the role of curse in Deuteronomy against the background of curse in the ancient Near East. Although the substance of the essay could have been written by a Jewish scholar, a Christian like Noth was more likely to foreground Deut 27:26 because of its Pauline recontextualization in Gal 3:10.

46. Babylonian Talmud Pesahim, 66a.

CHAPTER ONE
The European Background

In the year 1822, the *Zeitschrift für die Wissenschaft des Judentums*, edited by Leopold Zunz (1794–1886), soon to become a leading figure within German Jewry and a major scholar of the period, announced a program that would do nothing less than revolutionize the study of Judaica. Calling for the restudy of the literary and documentary sources of Judaism utilizing the critical methods employed in the European university, the scholarly movement known as *Wissenschaft des Judentums* would bring to the study of Judaism the same kind of academic respectability enjoyed by such traditional subjects as classics, history and philosophy. Initially, the *Wissenschaft* movement intended to encompass the totality of the Judaic heritage, from biblical to modern times.[1] This did not turn out to be the case. Instead, the leading European Jewish scholars of the nineteenth century chose to concentrate their primary attention on postbiblical Judaism. To the extent that biblical texts were restudied, prophecy and Hagiographa *(Kethubim)* received the most attention, not Torah literature. We may, in consequence, speak of a "cultural lag" between Jewish and Gentile biblical scholarship, whose effects are still in evidence. Simply stated, Jewish Bible scholars of the nineteenth century made relatively little headway in critical inquiry, at the very time when Christian scholars were revolutionizing the study of the Bible. How are we to explain this sharp contrast in the commitment of scholarly energies and resources? Why did the *Wissenschaft* movement neglect biblical studies?

This question has been discussed often, and reasons have been adduced to explain, at times to excuse, what hindsight teaches was a missed opportunity. Some have pointed to practical limitations of access to the requisite skills, which restricted Jewish scholars, citing quotas on Jewish enrollment in European universities as an example. The true answer to our question probably lies elsewhere however, and has more to do with intellectual and ideological currents within Jewry than with external factors.

Our search for an adequate answer takes us back to the last

quarter of the eighteenth century, to the age of Moses Mendelssohn. Often regarded as the founder of modern Judaism, Mendelssohn (1729–1786), a contemporary of Immanuel Kant, was a noted philosopher and a gifted writer. He gathered around himself a circle of adventurous Hebraists, and together between 1780–83 they produced the *Bi'ur,* a Hebrew commentary on the Pentateuch, accompanied by a German translation transcribed in Hebrew characters.[2] Mendelssohn also translated other biblical books, including the Song of Songs, Psalms and the fifth chapter of Judges (The Song of Deborah) into German, demonstrating his intense interest in Hebrew poetry. The Mendelssohn circle hoped that when utilized fully, the *Biur* and the German translation would produce a constructive change in the intellectual capabilities of contemporary Jews. The *Bi'ur* would enhance appreciation of the Hebraic heritage, whereas the German translation would stimulate the integration of European Jews into the mainstream of European culture. Whether either of these objectives was realized to any significant degree through the instrumentality of Mendelssohn's endeavor is open to question.[3]

The many studies treating the life and creativity of Moses Mendelssohn, most notably Alexander Altmann's book,[4] have emphasized his indebtedness to contemporary masters and to the intellectual environment in which he flourished. We may cite two of the most significant influences. In 1753 Robert Lowth had published a Latin tome on poetic parallelism in Hebrew poetry, which was to have a lasting impact on biblical studies, and which was well known to Mendelssohn.[5] In addition, Johann G. Herder, a personal friend of Mendelssohn, ignited him with his romantic adulation of ancient Hebrew poetry.[6] In fact, Herder and Mendelssohn, whose works appeared fairly simultaneously between 1780–83, had been discussing biblical literature for some years prior to that time.

Altmann observes that Mendelssohn was well aware of the problems raised by critical scholarship.[7] Indeed, about the same time that the *Bi'ur* appeared, the Christian scholar Johann Gottfried Eichhorn of Göttingen (1752–1827), whom Cheyne called the "founder of modern Old Testament criticism,"[8] was publishing his three-volume introduction to the Old Testament, where he boldly presented a radical critique of traditional doctrine on the unity of authorship of the Pentateuch, including a division of Genesis into a J and an E source.[9] In contrast, Mendelssohn intended his work to be "thoroughly imbued with the traditional reverence for the Pentateuch as

God's gift to Israel through Moses."[10] Accordingly, the critical approach was not allowed to intrude. Instead, the principles Mendelssohn followed in his translation were designed to operate within the assumption that the Pentateuch was Mosaic in its enirety.

Outside of the Pentateuch, Mendelssohn and his circle were open to a certain amount of text and source criticism. Nonetheless, the modernity often attributed to the collaborators in the *Bi'ur* had relatively little connection with the goal which, in time, became the main thrust of modern, critical biblical scholarship, namely the recovery of the literary history of the Hebrew Bible. Theirs was, instead, an attempt to free historical exegesis from its heavily midrashic, or homiletical character, by emphasizing the importance of *peshat,* the precise philological and contextual exegesis of the Hebrew text of the Bible.[11] If Mendelssohn was a modern, it was in the sense that he showed an interest in the realia of the biblical environment, and in the literary forms of biblical writing. Mendelssohn, like Herder, was captivated by the phenomenon of language.

Where Mendelssohn showed boldness was in the very readiness to engage Torah-literature in new ways, in his essential eagerness to elucidate the central text of Judaism afresh. As we shall note later, many subsequent Jewish scholars lacked similar courage. The Torah, which claimed to preserve the record of Mosaic revelation, was often considered off-limits to modern critical Jewish scholarship. Failing to realize that until the Torah itself had undergone critical investigation, all efforts at restudying the Judaic heritage would fall short of fulfillment, most Jewish scholars exhibited a timidity that seriously impeded scholarly progress.

Much as we may now regret that timidity, we should have been unrealistic, in retrospect, to expect a radical break with tradition in the Jewish scholarly world on the question of the unity of Torah literature so early in Judaism's modern period. True, Benedict Spinoza (1632–1677) had earlier broken with that tradition, but he was hardly a spokesman for Judaism or a leader of Jews. The fact is, that even by the close of the nineteenth century, a hundred years or so after Mendelssohn, Jewish scholars, even the liberals among them, had not yet come to grips with the challenge of source criticism. The problem was a persistent one. It reflected a deep apprehension that the authority of the Jewish religion might be undermined were the Torah, on which all subsequent Jewish practice claimed to depend, to be subjected to critical analysis. The liberal interpreters of Judaism in Europe at the end of the nineteenth century were still unable to formulate a rationale for the integration of the documentary hypothesis into the study of Torah literature, although by then traditional constraints had given way with regard to the other sections of Scripture.

A fine, if rare, example of a Jewish scholar of the period attempting to come to terms with biblical criticism may be found in volume IV (1892) of the *Jewish Quarterly Review (JQR)*, then published in England. There, Claude Montefiore, a liberal rabbi, philanthropist and New Testament scholar wrote an article articulating the need for a Jewish counterpart to Unitarianism; for a reasoned theology that would permit a professing Jew to accept higher criticism.[12]

Many of Montefiore's Christian countrymen had already engaged the problem. True, prior to 1880, English scholarship had been unreceptive to any type of criticism that might involve a radical reappraisal of the Old Testament's presentation of Israelite history. The appointment however, of S. R. Driver to the Regius Professorship of Hebrew at Oxford in 1883, showed that the tide of mainstream Anglicanism had turned in favor of criticism. By 1891, Wellhausenian criticism had come to dominate British biblical scholarship.[13] Writing in 1892, Montefiore could, understandably, be critical of Christian scholars for being unsympathetic to the theological plight of their Jewish counterparts on the same issue of criticism; but Montefiore himself was caught on the horns of a dilemma: In contrast to the situation in Christianity, no known version of religious Judaism had yet appeared capable of integrating higher criticism! Because he had no intention of removing himself from the context of Jewish religion, Montefiore remained in limbo.

In these same early issues of the British *JQR*, we find evidence of an intellectual irony: There was a surprising degree of communication across confessional lines in the area of biblical studies. The atmosphere of *fin de siècle England* was, in this respect, very similar to what we experience today in North America. Thus in the *JQR*, published under Jewish sponsorship, we find articles by W. Robertson Smith, S. R. Driver, T. K. Cheyne and other leading non-Jewish scholars. Heinrich Graetz, the noted Jewish historian, occasionally contributed articles on the Bible. But one searches the *JQR* of these years in vain for an article by either a Jewish or a Christian scholar, on the documentary sources of the Pentateuch. Indeed, in the very first issue of *JQR,* Solomon Schechter suggested that the higher criticism practiced by Christian scholars "might be guided by some modern Aryan reasons."[14]

What we observe was not unique to the Jews of England. *JQR* typifies a widespread failure of theological inquiry within Jewry; an inability, or at least a reluctance, to meet intellectual challenges. We note the tendency to protect tradition by insulating it; to avoid issues, rather than confront them directly. Nonetheless, it would be mistaken to paint an entirely gloomy portrait of nineteenth century European Jewish Bible scholarship. It would be more accurate to speak of measured progress. It behooves us to examine what amounts to a record of selective engagement and to give it proper weight.

We begin with S. D. Luzzatto (1800–1865), an Italian Jewish scholar, one of the first professors at the Instituto Convitto Rabbinico in Padua, and one of the traditionalist participants in the *Wissenschaft* movement. Luzzatto translated the Torah and the book of Isaiah into Italian, and wrote Hebrew commentaries on the books of the Torah, as well as on Isaiah, Jeremiah, Ezekiel, Proverbs and Job. He was influenced, or perhaps more precisely, motivated, by Mendelssohn's earlier endeavors, and like Mendelssohn was unprepared to apply to Torah literature the same critical apparatus that he would utilize in studying other books of Scripture.[15]

Luzzatto was of a very different intellectual and spiritual disposition from Mendelssohn, though he shared with him many points of emphasis. For one thing, Luzzatto also sought to retrieve the original sense of the scriptural text. He utilized targumic literature extensively, and made original contributions to that field.[16] Luzzatto was, of course, fully committed to *peshat,* and employed evidence from the Semitic languages, principally Arabic, in his studies. He often acknowledged his inability to fathom the true meaning of the biblical text. It is significant that, at times, he attributed this inability to the poor state of textual preservation, which reflects a distinctly critical attitude on his part. Thanks to his rabbinic background, Luzzatto appreciated the relevance of Rabbinic Hebrew to biblical exegesis. So long as he was not interpreting Torah literature, he was even prepared to depart from ancient inner-biblical, and rabbinic, traditions about the authorship of biblical books. By enlisting linguistic criteria in dating texts, Luzzatto concluded that King Solomon could not have written Ecclesiastes. One has the impression that Luzzatto was extremely close to a fully critical method of biblical study, and his works carry a modern flavor, even when read today.

Through the better part of the nineteenth century there were few modern Jewish biblicists at work. One might mention, for example, Joseph Perles (1835–1894), who worked on the Syriac versions,[17] but until quite late in the century little effort was exerted on biblical studies in the circles of *Wissenschaft*. The impressive start made by Luzzatto was followed only much later by another traditionalist, David Zevi Hoffmann (1843–1921), who wrote in German.[18]

Hoffmann was a noted talmudist, who had a secular education, and who was prompted to respond to biblical criticism by his zeal to defend Jewish tradition. In exegetical method, Hoffmann was a critical scholar who utilized ancient versions, rabbinic sources and comparative evidence. He refers to Luzzatto and the Mendelssohn circle, often disputing the latter, but hardly questioning the legitimacy of their method. Hoffmann wrote commentaries on Leviticus (1905–1906) and Deuteronomy (1913–1922), and other unpublished manuscripts have been reported. Though Hoffmann vehemently rejected higher biblical criticism,[19] his often lengthy disputations on documentary problems are articulate statements of historical and literary issues. In retrospect, Hoffmann may be regarded a forerunner of the Italian-Israeli scholar Umberto Moshe David Cassuto (1883–1957). Hoffmann's commentaries have been translated into Hebrew and continue to influence scholars, even those of a nontraditionalist bent.[20]

A discussion of modern Jewish Bible scholarship in nineteenth century Europe would hardly be complete without reference to the great historian Heinrich Graetz (1817–1891).[21] Graetz probably belongs with the traditionalist branch of the *Wissenschaft* movement. His greatest contribution was not as a biblical scholar, but as a pioneer historian,[22] and yet, his relationship to biblical studies was highly significant. Graetz wrote commentaries to Psalms, Song of Songs and Ecclesiastes. He freely applied critical method to most of Scripture, but not to Torah literature.

Graetz's multi-volume *History of the Jews*, originally written in German, was a remarkable achievement in its time. One item of biographical information relevant to the preparation of *History* is especially telling: Graetz delayed the first two volumes, which were to cover the periods of the first and second commonwealths, until he could undertake a personal visit to Palestine, which he ultimately managed to do.[23] Such was the mentality of this true historian that he sought reality at first hand. It was a similar interest in the Near East that motivated some of the greatest Christian scholars of the nineteenth century.

Before discussing the liberal wing of the *Wissenschaft* movement, we should make some reference to several rabbinic scholars of nineteenth century Europe; orthodox talmudic sages and heads of academies *(yeshivot)*, who devoted at least some of their energy to biblical studies, which, as we shall see in the next chapter, played only a minor role in the curriculum of the talmudical academy. Although these scholars were limited by their ideological commitments to pre-critical method, their very interest in the Bible represented at least a limited engagement with modernity, as we shall see presently.

The persons we shall discuss were consciously responding to a perceived threat emanating from reformist, and secular Jewish circles. Earlier scholars of like orientation had reacted violently to Mendelssohn's *Bi'ur,* variously seeing a greater threat in the Hebrew commentaries, which might lure the pious from traditional views, or in the German translations, which might reduce interest in the Hebrew original.

The most significant orthodox scholar of the old school contemporary with Mendelssohn was Elijah ben Solmon Zalman, the "Gaon"[24] of Vilna (Vilnius; 1720–1797), who had shown an unusual degree of interest in biblical studies. He wrote a critical work on the Targums, and frequently incorporated discussions of geography and ancient chronology in his writings. Elijah was particularly concerned with Hebrew grammar, with the phonology and vocalization of biblical Hebrew, and even with literary structure.[25]

The sage Jacob Zevi Meklenburg (1785–1865) was prompted to respond to reformist trends within European Jewry. He wrote a Hebrew commentary on the Torah, entitled *Ha-Ketav Veha-Qabbalah (Writ and Tradition),* published in 1835. Meklenburg concentrated on Hebrew grammar, and was strongly committed to *peshat.* It is noteworthy that Meklenburg utilized the work of Luzzatto extensively, although his viewpoint was emphatically much more traditional.[26]

The head of the Volozhin Yeshiva, Naphtali Zevi Judah Berlin (1817–1893), known as the Neziv, wrote commentaries on the Torah entitled *Ha-ameq Dabar (Penetrate the Word),* published in 1878/79, as well as a commentary on Songs of Songs, *Rinnah shel Torah (Song of Torah)*, published in 1886.[27]

Best known of the orthodox rabbinic commentators on the Bible was Meir Leibush, son of Yehiel Michel (1809–1879), known by the acronym, Malbim. His major work on the Torah was published in Hebrew in 1869. Like Meklenburg, Malbim was open in his opposition to reformist trends in European Jewry. At the same time however, he was critical of earlier generations of sages for abandoning the quest for the plain-sense of the text in favor of midrashic or homiletical interpretation. Malbim sought to bring Jews to greater understanding of the Hebrew language. He argued for the literary unity of Torah literature, adopting a strict position on the question. Malbim's influence was widespread and survives to this very day.[28]

The point to be made about these pre-critical orthodox scholars is that each reacted, in his own way, to the intellectual challenges of modernism. As communal leaders, they were keenly aware of what was occurring within European Jewry. The plausibility structure in which the sanctity and theological unity of Scripture could be assumed was being undermined. If Scripture were to continue to be viewed within an orthodox Jewish perspective, it would require the efforts of orthodox Jewish commentators.

One hardly knows what to make of the biblical work of Samson Raphael Hirsch (1808–1888). Hirsch, chief rabbi of the Orthodox community of Frankfurt,[29] was the ideological formulator of Neo-Orthodoxy. In contrast to the Paleo-Orthodox of his day, Hirsch raised the banner of *torah 'im derek'eretz*, literally: "Both Torah and the way of the world." Functionally, what Hirsch and his followers dedicated themselves to was observance of Jewish ritual law coupled with secular learning and with modernity in dress and manner. Hirsch proclaimed that traditional Judaism had nothing to fear from western civilization. On the contrary, university education would deepen one's committment to Judaism, because one would then have a solid basis from which to assert the superiority of Judaism.

Whereas contemporary readers of the commentaries produced by the orthodox commentators of the old school are likely to find the work of those scholars entirely consistent with their training, the same readers, knowing Hirsch's enthusiasm for secular learning, may find his Torah commentary astonishing in its dismissal of scientific analysis. The volumes of Hirsch's commentary, *Der Pentateuch übersetzt und erläutert*, appearing between 1867–1878, operate on the assumption that Judaism, as an entirely revealed religion, has no history and therefore may not be divided into different stages of development. Indeed, Hirsch attempts to demonstrate that the traditional laws and interpretations attributed to the talmudic sages of late antiquity are the necessary outcomes of the initial divine revelation contained in Scripture. Unlike the work of David Zevi Hoffmann, which confronted higher criticism by paying detailed attention to the biblical text, Hirsch's commentary has extensive recourse to special pleading, preaching[30] and highly dubious philology.[31] Despite these failings, Hirsch's fame in his own day as a brilliant orator, and his status as an outspoken, authoritative exponent of orthodox Judaism caused his Torah commentary to be widely read. It continues to be readily available in English[32] and Hebrew[33] translations.

What unites all these diverse personalities, the traditionalist members of the *Wissenschaft* school, the talmudic scholars who studied the Bible, and the Neo-Orthodox, is their common reaffirmation of traditional belief in the literary unity of Torah literature, and in the historical accuracy and authority of the biblical record. It would be unreasonable to expect any of them to have crossed too far over the line drawn by earlier traditional doctrines. It is less understandable why the liberal participants in the *Wissenschaft* movement failed to cross the same line. It is to this enigma that we now turn our attention. Leopold Zunz, with whom we began, edited a German translation of the Bible, published in 1837/38. He had a deep interest in Psalms, consistent with his absorption in the liturgy and history of the Synagogue. Nonetheless, Zunz's principal efforts were focused on post-biblical literature, rabbinic and medieval.[34]

Perhaps most enigmatic of the reformers in the left wing of the *Wissenschaft* movement with respect to the critical study of the Hebrew Bible was Abraham Geiger (1810–1874). Two recent papers, one by Nahum Sarna on Geiger's biblical scholarship,[35] another by Michael Meyer on Geiger's historicism[36] in studying the development of Judaism are relevant to our inquiry.

As portrayed by both Sarna and Meyer, Abraham Geiger, a true reformist, was an exceptional scholar, intellectually prepared to subject the entire Hebrew Bible, including Torah literature, to critical investigation, without reservation. Notwithstanding his promise to devote wholesale critical energy to biblical study, Geiger never confronted the central issues of criticism directly. His most important work in the biblical field, *Urschrift und Übersetzungen der Bibel*

(1857), focused instead on textual history.[37] Based primarily on the evidence of the ancient versions, Geiger's study concluded that the text of the Hebrew Bible was fluid in late antiquity, a theory that has gained support from recent discoveries, including the ancient writings from Qumran.

Geiger also wrote a historical work, entitled *Das Judentum und seine Geschichte* (1865–1871), the first volume of which was promptly translated into English in 1866.[38] Geiger's history provides an insight as to why the author himself and the *Wissenschaft* movement as a whole neglected the critical study of the Bible, turning instead to later phases of the Judaic heritage.

Sarna speculates that Geiger may have felt that Christian scholars were already studying the Bible critically with great success, and that he was thus free for other projects. In addition, Sarna intimates that Geiger subordinated certain of his scholarly goals to the ideological agenda of his time. This second insight of Sarna's may prove more significant than the first.

Near the conclusion of the first volume of his *History*, Geiger expressed the hope for a modern day Hillel the Elder who would guide European Jewry. (One suspects that he had himself in mind!) Geiger elaborates on the famous dictum of Hillel: "If I am not for my self, who will be for me?" by calling for a program for contemporary Jewry based on three principles: 1) It was vital to retrieve the splendid treasures of the Jewish past. 2) It was necessary to pare off of Jewish religious behavior what Geiger called, "the coat of mail,"—those features of Jewish religion which tended to insulate Jews from the life of the larger societies within which they lived. 3) Jews must cease looking to the past for inspiration, and instead draw guidance from the *Zeitgeist*, the living "Spirit" of the present.

The first principle is familiar from the program of the *Wissenschaft* movement. Interest in the past is hardly a reason, however, for neglecting biblical study. Nor is the second principle of great concern here. Reform attitudes that sought to pare off the coat of mail might, in fact, stimulate modern scholars to study Torah literature critically. It is the third principle which holds the key to our problem, because it effectively contradicts the first principle: Why study the ancient past of our people, when we are advised against looking to the past for guidance and inspiration?

Geiger posits a polarity between the living "Spirit" of the present and the dead past. In his *History*, he states his views on the subject of

Jewish nationalism and Jewish identity. Nationalism is a form of separatism, whereas Geiger advocated accommodation to the larger European culture. Strong national feeling and overbearing emphasis on the historical past might impede the full integration of the Jews of the nineteenth century within contemporary European society, a process Geiger believed that political liberalization within Europe might make possible. Geiger regarded Judaism as a religion. Essentially, but ironically, he even found it necessary to justify the continued practice of Jewish religion in the modern age.

Geiger was not a philosophical idealist, but as Meyer emphasizes, an advocate of historicism. Accordingly, all ideas, including religious ones claiming divine authority, must be introduced to humankind in the context of a body of believers, a collective organism of sorts; ideas must be realized in a social setting. A nation is one example of a collective body, but nationalism, as the spirit of a collective body, ceases to be relevant once a nation fulfills its mission and transmits its teachings and its ideas to the world. Inasmuch as the Jews have not as yet conveyed their singular message to the world, to humankind, in an effective manner, there is an honest justification for their continued existence as an identifiable collective. That collective for Geiger, however, could no longer be national, because Geiger and his contemporaries, including the Neo-Orthodox,[39] identified their nationality as German rather than Jewish. In consequence, the continued practice of the Jewish religion in some form was necessary for the preservation of the Jewish collective until such time as its mission could be fulfilled.

Geiger's negative evaluation of Jewish nationalism did not entail any degree of admiration for Christianity. Indeed, asserted Geiger, contemporary Christianity could not qualify as the ultimate fulfillment of historic Judaism. In its attempts to universalize the message of the Israelite prophets and bring it to all the nations of the earth, Christianity had failed because: "Its concepts and sentiments are characterized by great vagueness; they conflict with every definite national trait. . . . They widen the chasm between body and soul. . . . Christianity arose under the influence of the disintegration of noble civilizations, the Jewish and the Greek; it was garbed in decaying languages; it had the seeds of morbidity implanted in it, as it were—a morbid state under which it labors to this day."[40] If Christianity had failed, then the need for an identifiable Jewry persisted in modern times.

Geiger put the following words in the mouth of his modern-day Hillel the Elder:

"Thou beloved pilgrim, do not look back continually," thus he will speak, "do not cast thine eye continually toward the past! Jerusalem is a grave, which we honor, but new life springeth not from the grave; you must draw from the living present and turn it to profit."[41]

The conclusion is inescapable: For Geiger the national phase of Jewish history in the holy land belonged to the dead past. As such there was little point in reconstructing that past as historical reality. There was value in tracing the development of biblical monotheism, in appreciating the message of biblical prophecy, and in defining the norms of Mosaic law, all in historical context. For the most part however, the ancient biblical phase of Judaism was the least relevant to the realities of Geiger's present. It was more relevant as myth than as history. The hypothesis suggested here is that for Geiger and his *Wissenschaft* contemporaries, the degree of scholarly interest in the past was correlated very closely with the social and political agenda[42] of the scholarly community.

As a result, Geiger, who could have undertaken the critical investigation of the Torah literature by virtue of his scholarly view of Jewish tradition, had little interest in doing so! Here is the ironic situation: Traditionalists of the nineteenth century did more to engage Torah literature than did the liberals. Traditionalists were constrained by doctrine and prevented by their adherence to traditional forms of inquiry from freely adopting a critical view of the literary history of the Torah. Some of the liberals would have been able to legitimate a critical approach in their own eyes, but had their minds on other matters. As a result, we observe a flight from the inevitable controversy that critical engagement of Torah literature would later produce. To risk such a controversy would have required a genuine interest in the real history and in the political reality of ancient Israel, and that interest was lacking in Jewish liberal scholarly circles in the nineteenth century.

To test this hypothesis, that an overpowering interest in ancient reality would be needed to encourage scholars to break with traditional religious doctrine, we might review the career of one Christian scholar who did so. We refer to William Robertson Smith (1846–1894), whose classic work, *Lectures on the Religion of the Semites*, originally published in 1889, was reissued in 1969 with a prolegomenon by James Muilenberg. In his introductory essay, Muilenberg provides a fascinating description of the religious and intellectual environment of Robertson's Smith's day.[43] Robertson Smith lived in an era that had witnessed revolutionary studies in the physical sciences, social sciences and humanities, all of which were to have an impact on the modern study of the Bible. The works of August Comte, Charles Darwin, Herbert Spencer, James Frazer and Edward Tylor come readily to mind. As regards Bible proper, the German Julius Wellhausen (1844–1918) and the Dutch scholar Abraham Kuenen (1828–1891) who laid the foundations of critical study were Robertson Smith's contemporaries. The years 1835–1885 likewise witnessed the emergence of Egyptology and Assyriology, each fueled by massive discoveries of ancient texts by pioneers in archaeology.

As we survey the career of Robertson Smith, we are able to identify the factors at work in channeling his exceptional capabilities. Robertson Smith grew up and was educated in the Free Church of Scotland. It was through the Free Church that he held a chair of Old Testament until his dismissal on the grounds of unorthodoxy in 1881, despite his attempts to prove that critical study was compatible with Evangelical Christianity.[44]

But Robertson Smith was a paradigm of intellectual autonomy. Not only did he acquit himself well in antagonistic encounters with church spokesmen, but he continued to pursue his research interests with ever greater diligence. While the Free Church was trying to decide just how heretical was his article on the Bible published in *Encyclopedia Brittanica,* Robertson Smith was pioneering the fields of comparative religion and anthropology in Near Eastern context. He traveled widely in the Near East, in North Africa and in southern Spain. He devoted considerable time to the study of Arabic[45], and in all, endeavored personally to become familiar with the cultures of the Near East. In effect, Robertson Smith became more interested in the Bible as a window into ancient reality, than as a canonical document whose contents were to be accepted on faith.

Of course it would be misleading to compare Geiger and Robertson Smith in all respects. Nonetheless, partial comparison is extremely instructive. Robertson Smith was compelled to seek haven in the university world of late nineteenth century England after his expulsion from his church. Abraham Geiger, in contrast, would have had little, or no, difficulty in continuing to function within the reformist Jewish community in Germany had he subjected Torah literature to critical study.

For Robertson Smith the issue was religious legitimacy versus intellectual freedom; the individual versus the community. For Geiger the issue was different: He had to determine which aspects of the Judaic heritage were most relevant as he, Geiger, perceived it. To Geiger, the message of the biblical prophets was most relevant: Universalism and human brotherhood, social justice and equity, world peace and the war against superstition. Liberal Judaism tended to be anti-nationalist; or more precisely, against particularism. This tendency dampened interest in the historical investigation of the biblical period. Jewish national feeling was just beginning to burgeon in Geiger's time and had not yet had a serious effect on Jewish scholarship and letters.

The effect of nationalism was evident in the work of Graetz, as already noted. Early modern Hebrew poets and publicists were just beginning to generate a romantic attitude towards biblical antiquity. In contrast to the Berlin Haskalah (Enlightenment) of Mendelsssohn's day, the late nineteenth century East-European Haskalah would be, for the most part, passionately nationalistic. But its romanticism would stand in sharp contrast with the reformist wing of the *Wissenschaft* movement. In their unleashed creative energy these writers and poets would avail themselves of the inspiration furnished by biblical antiquity, voicing romantic hopes of restoration to the ancient homeland. But several decades of the twentieth century would pass before these stirrings would directly influence Jewish Bible scholarship.

This brief review of the European background of American Jewish Bible scholarship provides important retrospective insights. Perhaps most significant is one which, from the standpoint of logic, should have been obvious: Critical study of the Bible could not develop properly so long as it was fettered by textual limits, so long as one could not apply to Torah literature the same method that was considered legitimate in the study of Targum, Midrash, Psalms, Isaiah or Ecclesiastes. This was the problem faced by the orthodox as well as by traditionalists of the *Wissenschaft* movement. For the liberals, the matter was even more complex: Writings and teachings which would emphasize the historic relations between the Jewish people and its homeland, the land of Israel, and which might focus on the national phase of ancient Jewish history, were problematic for the reformists. Such intellectual pursuits might have clashed with the efforts of scholars like Abraham Geiger to promote the social and political acceptance of Jews within enlightened European society. The variable factor was the definition of Jewish identity as either a nationality or a religion. It is this problem of definition which explains the difference between Abraham Geiger and Heinrich Graetz, much more than their different attitudes towards Jewish religious practices or theological doctrine.

When the epochal events of recent Jewish history brought many Jewish scholars to Palestine, in the period before World War II, at a time when Hebraic culture was energetically being revived there, and when Jewish scholars in North America came under the tutelage of liberal Christian and humanistic mentors, the two indispensable preconditions for the pursuit of critical biblical scholarship were simultaneously present: There was sufficient liberalism to permit critical engagement, stimulated by the historical and comparative disciplines; there was an intense interest in rediscovering the biblical past as historical reality.

Notes to European Background

1. See the statement by Immanuel Wolf, "Über den Begriff einer Wissenschaft des Judenthums," in *Zeitschrift für die Wissenschaft des Judenthums* 1 (1822), 1–24. The term "Wissenschaft des Judenthums" was first coined by Eduard Gans. See M. Meyer, *The Origins of the Modern Jew* (Detroit: Wayne State University, 1967), 165.

2. The formal name of the *Bi'ur* was *Sefer Netivot Ha-Shalom*. The introduction was entitled *Or Lintivah*. The first edition contains the Hebrew text of the Pentateuch, a German translation in Hebrew characters, and a Hebrew commentary. Other books of the Bible were prepared, modeled on Mendelssohn's edition, by the group that became known as the "Bi'urists."

3. For a discussion of Mendelssohn's German translations and their impact on Mendelssohn's contemporaries see W. Weinberg, "Language Questions Relating to Moses Mendelssohn's Pentateuch Translation," *Hebrew Union College Annual* 55 (1984), 197–242.

4. A. Altmann, *Moses Mendelssohn: A Biographical Study* (Philadelphia: Jewish Publication Society, 1973), especially, 346–420.

5. Robert Lowth (1710–1787) had become Professor of Poetry at Oxford in 1741. His Latin work, *Praelectionis de Sacra Poesi Hebraerorum* (Oxford, 1753) appeared in English in 1787 as *Lectures on the Sacred Poetry of the Hebrews*. Mendelssohn reviewed Lowth's work in 1757. See Altmann, *Mendelssohn*, 84, and ibid, 409–413, for Mendelssohn's use of Lowth's insights.

6. See D. Baumgardt, "Herder, Johann Gottfried," in *EncJud* 8 343–344; For a summary of Herder's thought, see P. Gardiner, "Herder, Johann Gottfried," *Encyclopedia of Philosophy* 3, 486–489. For our purposes, Herder's most significant work is *Vom Geiste der ebräischen Poesie* (1782–1783). It is relevant to the general history of American biblical scholarship that the conservative American biblicist Moses Stuart was later to persuade his student James Marsh to translate *Geiste* into English as *The Spirit of Hebrew Poetry* (Burlington, Vermont: E. Smith, 1833). See J. Brown, *The Rise of Biblical Criticism in America, 1800–1870 The New England Scholars* (Middletown: Wesleyan University, 1969), 50.

7. Altmann's discussion, as he acknowledges, is largely grounded in the researches contained in the unpublished Ph.D. dissertation by E. Levenson, "Moses Mendelssohn's Understanding of Logico-Grammatical and Literary Construction in the Pentateuch: A Study of the German Translation and Hebrew Commentary, the *Bi'ur*," (Brandeis, 1972).

8. T. K. Cheyne, *Founders of Old Testament Criticism* (New York: Scribner's, 1893), 13.

9. J. G. Eichhorn, *Einleitung in das Alte Testament* (Leipzig, 1780–83). Altmann does not mention any contact between Mendelssohn and Eichorn, nor any correspondence between them.

10. See Altmann, *Mendelssohn,* 376; For details see Levenson, *"Bi'ur."*

11. The term *peshat* is employed here in its Modern Hebrew usage, which originated in the Middle Ages. In classical rabbinics, the term referred to "authoritative" or "generally accepted" meaning. See L. I. Rabinowitz, *EncJud 13, 330–331,* s.v. "Peshat," (with bibliography).

12. C. G. Montefiore, "Some Notes on the Effect of Biblical Criticism upon the Jewish Religion," *JQR 4* (O.S.; 1892), 293–306.

13. See J. Rogerson, *Old Testament Criticism in the Nineteenth Century England and Germany* (London: Fortress, 1985), 273–289.

14. S. Schechter, "The Dogmas of Judaism," *JQR* 1 (1892), 53–54. On Schechter and higher criticism see below.

15. See A. Tobias, "Luzzatto, Samuel David," *EncJud* 11, 604–607; See further, M. Margolies, *Samuel David Luzzatto: Traditionalist Scholar* (New York: Ktav, 1979).

16. Luzzatto's work on the Targum is entitled *Ohev Ger (Philoxenos;* Vienna, 1830). Incidentally, Luzzatto gave the name Philoxenos to his son.

17. See "Perles, Joseph," *EncJud* 13, 293–294. For a bibliography of Perles's work see W. Bacher, *JQR* 7 (O.S. 1895/95), 1–23.

18. See M. Herr, "Hoffmann, David Zevi," *EncJud* 8, 808–810; L. Ginzberg, "David Zevi Hoffmann," in Ginzberg, *Students, Scholars and Saints* (New York: Schocken, 1928), 252–262.

19. Ironically, Hoffmann's rabbinic researches make full use of higher critical method. It was Hoffmann who divided the Mekhilta, the legal midrash to Exodus, into Akiban and Ishmaelean sources.

20. For a recent example see B. Levine, *The JPS Torah Commentary Leviticus* (Philadelphia: Jewish Publication Society, 1989).

21. See I. Abrahams, "Heinrich Graetz: The Jewish Historian," *JQR*

(O. S.) 4 (1892), 165-194. For bibliography of Graetz's works see ibid., 194-203.

22. Graetz is best remembered for his eleven volume *Geschichte der Juden* (Leipzig: O. Leiner, 1860-1872). An English version in six volumes was published by Jewish Publication Society under the title, *History of the Jews*, between 1891-1898, and has since undergone several printings. The English version, regrettably, omits the notes of the original.

23. See N. Sarna, in Petuchowski (ed.), *Geiger*, 19-20.

24. The title "Gaon" had designated the heads of the Babylonian talmudic academies under medieval Islam. In Elijah's case, the term was a purely honorific testimony to his brilliance. In the last two centuries the term "Gaon" has become so abused that one encounters such honorifics as *hagga'on ha'amitti*, "the True Gaon, viz; a real genius," as opposed to pretenders.

25. See M. Kaddari and I. Klausner, "Elijah ben Solomon Zalman," *EncJud* 6, 651-658.

26. See T. Preschel, "Meklenburg, Jacob Zevi," *EncJud* 11, 1271-1272.

27. See Z. Kaplan, "Berlin, Naphtali Zevi Judah," *EncJud* 4, 660-661.

28. See Y. Horowitz, "Malbim, Meir Loeb ben Yehiel Michael," *EncJud* 11, 821-824; E. Hebert, "Hebrew Printing in Roumania," *Journal of Jewish Bibliography* 2 (1940), 110-116.

29. In general see S. Katz, "Hirsch, Samson (ben) Raphael," *EncJud* 8, 508-515. For a recent study of Hirsch and the Frankfurt community, with extensive bibliography, see R. Liberles, *Religious Conflict in Social Context The Resurgence of Orthodox Judaism in Frankfurt am Main 1838-1877* (Westport: Greenwood, 1985).

30. Perhaps the most interesting feature of these commentaries is their moralizing, hortatory style, which is highly reminscent of Luther.

31. For some good examples of typical Hirsch philology, see the commentary to the first three chapters of Genesis.

32. See S. R. Hirsch, *The Pentateuch Translated and Explained* (translated by I. Levy; London: Honig, 1955-1962).

33. S. R. Hirsch, *Hamishah Humshei Torah* (translated by M. Breuer; Jerusalem: Mossad Yitzhaq Breuer, 1966).

34. Zunz is best remembered for his major work on Jewish preaching entitled, *Die Gottesdienstlichen Vorträge der Juden, historisch entwinckelt* (Berlin, 1832). The book is the first example of the application of the *Wissenschaft* program to a specific area of Judaics. A Hebrew translation, *HaDerashot BeYisrael* appeared in 1947. For a good study of Zunz, with bibliography, see Meyer, "Leopold Zunz and the Scientific Ideal," in idem, *Origins*, 144-182.

35. Sarna, "Abraham Geiger and Biblical Scholarship," in Petuchowski (ed.), *Geiger*, 17-30.

36. M. Meyer, "Abraham Geiger's Historical Judaism," ibid, 3-16.

37. The full title is instructive: *Urschrift und Übersetzungen der Bibel in ihrer Abhängigkeit von der innern Entwicklung des Judenthums* (First edition, 1857; Heb. translation: *HaMiqra VeTargumaw*, 1949).

38. Abraham Geiger, *Judaism and Its History I*, translated by Maurice Mayer, London, 1866.

39. See M. Kaplan, *Judaism as a Civilization* (Philadelphia: Jewish Publication Society and Reconstructionist Press [Reprint], 1981), 145–150.

40. See Geiger apud R. Chazan and M. Raphael, *Modern Jewish History A Source Reader* (New York: Schocken, 1974), 66.

41. Geiger, *History*, 263.

42. Geiger's discomfort with Jewish nationalism also found expression in his opposition to the continued use of Hebrew as the language of Jewish liturgy. See J. Petuchowski in idem (ed.), *Geiger*, 45.

43. See William Robertson Smith, *Lectures on the Religion of the Semites*, third edition, with an introduction and additional notes by S. A. Cook, in Library of Biblical Studies, ed. H. M. Orlinsky, with a Prolegomenon by James Muilenberg. (New York: Ktav, 1969).

44. See Rogerson, *Criticism*, 275–280.

45. Robertson Smith became a professor of Arabic at Cambridge in 1883. See Cheyne, *Founders*, 217.

CHAPTER TWO
American Beginnings

Our sketch of the beginnings of modern Jewish Bible scholarship in Europe provides the necessary background for the primary topic; the history of Jewish Bible scholarship in North America. On the one hand, that history cannot be divorced from its European heritage. On the other hand, American Jewish biblical scholarship is inseparable from the larger political and social history of North American Jewry, a Jewry distinct, perhaps uniquely so, from all of its predecessors. The present chapter, which is devoted to the history of American Jewish Bible scholarship from its rudimentary beginnings until the outbreak of the First World War, outlines those features of American Judaism which either encouraged or impeded the serious study of the Bible by Jews.

American Jewish institutions and religious movements were shaped and formed more in response to pressing needs than by religious ideology.[1] Jewish Bible scholarship in America[2] was no exception. The community of 1500 Jews who lived in America on the eve of the Revolutionary War grew tenfold in the next half century but continued to be a tiny minority in the total population.[3] The Jewish settlement in Canada was even smaller.[4] Whereas the larger European Jewish communities had seldom lacked scholars, religious functionaries, well-trained teachers and educational materials, in America all of these were in short supply.[5] Schools conducted by Jewish congregations often made use of slightly reworded Protestant catechisms[6] and taught the Hebrew Bible to their students by means of the King James translation. Isaac Leeser (1806–1868) of Philadelphia[7] decried this state of affairs and attempted numerous solutions.

Leeser's contributions must be understood both against the background of the European Jewish community whence he came, and against the special circumstances of the United States. Born in Neuenkirchen in Prussian Westphalia, Leeser had received a good but limited gymnasium education. The same may be said of his Jewish education, which was greatly influenced by Abraham Sutro

(1784–1869), a somewhat enlightened orthodox rabbi. The period of Leeser's youth coincided with a period of revolutionary change in the structure and character of the Jewish communities. Until the late eighteenth century the nation states of Europe had related to Jews not as individual citizens of the state but as involuntary members of a corporate body, the Jewish community, which was generally autonomous in internal affairs. Individual Jews as members of the community were perforce governed by the traditional Jewish legal system *(halakah)*, which embraced all aspects of social, economic, political and religious life. Within these communities Rabbis functioned less as clergy than as communal officials and judges responsible for the interpretation and application of the all-encompassing law. Although synagogues fell within rabbinic jurisdiction, rabbis preached only rarely. Daily services were led by laics, that is, knowledgeable males at least thirteen years of age. Sabbath and holiday services, especially in larger communities, were usually conducted by a *hazzan* (cantor), a learned layman with professional or semi-professional musical training. The Emancipation of much of Western and Central European Jewry between 1770 and 1870 enabled Jews to move out of the ghetto and, in varying degrees, to become included in the society at large.[8] Emancipation amounted to a social revolution, which provided Jews as individuals with greater freedom, but at the same time narrowed the jurisdiction of the collective Jewish communities and consequently undermined the authority of those officials who had traditionally filled leadership roles. In effect, the jurisdiction of the ordained rabbi became limited to the specific realm of Jewish religious practice, which with the decline of the power of the community to enforce a uniform pattern of observance, had been transformed into a matter of individual conscience. At the same time, as emancipated Jews increasingly took advantage of opportunities for general education, their knowledge of Hebrew and of Jewish ritual declined to the extent that synagogues increasingly came to require the services of professional clergy. Modernist seminaries[9] soon arose to produce rabbis who, despite numerous differences among themselves in theology and religious observance, were in essential agreement with the increasingly cosmopolitan laity that Jewish clerics should function much like Protestant ministers.[10] These rabbis of the newer breed, who usually had some university education, preached regularly and, if orthodox, left the adjudication of fine points of ritual law to their more traditionally-schooled colleagues. Early nineteenth century American Jewry likewise required professional clergy. Given however its small size, low level of education and general lack of concern for the finer points of Jewish ritual law, the American Jewish community had little need for ordained rabbis, and indeed engaged none until the 1840's. Required instead were cantors to lead services, ritual slaughterers to provide kosher meat and ritual circumcizers to initiate baby boys into the Abrahamic covenant. Often one man would serve simultaneously in all these capacities. He would also be expected to teach synagogue Hebrew to the children and on the model of the American Protestant minister, to preach regularly in the synagogue.[11]

Isaac Leeser was just the kind of clergyman required in the American synagogue of his time. At the age of twenty-two, he became *hazzan* (cantor) of Congregation Mickveh Israel in Philadelphia, a position he occupied for twenty-one years. Leeser, like his contemporary occupants of the post of *hazzan*, lacked rabbinic ordination and had no doctoral degree.[12] Nonetheless, American historical circumstances combined with the man's personal vision and sense of purpose to make Leeser the primary architect of American Jewish institutional life. Bertram Korn has written: "Practically every form of Jewish activity which supports American Jewish life today was either established or envisaged by this one man."[13] Among Leeser's pioneering accomplishments were the establishment of the English sermon as a fixture of the American synagogue, and the editing and publication of *The Occident,* the first successful Anglo-Jewish newspaper in the United States. Leeser also founded the first American Jewish Publication Society and the first American rabbinic school, Maimonides College, neither of which long survived Leeser's death,[14] although his personal example inspired others to succeed where he had failed. What survived him for more than a half century was the Leeser translation of the Bible, a project that took seventeen years. The English translation of the Pentateuch appeared in 1845[15] followed in 1853 by an entire Hebrew-English Bible.[16] Leeser, unlike his Reform opponents, was personally committed to the observance of Jewish ritual law. Although Leeser's orthodoxy impelled him to forswear American citizenship, which he regarded as a compromise of the ancient Jewish messianic redemptive hope, he had *volens nolens* become an American influenced by American religion. In his own words, "If ever a country other than the blessed commonwealth of Israel, had especial cause for glorifying the most holy Name, it is surely the republic of the United States."[17] In the first half of the nineteenth century, religious traditions in the American republic were evaluated according to Protestant criteria and Protestantism itself was centered in the Bible. Between 1816–1820 the American Bible Society, itself a product of that revival movement known as the "Second Great Awakening," had distributed about one hundred thousand Bibles in the United States.[18] Leeser's bibliocentrism in religion, itself an unacknowledged departure from European Jewish orthodoxy, was complemented by his anglophilism and his admiration of the Episcopalian style of worship.[19] Accordingly, Leeser looked for his model of Bible translation to the English Authorized Version, whose translators he described "as honest as men writing for their sect are likely to be."[20] Nonetheless, because "persons differing from us in religious ideas make use of Scripture to assail Israel's hope and faith,"[21] it was Leeser's conviction that Jews required an English Bible[22] that would retain the dignity of the King James Version while abandoning its Christology. On the one hand, Leeser can hardly be faulted for his frank attempt to give his English version a Jewish coloring by translating biblical passages in accord with the Aramaic Targums, the medieval Jewish exeges and the "modern German Israelites" among them, Mendelssohn, Wessely, Zunz and Fürst."[23] On the other hand, it must be admitted that in his avoidance of christological interpretation Leeser often went to the other extreme by rendering biblical passages according to later Jewish law or theological doctrine while at the same time insisting that he was translating literally. In this approach Leeser differed from such outstanding medieval Jewish exegetes as Rashi who had regularly acknowledged that the plain sense of Scripture might differ from rabbinic interpretation. In the same vein, Leeser often attempted to harmonize conflicting biblical passages even when sufficient textual warrant was lacking, in order to demonstrate the unity of Scripture.[24] There can be no doubt that these flaws in his work stem from Leeser's bibliocentric agenda. In the manner of some of its Protestant counterparts, early nineteenth century American Judaism had to justify itself by Scripture alone.

As regards style, Leeser's translation faithfully followed the King James Version in its elegant, if archaic language, as well as in the pursuit of extreme literalness when such did not impede the translator's religious objectives. All *waws* were mechanically rendered "and;"[25] protagonists invariably "lift up their feet" before walking and "lift up their voices" before speaking. The Judaized King James produced by Leeser proved extremely popular among the Jews in America if not among their coreligionists in England.[26] There can be no doubt that the style and format of the Leeser Bible captured the "specific synthesis" of American Jewish life in the mid-nineteenth century.[27] In the United States the Leeser translation served as the English Bible of the Jews until its replacement by the translation of the Jewish Publication Society in 1917.

Whereas Leeser succeeded admirably in his goal of translating the Bible for American use, his failure at Maimonides College provides a partial explanation of why serious American Jewish Bible scholarship took a long time to develop. In the New World, Jews were freer than they had been throughout most of their history. For much of the nineteenth century their low population[28] served to shield American Jews from much of the religious discrimination suffered by Roman Catholics[29] and the racial abuses to which Chinese, blacks and American Indians were subjected.[30] Internally, there was no autonomous Jewish governing body to coerce its members into conformity of belief and practice. But if the American Jewish community was freer than its European antecedents, it was far less schooled in the law and lore of Judaism. The lack of Jewish libraries, the scarcity of Hebrew type and the relative smallness of the American Jewish community were responsible only in part for this cultural lag. More important was the social and educational position of the Jewish community.

The Jews who had come to American were predominantly peddlers and traders rather than scholars and students.[31] For the first seventy-five years of the nineteenth century, educational and rabbinic leadership came from abroad,[32] trained according to the traditional European Jewish curriculum. It must be emphasized that whereas the Reformation had made the Bible fundamental to Protestant seminary education, Scripture played a very minor role in the training of traditional rabbis. The European Jewish curriculum prescribed Bible solely for early elementary education in the *heder* (one-room schoolhouse). Older boys with the desire for higher learning whose families or communities were able and willing to support them, were spared the pressures of earning a living, so that they might continue their studies in a talmudical academy *(yeshivah)* where they concentrated on the Babylonian Talmud and its commentaries.[33] Students who desired rabbinic ordination were given the further requirement of mastering the late medieval Jewish law codes.[34] In contrast, Bible study in the talmudical academy generally consisted of little more than following the public reading of the Torah during the synagogue service. In some pietistic circles, study of the Bible by adults, especially when unmediated by the proper medieval commentaries and the talmudic traditions, was construed, with good cause,[35] as a mark of heterodoxy. Needless to say, critical study of the Bible, which questioned the accuracy of the received text, challenged traditional attributions of authorship and discovered disparate sources where tradition claimed unity of composition, was anathema to the orthodox. But even in the circles of nineteenth century *Wissenschaft des Judentums*, there was very little attention paid to critical study of Bible for a number of reasons. First, and most significant as explained in the previous chapter, scholars associated with *Wissenschaft des Judentums* sought citizenship rights in their native or adopted countries. For them, reconstruction of the history of the Jew in the gentile world was a scholarly task with contemporary and personal relevance. In contrast, the serious study of historic ancient Israel in its own land had embarrassingly nationalistic overtones. Second, critical Christian Bible scholarship since the days of Herder had often been couched in language highly critical of Jews and Judaism.[36] Wellhausen, for example, was notorious in Jewish circles for his negative evaluation of the late Jewish "church" to which he attributed the final form of the Pentateuch, a work he considered overly legalistic and ritualistic.[37] To be sure, Wellhausen's antipathy to legalism as expressed in his biblical scholarship was largely meant as an assault on his own German Protestant contemporaries who practiced what Wellhausen considered an unduly legalistic Christianity.[38] Nonetheless, his comments could be, and were, regarded as anti-Semitic by many Jewish scholars.[39] Third, we must recall that critical study of the Bible remained a sensitive topic even for educated American Christians throughout the nineteenth century.[40] American Presbyterian authorities for example, convicted of heresy both Henry Preserved Smith (1891) and C. A. Briggs (1893) because of their espousal of biblical criticism.[41]

In consequence, even when American Jewry began successfully to train its own leaders, critical study of the Bible was at first discouraged.[42] Isaac Mayer Wise (1819–1900),[43] against whose reformist approach much of Isaac Leeser's activity was directed, serves as a notable example of one who encouraged the scientific study of Judaism while at the same time institutionalizing a sentimental attachment to the Bible of his own early childhood. German-born and despite his own claims to the contrary, largely self-taught,[44] Wise compensated for his lack of formal training with ambition, vision and apparently boundless energy. In 1875, after an earlier failure[45] Wise founded the first American rabbinic seminary to survive its infancy, Hebrew Union College (HUC) in Cincinnati, Ohio. Although Wise was a religious reformer who considered such matters as the dietary laws "purely national laws for Israel, local and temporary,"[46] and denied or questioned the hallowed beliefs in resurrection and a personal god, he continued at HUC the traditional practice of moving students quickly from Bible to Talmud.[47] Wise was unwavering, if behaviorally and ritually inconsistent, in his faith that the Pentateuch had been revealed to Moses by the hand of God. For Wise it was "Mosaic and Sinaitic . . . or nothing."[48] In 1891 Wise published *Pronaos to Holy Writ*[49] with the aim of demolishing what the author repeatedly termed "negative criticism," in order to demonstrate the antiquity of the Pentateuch and the fact of its Mosaic authorship. According to Wise, negative criticism was to be shunned because it depicted the Bible as "a compendium of pious or even impious frauds, willful deceptions [and] unscrupulous misrepresentations."[50] Although tendentious and idiosyncratic, *Pronaos* is a much better book than one might expect. On the negative side of the ledger, Wise departs from accepted convention by never quoting any other scholar by name. In addition, Wise inconsistently, but in a manner hardly unique in Jewish scholarship,[51] accepts the critical method when its conclusions do not undermine the authenticity and Mosaic origin of the Pentateuch. Thus, Wise avers that Isaiah 40–66 is exilic (*Pronaos,* 72) and that Psalm 118 is Maccabean (ibid, 90). On the positive side, *Pronaos* depends for its argumentation on a very detailed knowledge of the Hebrew Bible, which Wise possessed in abundance. Indeed, the work rewards its readers by demonstrating that Wise was both a man of superior intellect and a very close reader of the biblical text. In sum, Wise had the potential to make lasting contributions to biblical scholarship but lacked that openness of mind which might have accompanied a better formal education. *Pronaos* reflected a view of the Bible that other HUC faculty, better educated than Wise, and more sympathetic to critical Bible scholarship, could not accept. Nonetheless, Wise's view, that biblical instruction should concentrate on "exegesis," prevailed in the first quarter-century of HUC's existence.[52] By "exegesis," Wise meant that students should study Bible primarily in the light of the Jewish medieval commentaries and the Aramaic targums.[53] In Wise's lifetime professors were prohibited from suggesting textual emendations of the Pentateuch in class. During one visit to a classroom Wise heard a professor expounding Wellhausenian biblical criticism and ordered him to discontinue the lecture.[54]

A similar institutional position was taken by the Jewish Theological Seminary (JTS), organized in 1886 by the centrist forces, which had begun to coalesce in American religious Judaism as early as the 1870's and especially in the 1880's. On the left wing were scholarly rabbis such as Alexander Kohut,[55] Marcus Jastrow and Benjamin Szold who were considered by many to be Reform,[56] but who could not support the radical Reform[57] stance of the Philadelphia Conference of 1869[58] and especially, the Pittsburgh Platform of 1885.[59] On the right wing were clerics more committed to traditional Jewish observance, notably the Sephardim Sabato Morais and H. Pereira Mendes, who along with like-minded German and early East and Central European immigrants who had grown up in America, were too acculturated to the United States and too disdainful of the newer immigrants[60] to be accepted by them as authentically orthodox.[61] These men and others who identified themselves with the "the Historical School" founded The Jewish Theological Seminary Association in New York in 1886 "for the preservation in America of the knowledge and practice of historical Judaism." The JTS itself was opened formally in 1887. Because the Seminary's natural constituency of "acculturated East European immigrants and their children had not yet come into being," JTS barely survived into the twentieth century.[62] By 1902, when the Seminary was reorganized with Solomon Schechter as president, the American Jewish demographic situation had begun to change considerably. There were now increasing numbers of Jews, mainly of East-European origin, who were alienated from old-style orthodoxy but unwilling to reject its forms completely. These Jews favored the retention of Hebrew as their language of prayer, but at the same time demanded decorous services with frequent English accompaniment. In Orthodox fashion they preferred to cover their heads during worship. In Reform fashion and in keeping with American church style, they preferred family pews to the Orthodox requirement of separate seating for men and women. United in opposition to Reform and largely unwelcome in

Reform synagogues, such people differed considerably in their own forms of personal observance and belief. It was from JTS that the rabbinic leadership of this new constituency was to come. Although the members of the "Historical School" who served on the faculty of JTS during the Schechter years and later, differed from their genuinely orthodox adversaries in their advocacy of the scientific approach to the study of Judaism, they generally adhered to the personal observance of Jewish law in greater or lesser degrees and were not entirely committed to the creation of a new religious movement within Judaism.[63] Nonetheless, the self-definition of JTS as traditionalist in opposition to Reform, was insufficient to win the support of the Orthodox who maligned JTS as "Schechter's seminary."[64] In consequence, a new Conservative[65] movement gradually emerged with JTS as its primary source of synagogue professionals.[66]

The man behind "Schechter's seminary", Solomon Schechter[67] (1847–1915), grew up in a family of Habad-Lubavitch Hassidim.[68] His given name was Shneur Zalman,[69] while the Yiddish surname "Schechter" attests to his father's position as a Jewish ritual slaughter. Schechter had studied in traditional *yeshivot* in Galicia and Rumania before attending universities in Vienna and Berlin. Claude Montefiore (1858–1938), the British Jewish philanthropist and New Testament scholar brought Schechter to England as his private tutor. Although Schechter had not earned a doctorate,[70] a position was created for him as reader in rabbinics at Cambridge University. It was Schechter who realized the significance of the contents of the Genizah[71] in the Ezra synagogue in Cairo. Thanks to him, some 140,000 fragmentary documents, invaluable for the reconstruction of Jewish history and culture, were brought to Cambridge. The subsequent publication of many of these finds, including a Hebrew manuscript of Ecclesiasticus, not only earned Schechter his scholarly reputation but brought him to the attention of the most prominent American Jewish lay leaders.

Leading American Jews, including Louis Marshall, Jacob Schiff, Felix Warburg, the Lewisohns and the Guggenheims had been increasingly concerned about the breakdown of traditional Jewish life in immigrant families. To be sure, these leaders, members of the Reform Temple Emanuel, who themselves were not ritually observant, did not agonize over the alienation of the immigrants from such identifiably East European traits as strict Sabbath observance and adherence to the Jewish dietary laws. They were mostly concerned with the crime rate among the immigrants and the attraction of their young to socialism and anarchism, all of which reflected negatively on their more prosperous and acculturated coreligionists. Thanks to the efforts of such Philadelphia Jewish intellectuals as Cyrus Adler, his cousin Mayer Sulzberger, and Solomon Solis-Cohen, the New York "Uptown Jews" were persuaded that the ideology of the "Historical School," which valued both secular learning and Jewish ritual law in moderation, coincided with their own social goals. The Jewish philanthropists supported JTS financially because of its potential to train American rabbinic leaders who might build stability among the East European immigrants and westernize them at the same time.[72] Schechter, a charismatic personality, combined traditional East European Jewish learning and a tolerable amount of its religious commitment with some university training, and no less important, with a fine command of written English. To this day, his essays serve as models of scholarly popularization.[73] For his part, Schechter wanted very much to come to America. He felt the need for more money for the support of his family than he could ever hope to make at Cambridge.[74] He also desired a more observant Jewish atmosphere in which to raise his children.

A far stronger scholar than Isaac Mayer Wise, but like him a man of daring and vision, Schechter succeeded in placing JTS on a firm academic foundation by actively recruiting promising young European trained scholars to its faculty.[75] Ironically, the first, and ultimately the most significant, appointment made by Schechter was that of Louis Ginzberg (1873–1953), an outstanding talmudist, whose earlier appointment to HUC had been precipately withdrawn, in part because he accepted the views of higher criticism to which he had been exposed in his university studies.[76] JTS emulated its namesake the *Jüdisch—Theologisches Seminar* of Breslau, Germany in its commitment to the "positive-historical Judaism",[77] preached by Zacharias Frankel (1801–1875) and his circle, which attempted to combine a somewhat lenient orthopraxy with the *Wissenschaft* approach[78] to all of the sources of Judaism, including, in theory, the Bible.[79] Schechter nonetheless, once characterized by an angry Ginzberg as "a Rumanian who never had a proper modern education,"[80] equated biblical criticism with "higher anti-Semitism."[81] Accordingly, his search for a Bible professor led him to orientalists whose primary focus was outside of biblical studies. In 1903 the position in biblical literature and exegesis was first offered to Samuel Posnanski (1864–1921), a Polish-Jewish medievalist especially remembered for his scholarly contributions to the study of the Karaite movement. When Poznanski rejected the offer, Schechter turned to Israel Friedlaender (1876–1920),[82] a graduate of the (Orthodox) Hildesheimer Seminary in Berlin. Friedlaender held great promise in Semitics. He had studied under Theodor Nöldeke, as had Ginzberg at an earlier date, and had come to America recommended by Nöldeke as well as by the great Islamicist Ignaz Goldziher.[83] Although Friedlaender had attended lectures given by the Assyriologist Friedrich Delitzsch and studied Bible with David Zvi Hoffmann,[84] the only orthodox Jew to engage the Wellhausenian hypothesis and attempt its rebuttal, his scholarly interests were in Arabic and Judeo-Arabic.[85] Fully aware of the lacunae in his biblical training, Friedlaender appended to his acceptance of Schechter's offer the following promise:

"I shall seek to familiarize myself with the problems of Biblical scholarship. . . . I intend to make a modest contribution to their clarification and solution."

Friedlaender did not fulfill his promise. It appears that his real interest was the Jewish community rather than the academy.[86] Friedlaender was a tireless worker for Zionism, for Jewish education for children and adults and for the amelioration of the suffering of East European Jewry. Although Friedlaender devoted much time to lecturing and writing popular articles, he nonetheless managed to complete scholarly projects begun in Europe. During his brief lifetime Friedlaender made significant contributions to medieval studies[87] but wrote little in biblical scholarship. We may cite: "The Present Position and Original Form of the Prophecy of Eternal Peace in Isaiah 2:1–5 and Micah 4:1–5."[88] In popular essays, notably in a review of C. Briggs" *Psalms* (New York, 1906–07), Friedlaender polemized against higher biblical criticism.[89] Nonetheless, in other popular pieces of an ideological cast, Friedlaender regularly advocated adherence to "ceremonalism," i.e., observance of ritual law, on the grounds that Ezra:

"understood that prophetic Judaism was indispensible as an ideal . . . but that it was too lofty . . . to serve . . . in everyday existence . . . He therefore proceeded to turn the solid gold bars of prophecy into small coin."[90]

The "small coin" which Ezra made available for everyday use was the law. As Shargel correctly observes:

"Friedlaender's . . . metaphor implies a Wellhausian (sic) conception . . . that the prophets preceded and were in part responsible for the composition of the Pentateuch."[91]

Accordingly, it seems that Friedlaender was more opposed to the tone of classical criticism than to its content. Classical criticism maintained that the encapsulation of prophecy in the law of the Pentateuch had killed prophecy by transforming it into "legalism." Friedlaender, along with the critics and in contrast to traditional Jewish teaching, agreed that the law had chronologically followed prophecy but as a proudly observant Jew[92] applauded the process by which that law had enabled prophecy to become common property. That the form taken by Christian Bible criticism rather than its substance was at issue, may also be seen in Friedlaender's tribute to Arnold Ehrlich, a proponent of both lower and higher criticism.[93]

Neither Schechter's death in 1915 nor Friedlaender's tragic demise at the hand of bandits while on a relief mission in the Ukraine in 1920,[94] brought about a change in the orientation of biblical studies at JTS. Although Schechter was succeeded as President by Cyrus Adler (1863–1940), who had earned his doctorate under the great orientalist and biblicist Paul Haupt,[95] editor of a classic of source-criticism, the *Polychrome Bible,* higher biblical criticism at JTS continued to be viewed with some disdain. Pentateuch criticism was avoided altogether and not taught officially at JTS rabbinical school until 1966.[96]

The negative attitude to critical Jewish biblical scholarship shown by the administration of the two modernist non-orthodox rabbinic schools[97] in America was, fortunately, not unanimous. It is of interest that the Society of Biblical Literature, then the Society of Biblical Literature and Exegesis, founded in 1880, had three Jewish members by 1886,[98] Rabbi Marcus Jastrow, (1829–1903) Rabbi of Temple Rodeph Shalom of Philadelphia, who had taught at Leeser's Maimonides College and was later to produce the standard English language talmudic and targumic dictionary,[99] Gustav Gottheil, Rabbi of Temple Emanuel of New York[100] and his son Dr. Richard Gottheil (1862–1936), professor of Semitic languages at Columbia University.[101]

Coincidentally, in that same year, 1886, Benjamin Szold (1829–

1902), published a Hebrew commentary on Job. Szold, born in Hungary, was expelled from Vienna for his political activities in the revolution of 1848. A former student of Zacharias Frankel and Heinrich Graetz at the Jüdisch-Theologisches Seminar in Breslau, Szold became rabbi of Congregation Oheb Shalom in Baltimore in 1858.

Szold, father of the far better known social activist Henrietta Szold, did not teach at a university or seminary, but was very much involved in communal affairs. As a progressive in religious matters, he often found himself opposed by the left and right wings of American Judaism.[102] Despite his activism, Szold found time for important scholarly contributions, including biblical studies. Of particular interest and still valuable is his commentary on Job.[103] The reader willing to engage the nineteenth century scholarly Hebrew in which the commentary is written will be rewarded with important insights and observations. Szold makes full use of the medieval Jewish commentators but also specifically acknowledges his recourse to Christian scholars including Delitzsch, Ewald and Hitzig. Szold's approach may be characterized as conservative criticism. Textual emendation, although rare, is employed, and higher criticism is cautiously offered. Note his summary statement: "The book [of Job] is a complete whole.... It was not composed at one time.... [Yet] there is no doubt that it was entirely complete in its sections and in its present shape before it entered the Covenant of Scripture and has not been altered since."[104]

A younger contemporary of Szold was Arnold (b. Abraham) Bogumil Ehrlich (1846–1919),[105] who likewise held no academic institutional position in America. An "utterly egocentric personality"[106] who weighed three hundred pounds[107] Ehrlich affected the persona of a recluse, signing his name Shabbetai ben Yom Tob ibn Boded (i.e. "Mr. Lonely-[even] on-Sabbaths-and-Festivals") to his *Mikrâ ki-Pheschutô*. Born in Polish Russia, Ehrlich studied in *heder* and then in *yeshivah*. But his narrow Jewish world held too little for him. Ehrlich's wife did not share his need to experience the larger world. Accordingly, he divorced her and made his way to Leipzig, where under the influence of Christian missionaries and "tempted by prospects of a better position than I could ever attain as an Israelite," he converted to Christianity at the age of twenty-three.[108] In Leipzig, Ehrlich worked with Franz Delitzsch (1813–1899) in his missionary Institutum Judaicum, helping to translate the New Testament into

Hebrew for the purpose of Christian mission to the Jews.[109] After arriving in America in 1876, Ehrlich sought out Rabbi Gustav Gottheil who convened a rabbinic court which accepted him back into the Jewish faith.[110] Although Ehrlich loved America and was an intimate friend of the influential Louis Ginzberg, he could never attain a real academic post. Jews with academic influence suspected his Christian missionary connections. At the same time, Christians probably thought him too much a Polish Jew.[111] In order to support himself and his family, Ehrlich worked at various jobs, including social work, portraiture and private Hebrew teaching. A major scholarly work of Ehrlich's was the three volume commentary *Mikrâ ki-Pheschutô* (German title: *Die Schrift nach ihrem Wortlaut*), which appeared between 1899–1901.[112] Ehrlich derived the title from the hermeneutic dictum recorded in Babylonian Talmud Shabbat 63a: "(Despite the numerous meanings that might be teased out of it,) no scriptural verse (Heb *miqrâ*) may be permitted to escape its plain sense (Heb *pěšûtô*)." Ehrlich chose to write in Hebrew as had Szold. Unlike Szold, Ehrlich explained his choice. With an almost missionary zeal, Ehrlich expressed in the preface his hope that the book would reach "my brethren and my people who understand only Hebrew . . . and demonstrate that its author was a Jew in origin and education." The author first chastises the old style Jewish scholars who worry about the minutiae of Jewish law to the exclusion of all worldly matters. He then directs his ire against the *Wissenschaft* practitioners who "waste their days studying worthless medieval rhymes and rhymesters." Ehrlich laments the absence of Jews from biblical study, an absence attributable in his thinking, to the talmudic dictum that all intellectual development since the days of the early rabbis has been from higher to lower forms.[113] Observing that the allegedly superior ancient rabbis believed in demons and incantations, "which only fools believe in nowadays,"[114] Ehrlich faults his coreligionists for abandoning Bible study to the Christians. Needless to say, Ehrlich does not spare the Christians either. In his opinion, Christian scholarship since Reuchlin's day has benefitted from linguistic advances coupled to the spirit of inquiry. Unfortunately, Christian understanding has been limited, because Christian scholars do not respect the Old Testament on its own terms, but only as a precursor of the New Testament. In addition, because Christians are largely ignorant of post-biblical Hebrew and of the conservatism and continuity of Jewish tradition, they are unable to employ the valuable rabbinic sources in their biblical research. Unlike the Jews, Christian scholars are compelled to rely for comparative philology on the languages of ancient Israel's gentile contemporaries. Ehrlich faults such comparisons because:

"just as the resemblance between fathers and sons is greater than that among brothers, so are the later stages of a language more illuminative of the earlier than is the evidence drawn from the contemporary related languages."[115]

This linguistically dubious statement justifies Orlinsky's suspicion[116] that Ehrlich thought it necessary to defend his frequent recourse to rabbinic Hebrew and Arabic[117] as compensation for his ignorance of Akkadian and the newer discoveries in Northwest Semitic. In addition, *Mikrâ* may be faulted substantively for containing numerous scattered higher critical statements about "early" and "late" sections of the Bible, but no forthright statement about the documentary hypothesis as a whole, as well as for falsely claiming originality for interpretations already offered in medieval Jewish commentaries.[118] Despite these shortcomings and Ehrlich's overly polemical tone, *Mikrâ* demonstrates both its author's enormous talent as a philogist and his fervent desire to attract Jews to Bible study. Non-Jewish scholars are more familiar with Ehrlich's German Bible commentary, *Randglossen zur hebräischen Bibel* (1908–1914), a work that continues to be consulted. *Randglossen* follows the form of *Mikrâ*, but often differs in particulars. Ehrlich's scholarship has been very influential. The preface to the 1917 Jewish Publication Society Bible translation, *The Holy Scriptures,* singles Ehrlich out for special mention together with the medievals Rashi, Kimhi, ibn Ezra, and the modern conservatives, Luzzatto, and Malbim.[119] Later Jewish biblicists, notably the Israeli scholar N. H. Tur-Sinai (Harry Torczyner; 1886–1975), and H. L. Ginsberg, have acknowledged their debt to him.[120] The translators who produced NJV were likewise greatly indebted to Ehrlich.[121]

Unlike Szold and Ehrlich, Morris Jastrow (1861–1921),[122] a son of Rabbi Marcus Jastrow, was very much a professional academician. The elder Jastrow, although not a Bible scholar, served as first editor of the bible translation project undertaken by the Jewish Publication Society to replace the Leeser Bible.[123] Morris Jastrow was brought by his father to Philadelphia as a child but returned to Europe to earn the doctorate at Leipzig in 1884 with a thesis on the medieval Jewish grammarian Judah Hayyuj. Jastrow began teaching at the University of Pennsylvania in 1885 and remained there until his death in 1921. Together with Richard Gottheil of Columbia, likewise the son of a prominent rabbi, Jastrow edited the Semitic Study Series. Although his primary field of interest was Assyriology and especially Mesopotamian religion, Jastrow devoted a great deal of study to the Bible, often bringing Mesopotamian material to bear on biblical interpretation, as in his *Hebrew and Babylonian Tradition* (1919). Jastrow's publications include some forty items in biblical studies, notably books on Ecclesiastes, Job and Canticles.[124] Jastrow also served as Bible editor of the *Jewish Encyclopedia*.[125] He was President of the Society of Biblical Literature in 1916. A great admirer of Keunen and Wellhausen,[126] Jastrow was an outspoken champion of higher criticism, maintaining that "criticism has usurped the place once taken by tradition."[127] Methodologically, Jastrow was consistent, if overly rationalistic, in his higher criticism: "Instead of assuming a combination of many documents, . . . it is a sounder method to assume in many cases a single document extended by glosses, explanatory comments and other kinds of additions by later editors."[128] Jastrow's application of this method may be seen in his Ecclesiastes commentary whose full title is: *A Gentle Cynic, being a translation of the Book of Koheleth, commonly known as Ecclesiastes, stripped of later additions, also its origin, growth and interpretation*.[129] Jastrow accounts for the numerous inconsistencies in Job and Ecclesiastes by arguing that both books originated as short unorthodox works, which were later enlarged by pietists.

Max Margolis (1866–1932) was the most important American Jewish Bible scholar before the First World War in his role as Editor-in-Chief of the 1917 Jewish Publication Society translation of *The Holy Scriptures*.[130] Born in Meretz in Polish Russia into an enlightened rabbinic family, Margolis was tutored as a boy by a Greek Orthodox priest. After completing gymnasium in Berlin, he came to America in 1889 and studied at Columbia University under Richard Gottheil. Margolis earned the Ph.D. in Oriental Studies with a thesis, in Latin, on the use of Rashi's commentary to Babylonian Talmud Erubin to restore its original text.[131] Margolis' first academic position was as Assistant Professor of Hebrew and Biblical Exegesis at Hebrew Union College from 1893–1897. On higher criticism he seems to have agreed with I. M. Wise (see below). Margolis left HUC in 1897 to teach Semitics at Berkeley where he remained until 1905. He enjoyed Berkeley's academic atmosphere greatly. In addition, while teaching there, Margolis met Evelyn Aronson, a member of one of California's oldest and most prominent Jewish families, whom he was later to marry. Nonetheless, he felt the absence of Jewish community[132] and was happy to return to HUC in 1905 as Professor of Biblical Exegesis. His happiness was short-lived. Kaufmann Kohler, president of HUC, who had enthusiastically[133] invited Margolis to return to HUC, was like him, an extremely strong willed individual. On the small HUC faculty constant clashes between the two men were inevitable. To be sure the differences were often clothed in ideological garb. Thus Kohler advocated the lecture method while Margolis maintained that the inductive textual method was more effective. More significant was the issue of Zionism. Kohler had codified the classic anti-Zionist stance of early American Reform Judaism in the Pittsburgh Platform.[134] During the Kohler presidency, chapel sermons advocating Zionism were strongly discouraged or forbidden outright.[135] Margolis, previously opposed to Jewish nationalism, had become converted to Zionism shortly before returning to teach at HUC. Tensions between Kohler and Margolis finally resulted in Margolis' resignation in 1907.[136] Margolis then spent a year in Europe where he completed his *Manual of the Aramaic Language of the Babylonian Talmud*.

In the meantime, the death of editor-in-chief Marcus Jastrow[137] in 1903 had effectively halted the translation project begun in 1892 by the Jewish Publication Society with the goal of replacing Lesser's Bible. Progress had been slow because individual books were first delegated to scholars in England and America and then studied by an editorial committee, which returned their comments to the original translators. In 1908 the Society in cooperation with the Central Conference of American Rabbis (Reform) agreed on the more efficient procedure of translation by which by an editorial board would revise a draft translation to be prepared by its new editor-in-chief. The new board chose Margolis, the only professional Bible scholar among them,[138] to assume the posts of secretary to the Board of Editors and editor-in-chief of the Bible translation.[139] Margolis shared Leeser's high estimation of the Authorized Version but had the further advantage of access to the Revised Version produced by the Church of England in 1885.[140] Margolis, along with his wife who served as his secretary, proceeded to immerse himself in the literature of Elizabethan and Restoration England before beginning the work proper.[141] Far better trained as a text-critic than Lesser had been, Margolis took less than a year[142] to produce a draft translation of the entire Hebrew Bible for the use of the editors. At the same time that Margolis was working on the translation he was also carrying out extensive text-critical researches in the Septuagint, Aquila, Symmachus, Theodotion, the Targums, the Peshitta, the Vulgate and Saadia. The results of Margolis' research were made available to the members of the translation committee in a privately circulated 646 page manuscript of Notes on the New Translation of the Holy Scriptures.

In 1909, while still the beneficiary of one Lesser legacy, the JPS translation project, Margolis became heir to a second, the professorship in Biblical Philology at the Dropsie College for Hebrew and Cognate Learning. Oganized in 1907 in Philadelphia and chartered in 1909, the school was funded by money provided by the will of Moses Dropsie (1821–1905), a Philadelphia lawyer and one-time disciple of Isaac Leeser. Dropsie had desired the creation of a nonsectarian[143] and nontheological school devoted to the study of Hebrew, Biblical and Rabbinic Literature, the Middle East and cognate fields.[144] Leeser's personal library became the basis of the Dropsie collection. The school's first president[145] was Cyrus Adler who had been deeply involved in the reorganization of JTS and would later serve as its president.[146] It was Adler together with Solomon Schechter, who in 1910 revived the moribund British scholarly journal, *Jewish Quarterly Review,* which had been founded in London in 1889. Under the auspices of Dropsie, *JQR* provided an important American outlet for Jewish scholarly publication. The independent, non-denominational character of Dropsie College was a great boon to Margolis who taught there until his death.

Margolis' scholarly contributions were mainly in textual criticism. Some twenty years of his life were dedicated to the goal of producing a true critical edition of the Septuagint, of which only the Greek Joshua actually materialized. Margolis also contributed commentaries on Zephaniah and Malachi to the first Hebrew multi-volume collaborative critical commentary to the Bible, A. Kahana's *Tanak ʿim Perush Madaʿ i*.[147] Naturally, Margolis made use of the versions and of medieval and modern Jewish and Christian scholarship. In these brief commentaries, Margolis is conservative with regard to emendations and rationalistic in approach. Thus, for example, he explains biblical prophecies of total earthly destruction as poetic exaggerations or symbols. Margolis' characteristic attitude to higher critical problems is illustrated by a comment to Malachi 3:22: "Because 'Horeb' is mentioned, Wellhausen has claimed that this is proof that Malachi had only Deuteronomy before him and that the Priestly Code had not yet appeared. But this is insufficient proof. In fact one scholar who assigns a later date [than the rest of Malachi] to verses 22–24 has stated that even after the appearance of the Priestly Code, expressions based on Deuteronomy continued to be employed. If so, we may say that **Malachi had before him the entire Torah just as we have it** [emphasis added]." Margolis' conservatism in matters of higher criticism mars the sections devoted to the history of the biblical period in the classic one-volume *History of the Jewish People*[148] written mostly by Margolis, in collaboration with Alexander Marx. In these chapters, Margolis essentially paraphrases the biblical account, alluding occasionally to "corroborative" archaeological data. Thus, we read (ibid, 15) that "the exodus took place in the spring of the year 1220," undoubtedly because of the famous reference to "Israel" in the stele that dates from Pharaoh Merneptah's fifth regnal year. It is likewise instructive to read Margolis' discussion of the differences between Deuteronomy and the Book of the Covenant (Exodus 21–24), on the issue of centralization of worship (ibid, 19): "Moses now realized the danger to the new and spiritual religion of his foundation, when local habits and pagan superstitions of the former inhabitants might creep in. He accordingly revised his earlier legislation in a new Book of the Covenant issued on the eve of his death in the plains of Moab opposite Jericho."

Among his many distinctions, Margolis served as editor of the *Journal of Biblical Literature* from 1914–1922 and as President of the Society of Biblical Literature in 1923. He was editor of the *Journal of the American Oriental Society* from 1922–1932.

Mention must be made here of Margolis' successor at Berkeley, William Popper (1874–1963).[149] Before coming to Berkeley, Popper had served as acting head of the Oriental Department of the New York Public Library and as an associate editor of the *Jewish Encyclopedia*. A native of St. Louis, Popper had, like Margolis, earned his doctorate at Columbia under Richard Gottheil in 1899, with a dissertation entitled, "The Censorship of Hebrew Books." Subsequently, Popper studied in Europe with the Semiticists J. Euting, T. Nöldeke and H. Derenbourg. Early in his career, Popper devoted several studies to biblical parallelism, which can still be consulted with profit.[150] The bulk of his research however, gradually shifted to Arabic, primarily the historical writings of Yusuf ibn Taghri-Birdi.

Shortly after Margolis' departure from Berkeley provided an opening for Popper, his departure from HUC made way for Julian Morgenstern (1881–1976), whose productive career spanned two generations. Morgenstern joined the HUC faculty in 1907.[151] Born in St. Francisville, Illinois, Morgenstern was ordained at HUC in 1902. He then studied Assyriology in Germany with such luminaries as Friedrich Delitzsch, Bruno Meissner and Carl Bezold, earning a Ph.D at Heidelberg in 1904 with a dissertation on "The Doctrine of Sin in Babylonian Religion." Assyriology however, was soon replaced by Bible as the focus of Morgenstern's scholarly interests. Indeed, Morgenstern was the first American Jewish scholar with a primary scholarly interest in Bible, to practice higher biblical criticism systematically. In some respects, Morgenstern may be considered a Jewish bridge to what was then a gentile discipline. A firm adherent of the documentary hypothesis in the European tradition of critical Christian Bible scholarship, Morgenstern added a K(enite) source of his own. Morgenstern denied the Mosaic authorship of the Torah. Indeed, he called on the Reform rabbinate to take a public stand against Mosaic authorship because that would help justify Reform's stand against the binding character of Jewish law.[152] Kaufmann Kohler was himself a staunch advocate of higher criticism. Accordingly, the triumph of critical biblical study at HUC was assured. Morgenstern, unlike his predecessors of the Wise years, had no reason to be reticent. He wrote voluminously on such matters as calendar studies, Pentateuchal law, prophecy and the history of the cult.[153] Because Morgenstern contributed annually to *HUCA*, one of his articles appeared in a volume that turned out to be his own Festschrift.[154] Morgenstern's work is quite free in regard to textual emendations and rearrangements of verses and chapters. Although he began as an ardent Wellhausenian, later in his career Morgenstern began to realize the insufficiency of literary criticism alone to reconstruct the biblical world. In his presidential address to the SBL in 1941, Morgenstern referred to the "increasingly outmoded documentary techniques,"[155] and called for a synthesis of classical biblical study with archaeology, folklore studies, and religious phenomenology. As President of HUC from 1922–1947, Morgenstern was responsible for its major institutional growth. In that same capacity he was able to save many Jewish scholars from the Nazis by bringing them to HUC. Although Morgenstern's actual writings have not been very influential in recent years, the programmatic synthesis he called for in 1941 is now a universally accepted goal of Bible scholarship.

Less productive than Morgenstern but nevertheless worthy of mention, is Moses Buttenwieser (1862–1939), first a teacher and later a colleague of Morgenstern's at HUC. Born at Beerfelden, Hessen Darmstadt, Buttenwieser studied at Wurzburg and Leipzig, earning his Ph.D. in 1896 at Heidelberg with a dissertation on the Hebrew Elijah Apocalypse. A year later Buttenwieser became Assistant Professor of Biblical Exegesis at HUC. Although Buttenwieser accepted Wellhausenian theory, he did not have to clash with I.M. Wise because his interests were outside of Pentateuch. In his personal life, Buttenwieser was known as a consistent champion of social justice who took the prophets as role models.[156] His major scholarly works were: *The Prophets of Israel* (1914), *The Book of Job* (1922) and *The Psalms, Chronologically Treated with a New Translation* (1938).[157] Blank has aptly noted, if understated, that "a fair amount of subjectivity"[158] attaches to Buttenwiser's method. Indeed, Buttenwieser believed that he could precisely date specific passages in the books he treated. Although contemporary scholars would consider his historical approach arbitrary, it must be acknowledged that Buttenwieser was a superior Semitic philologist and grammarian whose translations of poetic passages may still be consulted with benefit.[159]

We have thus far surveyed the contributions of individual American Jewish Bible scholars. It remains to comment on the most important collective effort of early twentieth century Jewish scholarship, *The Jewish Encyclopedia*.[160] A private undertaking, not sponsored by a university or a seminary, *JE* was originally conceived by Isidore Singer, a journalist and promoter who hoped to enrich himself by soliciting Jewish sports figures and businessmen who might be flattered by having their biographies in print and willing to pay for the privilege.[161] Ironically, *JE* turned out to be an invaluable contribution to scholarship, with many articles that may still be consulted with profit eighty years later. The twelve volume work contained contributions from scholars all over the world, mostly, but not exclusively Jewish. To a great extent, *JE* was a summation of nineteenth century *Wissenschaft des Judentums*.[162] We have seen that Morris Jastrow served as Bible editor.[163] Nonetheless, characteristically, non-Jewish scholars predominated in the area of Bible, among them Barton, Budde, Buhl, Conybeare and Torrey. Characteristic as well was the arrangement of Bible articles in the encyclopedia. These were divided in three sections: a) biblical data, i.e. text summaries; b) comments on the particular biblical topic drawn from rabbinic literature; c) critical view, as held in contemporary scholarship. Readers were thus enabled to ignore the offending section, which for most, was the third.

On the eve of the First World War, various historical factors had conspired to make Philadelphia and Cincinnati the two institutional centers of American Jewish Bible scholarship. Jewish scholarship in America, to a greater extent than Christian, remained dependent on Europe. The simple fact that Jews were a minority meant that there were many more Christian than Jewish seminaries in the United States and in consequence more opportunities for Christian scholars to study and teach. University appointments in Bible were generally held by Christians. The Jewish scholars whose work we have described thus far were few in number and either European born or European trained. Only during the next generation would the situation begin to change.

Notes to American Beginnings

1. See A. Karp, *Haven and Home A History of the Jews in America* (New York: Schocken, 1985), 51–83. As one succinct formulation has it: "The intellectual and religious traditions of American Jewry . . . have shallow roots." See A. Hertzberg, *The Jews in America* (New York: Simon and Schuster, 1988), 13.

2. For a comprehensive survey of American Jewish biblical scholarship until 1972 see the necrology by H. M. Orlinsky, "Jewish Biblical Scholarship in America," in idem, *Essays in Biblical Culture and Bible Translation* (New York: Ktav, 1974), 287–332; Cf. idem. "Old Testament Studies," in P. Ramsey (ed.), *Religion* (Englewood: Prentice-Hall, 1965; In the *Princeton Studies: Humanistic Scholarship in America*), 51–109. In addition to Orlinsky's surveys, see I. Abrahams, "Bible: Exegesis among Jews in the Modern Period," *Encyclopaedia Judaica* 4, 899–904; S. Blank, "Bible" in S. Karff (ed.), *Hebrew Union College-Jewish Institute of Religion at One Hundred Years* (Cincinnati: Hebrew Union College, 1976), 287–316; S. David Sperling, "Judaism and Modern Biblical Research," in L. Boadt and L. Klenicki (eds.), *Biblical Studies: Meeting Ground of Jews and Christians* (New York: Stimulus, 1980) 19–44; B. Levine, "A Decade of Jewish Bible Scholarship in North America," *Jewish Book Annual* 39 (1981–1982), 9–29; S. D. Sperling and B. Levine, "Biblical Scholarship, Modern," in G. Abram-

son (ed.), *Blackwell Companion to Jewish Culture From the Eighteenth Century to the Present* (Oxford: Basil Blackwell, 1989), 87-91.

3. The figure is from Karp, *Haven*. See ibid, Appendix 1-4 for American Jewish population tables from 1790-1980. For the slightly larger figure of "perhaps 2,000." See Hertzberg, *Jews*, 49.

4. In 1871, the first census after confederation showed 1,115 Jews in Canada. For population figures see B. Kayfetz, "Canada," *EncJud* 5, 104-105.

5. Both Karp, *Haven* and Hertzberg, *Jews* offer excellent detailed narrative histories of the American Jewish community from its beginnings to the present. For a briefer sketch of American Jewish history with extensive bibliography, see M. Atkin, "United States of America," *EncJud* 15, 1585-1671; See further, A. Hertzberg, "The American Jew and his Religion," in J. Neusner, (ed.), *Understanding American Judaism* (New York: Ktav, 1975) I, 5-24; On the paucity of Jewish books and educators in mid-nineteenth century America, see M. Davis, *The Emergence of Conservative Judaism* (Philadelphia: Jewish Publication Society, 1963), 47-55. Davis notes (ibid, 55) that in the eighteen-forties some sixty men served as congregational rabbis and *hazzanim*. Of these, only the Reform Max Lilienthal and the Orthodox Abraham Rice (Reiss) were known to have genuine rabbinic ordination; cf. the material assembled in the somewhat overly-polemical biography of Rice by I. H. Sharfman, *The First Rabbi* (Malibu: Joseph Simon Panngloss, 1988). See further, E. Silberschlag, "The Primacy of Hebrew in Early America," in *Hebrew Studies* 16 (1985; Katsh volume), 123.

6. See L. Sussman, "Isaac Leeser and the Protestantization of American Judaism," in *American Jewish Archives* 38 (April, 1986), 20, n. 49.

7. For a recent bibliography of studies on Leeser, see L. Sussman, "Isaac Leeser and the Protestantization of American Judaism," *American Jewish Archives* 38 (April, 1986), 16, n. 4. For much of what follows we are indebted to idem, "Another Look at Isaac Leeser and the First Jewish Translation of the Bible in the United States," *Modern Judaism* 5 (1985), 159-190. For a reliable biography of Leeser see now idem, "The Life and Career of Isaac Leeser (1806-1868): A Study of American Judaism in its Formative Period," (unpublished Ph.D. thesis, Hebrew Union College-Jewish Institute of Religion; Cincinnati, 1987).

8. See J. Katz, *Out of the Ghetto* (New York: Schocken, 1978).

9. The earliest modernist rabbinical seminary was the Instituto Convitto Rabbinico founded in 1829 in Padua. A year later the École Centrale Rabbinique opened in Metz. Other significant seminaries were the Jüdisch-Theologisches Seminar of Breslau, founded in 1854; Jews' College in London (1855); Israelitisch-theologische Lehranstalt in Vienna (1862); Hochschüle für die Wissenschaft des Judentums in Berlin (1873); Rabbiner Seminar für das Orthodoxe Judentume in Berlin (1874); and Orzságos Rabbiképzö Intézet (= Franz-Josef Landesrabbinerschule) in Budapest in 1877. For a historical outline with bibliography see L. Rabinowitz, "Rabbinical Seminaries," *EncJud* 13, 1463-1466.

10. The radically innovative character of the modernist seminaries may

be appreciated by observing with Rabinowitz, ("Rabbinical Seminaries," 1464), that such institutions never took root in Russia, Poland, or for that matter in modern Israel, where the old style talmudical academy *(yeshivah)* retained its predominance.

11. See Sussman, "Protestantization," 10–11. The job of the factotum sometimes required him to teach the native European language of the synagogue's adult members to the children. See the synagogue advertisements cited by Sussman, ibid, 19.

12. In Karp's *(Haven,* 67) felicitious formulation: "Leeser . . . had the grace never to call himself 'Rabbi'. Others readily conferred ordination and doctorates upon themselves." Nonetheless, the introduction to the authoritative *TANAKH A New Translation of the Holy Scriptures According to the Traditional Hebrew Text* (Philadelphia: Jewish Publication Society, 1985), xvii persists in referring to Leeser as "the American rabbi."

13. B. Korn, apud, Sussman, "Another Look," 159.

14. Maimonides College enrolled four students in 1867. By the time it closed its doors four years later, it had trained three men for the rabbinate. See Davis, *Emergence,* 59–64.

15. I. Leeser, *The Law of God. Edited, with Former Translations Diligently Compared and Revised* (Philadelphia: C. Sherman, 5605 [=1844–1845]).

16. I. Leeser, *The Twenty-Four Books of the Holy Scriptures: Carefully Translated According to the Massoretic Text, on the Basis of the English Version, after the Best Jewish Authorities; and Supplied with Short Explanatory Notes* (Philadelphia, 5614 [=1853–1854]).

17. Thanksgiving Day sermon, December 21, 1843, quoted by Sussman, "Another Look," 171. The very act of preaching a sermon on Thanksgiving Day exemplifies Leeser's Americanization as well as his acceptance of a Protestant model.

18. Sussman, *Modern Judaism* 5, 161.

19. See Sussman, "Protestantization," 4–6. It is of interest that Leeser in collaboration with Joseph Jaquett, an Episcopalian cleric, published an untranslated *Biblia Hebraica* in 1848. See Sussmann, "Another Look," 166.

20. Leeser, *Twenty-Four Books,* iii. Note the words "on the Basis of the English Version," in the full title.

21. ibid, vii.

22. Their lack of Hebrew fluency also required the production of English prayer books. Solomon Jackson had published a prayer book in Hebrew and English in 1826. Leeser provided an edition of the Spanish and Portugese rite with translation in 1836, and a corresponding German rite version in 1848. See Karp, *Haven,* 37–38.

23. ibid, vii–viii.

24. For numerous examples of such tendentious renditions along with a detailed appreciation and critique of Leeser as translator see M. Tsevat, "A Retrospective View of Isaac Leeser's Biblical Work," in J. Marcus (ed.), *Essays in American Jewish History* (Cincinnati: American Jewish Archives, 1958), 295–313.

25. See the remarks about "'And Bibles'," in Orlinsky, *Essays*, 410–411.
26. See I. Abrahams apud Tsevat, "Retrospective," 296, n. 4.
27. See Sussman, "Another Look," 169.
28. See Karp, *Haven*, Appendix 1.
29. See Hertzberg, *Jews*, 121.
30. This is not to say that that Jews had suffered no ethnic prejudice before the mass immigrations. See M. Selzer, *Kike* (New York: Meridian, 1972), 9–39.
31. See Orlinsky, "Scholarship," 288; cf. E. Silberschlag, "The Primacy of Hebrew in Early America," in *Hebrew Studies* 16 (1985; Katsh volume), 123. Hertzberg notes (*Jews*, 50) that in the 1770's when Rhode Island College, now Brown University, offered to establish a chair in Hebrew and Oriental Languages the wealthy Jewish merchants declined to contribute funds.
32. See Hertzberg, "American Jew," 9.
33. On the history, structure and curriculum of the *yeshivah* see I. Assaf, W. Brickman et al, "Yeshivot," *EncJud* 16, 762–773. No less an authority than Elijah b. Solomon of Vilna (1720–1797), "the Gaon of Vilna" had failed in his attempt to reform the curriculum so that students might learn Bible properly before turning to Talmud. See E. Ginzberg, *Keeper of the Law: Louis Ginzberg* (Philadelphia: Jewish Publication Society, 1966), 24. Ginzberg (ibid) quotes the saying that "Jews learned their Bible from Talmud."
34. In nineteenth century eastern Europe it was the practice to ordain only married students. Because the *yeshivot* had facilities only for unmarried students, married men seeking ordination united in a study-community known as a *kolel*, where they and their families were supported out of communal funds for the three to four years needed to master the code literature. See Assaf, "Yeshivot," 769–770.
35. See Katz, *Ghetto*, 129–130.
36. Herder, writing in the eighteenth century, set the tone for the common nineteenth century view that the restoration community of the sixth century B.C. was degenerate in comparison with pre-exilic Israel: "When the Jews . . . returned from bondage . . . they built a temple, as if this would have revived the times of Moses and Solomon: their religion was pharisaical; their learning a minute nibbling at syllables." (cited from J. Rogerson, *Old Testament Criticism in the Nineteenth Century England and Germany*, London: Fortress, 1985], 43). Similarly, in the first decade of the nineteenth century de Wette wrote: "Das Judenthum ist das Unglück, das Christenthum der Trost dafür." (Rogerson, ibid, 41, n. 57). In describing the literature of the post-exilic period Wilhelm Gesenius wrote: "Die Bücher Daniel, Esther, Jona enthalten Legenden in einem gesunkenen jüdischen Geschmacke." (See Rogerson, ibid, 53, n. 16).
37. See references in Sperling, "Judaism," 23.
38. See L. Silberman, "Wellhausen and Judaism," *Semeia* 25 (1983), 79–82. On Silberman's analysis, we must include Wellhausen in the tradition of

Christians whose characterization of their opponents as "Judaizers" has little or nothing to do with Jews or Judaism. It was Wellhausen who personally encouraged Silberman's teacher Jacob Lauterbach in the study of rabbinics in which he was to excel. It must be said nonetheless, that Jewish readers of Wellhausen and his colleagues in biblical studies might readily be discouraged from pursuing a field in which scholarly literature abounded in rhetoric inimical to Judaism.

39. Jews could easily take offense with such summaries of their religion as the following: "Judaism . . . is a mass of antinomies. We are struck with the free flight of thought and the deep inwardness of feeling which are found in some passages in the Wisdom and in the Psalms; but, on the other hand, we meet with a pedantic asceticism which is far from lovely, and with pious wishes the greediness of which is ill-concealed; and these unedifying features are the dominant ones of the system. . . . The Creator of heaven and earth becomes the manager of a petty scheme of salvation. . . . The Law takes the soul out of religion and spoils morality. . . . The labour is done for the sake of the exercise; it does no one any good, and rejoices neither God nor man." The above is taken from Wellhausen's article "Israel" appended to J. Wellhausen, *Prolegomena to the History of Ancient Israel* (Cleveland: Meridian, 1961 [originally published in 1878]), 509.

40. This was true in Europe as well. See Rogerson, *Criticism*.

41. See E. W. Saunders, *Searching the Scriptures, A History of the Society of Biblical Literature, 1880–1980* (Chico: Scholars, 1982), 17–18. For earlier nineteenth century American controversies over Bible study see J. Brown, *The Rise of Biblical Criticism in America, 1800–1870, The New England Scholars*. Middletown: Wesleyan, 1969.

42. At the ill-fated Maimonides College, Bible had been taught by Sabato Morais, a man of strong conservative bent. See Davis, *Emergence*, 61, and see below.

43. On Wise see M. Meyer, "In the Days of Isaac Mayer Wise," apud Karff, *Hebrew Union College*, 7–47; For further bibliography see ibid, 248, n.4.

44. See Meyer, ibid, 11; Cf. W. Jacob, "The Influence of the Pittsburgh Platform on Reform Halakhah and Biblical Study," in idem (ed.), *The Pittsburgh Platform in Retrospect* (Pittsburgh: Rodef Shalom, 1985), 28.

45. Wise had established the Zion Collegiate Institute in 1855. It fell victim to apathy and lack of financial support. See Davis, *Emergence*, 56–67.

46. ibid, 42.
47. ibid, 20.
48. ibid, 44.
49. I. M. Wise, *Pronaos to Holy Writ Establishing on Documentary Evidence the Authorship, Date, Form and Contents of Each of the Books and the Authenticity of the Pentateuch* (Cincinnati: Robert Clarke and Company, 1891). For a detailed critique see S. Sandmel, "Isaac Mayer Wise's Pronaos to Holy Writ," in B. Korn (ed.), *A Bicentennial Festschrift for Jacob Rader Marcus* (New York and Waltham: American Jewish Historical Society and Ktav, 1976), 517–525.

50. *Pronaos*, iv.
51. See below.
52. Blank apud Meyer, 288-289.
53. Such courses in "Commentaries" are now offered at HUC under the aegis of the Rabbinics Department.
54. Meyer apud Karff, 194.
55. Alexander Kohut (1842-1894) contributed significantly to Semitic lexicography with his eight volume edition of the medieval talmudic dictionary of Nathan ben Jehiel (1035-ca. 1110), which appeared as *Aruch Completum* (8 volumes, reprint New York, 1955).
56. According to Karp, (*Haven*, 59) Szold's Oheb Shalom in Baltimore "may well have been the "first . . . Conservative (although this term began to be used only later) congregation." Nonetheless, both Oheb Shalom and Jastrow's Rodeph Shalom in Philadelphia were members of the Union of American Hebrew Congregations organized by I. M. Wise. See Meyer apud Karff, *Hebrew Union College*, 39. Szold gave the opening address at the first HUC ordination in 1883 (ibid, 38). Hertzberg, *(Jews)* refers to Szold as a "Reform rabbi." Davis, *(Emergence,* 17) characterizes Szold as theologically more radical than I. M. Wise.
57. Wise had always favored unity over ideology (Jacob, *Pittsburgh Platform*, 26). Indeed the Cleveland Conference called by Wise in 1855 included Leeser as a participant. (Meyer apud Karff, *Hebrew Union College,* 38). Among the Cleveland declarations of principle were the following: "The Bible as delivered to us by our fathers and as now in our possession is of immediate divine origin and the standard of our religion. The Talmud contains the traditional legal and logical exposition of the biblical laws, which must be expounded and practiced according to the comments of the Talmud." (Jacob, *Pittsburgh Platform,* 26) The fact that the call for the Pittsburgh Conference came from Kaufmann Kohler demonstrated that the radical wing was in control and prompted the more traditional elements to avoid the conference entirely (Jacob, ibid, 28-29).
58. Among other things, the Philadelphia conference repudiated Davidic Messianism and maintained that the dispersion of the Jews was not a "punishment for the sinfulness of Israel" but a "realization of their high-priestly mission, to lead the nations to the true knowledge and worship of God." See D. Polish, "The Changing and the Constant in the Reform Rabbinate," in *American Jewish Archives* (November, 1983), 270.
59. In general see the studies in Jacob (ed.), *Pittsburgh Platform*. No direct transcript of the Pittsburgh meetings has survived. See Jacob, ibid, 28.
60. When questioned by a reporter about the plan to bring Rabbi Jacob Joseph of Vilna to New York as chief rabbi of the Association of American Orthodox Congregations, Sabato Morais stated: "I never before heard of Rabbi Joseph. I am familiar with the manner in which the Hebrews in the place when he comes are educated, and I know he is not a cultured man. He does not possess the knowledge nor the literary attainments which a rabbi should possess." See A. Karp, "The Conservative Rabbi—'Dissatisfied But Not Unhappy'," *American Jewish Archives* 35 (1983) 199-200.
61. See Karp, "Conservative Rabbi," 196. On the question of Morais'

orthodoxy see ibid, 195–196. See further the discussion and bibliography in J. Gurock, "Resisters and Accomodators: Varieties of Orthodox Rabbis in America, 1886–1893," ibid, 162–163.

62. Karp, "Conservative Rabbi," 201. Financial difficulties at both JTS and HUC had led two of New York's wealthiest Reform Jews, Jacob Schiff and Louis Marshall, to advocate a merger of the two institutions. See Meyer, apud Karff, *Hebrew Union College,* 51–52.

63. It is significant that the Reform HUC consciously arrogated to itself the authority of the classical *yeshivah* by granting its rabbinic graduates the traditional *semikah* "judicial authorization" whose central clause is the talmudic formula: *yoreh yoreh yadin yadin* "Shall he rule? He shall rule! Shall he judge? He shall judge!" In contrast, although the English version of the JTS ordination confers the degree of "Rabbi, Teacher and Preacher" on rabbinic graduates, the Hebrew version withholds the traditional *semikah* because students are not required to master the law codes. In a similar vein, the Seminary synagogue differed from nearly all other Conservative synagogues in requiring separate seating for men and women in pseudo-Orthodox fashion (no physical partition or separate gallery as required by classical Jewish law) and in the use of prayer books produced under Orthodox auspices.

64. The derogation was employed at least until the nineteen sixties, long after Schechter's death. A more extreme form was "Schechter's cemetery," i.e., the place to bury one's Judaism.

65. "Schechter emphatically deprecated all attempts to have the movement which he inaugurated labelled 'Conservative'." So, Mordecai Kaplan, *Judaism as a Civilization* (New York, 1934), 163.

66. For details of early JTS history see Davis, *Emergence*. As yet, there is no standard history of JTS and the Conservative movement from 1902 onward. Of great value however, is A. Karp, "A Century of Conservative Judaism in the United States," *American Jewish Yearbook* 86 (1986), 3–61; See also idem, "Conservative Rabbi;" Much useful information about JTS until the 1950's can be found readily in Ginzberg, *Keeper*. See also M. Waxman (ed.), *Tradition and Change; The Development of Conservative Judaism* (New York: Burning Bush, 1958); A. Hertzberg, "Conservative Judaism," *EncJud* 5, 901–906; A. Kass, "Jewish Theological Seminary of America, The (JTS)," ibid, 10, 95–97.

67. A critical biography of Schechter remains a desideratum. For a basic chronological account see N. Bentwich, *Solomon Schechter a Biography* (Philadelphia: Jewish Publication Society, 1938).

68. For an outline of the tenets of this sect see R. Elior, "HaBaD: The Contemplative Ascent to God," in A. Green (ed.), *Jewish Spirituality II* (New York: Crossroad, 1987), 157–205.

69. To this day it remains customary within Habad Lubavitch to name male children after the cult's founder Shneur Zalman of Lyady (1745–1813).

70. Schechter claimed rabbinic ordination from both I. H. Weiss of Vienna and Z. Frankel of Berlin. In 1892 Cambridge awarded Schechter the M.A. *honoris causa*. See A. Karp, "Solomon Schechter Comes to America," *American Jewish Historical Quarterly* 53 (1963), 44–62.

71. For a brief description see A. Habermann, "Genizah," *EncJud* 7, 403-407.

72. See Karp, *Haven,* 99-102; For a list of the largest contributors to the endowment of the new JTS see Ginzberg, *Keeper,* 91.

73. See e.g. S. Schechter, *Studies in Judaism* (Reprint Philadelphia: Jewish Publication Society and Meridian, 1958).

74. In Cambridge, Schechter was dependent on the private support of Claude Montefiore, who in contrast to Schechter, was opposed to Zionism, favored Sunday Sabbaths and preferred English language religious services. See Karp, "Schechter," 56-57.

75. See Karp, *Haven,* 210.

76. Ginzberg,; *Keeper,* 60-63. Ginzberg had earned his Ph.D. studying under Nöldeke at Strassburg and Bezold at Heidelberg. See ibid, 47-58. For Ginzberg's acceptance of the documentary hypothesis see L. Ginzberg, "Law, Codification of," in *Jewish Encyclopedia* 7, 635-647.

77. See "Juedisch-Theologisches Seminar, Breslau," in *EncJud* 10: 465-466. The buildings of JTS bear a striking resemblance to the Breslau Seminary. Cf. the respective photographs in ibid. 97 and 465. It is of interest that Ismar Schorsch, current chancellor of JTS, in an address delivered on December 10, 1986, spoke of JTS as "founded first in Breslau and then in New York." See I. Schorsch, *Thoughts from 3080 Selected Addresses and Writings* (n.d., n.p.), 24; cf. ibid, 17, 49.

78. The ideology of positive-historical Judaism as advocated by Frankel and emulated by the JTS of America is quintessentially expressed in Z. Frankel, "On Changes in Judaism," in Waxman, (ed.), *Tradition and Change,* 43-50.

79. According to its original preamble adopted on May 6, 1886, JTS was to be a "seminary where the Bible shall be impartially taught." See Karp, *Haven,* 97.

80. Ginzberg, *Keeper,* 89.

81. See S. Schechter, "Higher Criticism—Higher Anti-Semitism," in idem, *Seminary Addresses and Other Papers* (Cincinnati: Ark, 1915), 36-37. On March 26, 1903, Schechter delivered an address in which he said: "Wellhausen's *Prolegomena* and *History* are teeming with aperçus full of venom against Judaism." See Silberman, "Wellhausen," 26.

82. For biographical details see B. Shargel, *Practical Dreamer: Israel Friedlaender and the Shaping of American Judaism* (New York: Jewish Theological Seminary, 1985).

83. See Shargel, *Dreamer,* 192.

84. See Shargel, *Dreamer,* 45.

85. Friedlaender's thesis was published as *Der Sprachgebrauch des Maimonides. Ein lexikalischer und grammatischer Beitrag zur Kenntnis des Mittelarabischen* (Frankfurt am Main, 1902).

86. For details of Friedlaender's communal activities see Shargel, *Dreamer.* In addition, see Ginzberg, *Keeper,* 150; Karp, *Haven,* 167-169.

87. See Orlinsky, "Scholarship," 313-316. For a complete bibliography see Shargel, *Dreamer,* 202-204.

88. *Jewish Quarterly Review* N.S. 6 (1916), 405-413. Although

Friedlaender refers to Christian scholars, including Wellhausen, he does not seriously engage the critical issues of the prophetic doublet. More incisive is the brief note, "Das hebräische *seper* in einer verkannten Bedeutung," *JQR* O.S. 15 (1903), 102–103. In all likelihood, Friedlaender had written the note in Europe, because he did not arrive in America until September, 1903. See Shargel, *Dreamer*, 6.

89. I. Friedlaender, "A New Specimen of Modern Biblical Exegesis," *American Hebrew and Jewish Messenger* 81 (July 5, 1907): Literary Supplement, 3–7.

90. Friedlaender apud Shargel, *Dreamer*, 57.

91. Shargel, *Dreamer*, 61.

92. Like Schechter, Friedlaender was not punctilious in observance. It was known that he somehow managed to come to Sabbath morning services at JTS in Manhattan from far-off Staten Island.

93. See the eulogy by Friedlaender, "A Great Bible Scholar, Arnold B. Ehrlich," *Nation*, January 10, 1920, 41. On Ehrlich see below.

94. See Shargel, *Dreamer*, 32–35.

95. See Orlinsky, "Scholarship," 304–305.

96. Louis Finkelstein (b. 1895; Friedlaender's brother-in-law), who succeeded Adler as President (later: Chancellor) of JTS in 1940, remarked on several occasions that "what was good enough for Schechter" as regards the avoidance of higher criticism was good enough for Finkelstein. This is not to say that classical Pentateuch criticism went unnoted. Students in classes dealing with the history of the biblical period were often assigned secondary sources referring to the documentary hypothesis. Nonetheless, the first course in Pentateuch employing the critical method to be offered officially in the Bible Department of JTS rabbinical school was "Exodus," given in 1966–67 by Moshe Greenberg, then visiting from the University of Pennsylvania. Previously, there had been offered only a pre-critical preparatory course entitled "The Pentateuch with Rashi's Commentary," for students insufficiently prepared to enter the rabbinic program proper. In an oral communication (June 20, 1987), Professor Abraham Karp and Mrs. Deborah Karp recalled that Mordecai Kaplan (1881–1983), the founder of the Reconstructionist movement, had regularly taught Pentateuch criticism in his homiletics classes at JTS as background for preaching from the Bible. Kaplan, a member of the 1902 graduating class of JTS, had been introduced to higher biblical criticism by Arnold Ehrlich who belonged to the personal circle of Kaplan's father the Orthodox Rabbi Israel Kaplan, himself brought to America at the invitation of Rabbi Jacob Joseph. See A. Hertzberg in the Introduction to Kaplan, *Judaism as a Civilization*, xxii–xxiv.

97. The first modern Orthodox rabbinic school to survive and flourish in America was Rabbi Isaac Elhanan Theological Seminary (RIETS), organized in 1897. On its background see J. Gurock, "Resisters," 129–130. RIETS eventually grew into what is now Yeshiva University. On Yeshiva's contribution to biblical study see Chapter Seven below.

98. Saunders, *Searching*, 6–7.

99. M. Jastrow, *A Dictionary of the Targumim, the Talmud Babli and Yerushalmi, and the Midrashic Literature*. New York, 1903.

100. Gottheil served as superintendent of an ill-fated rabbinic school in New York City known variously as the Emanu-El Theological Seminary, The American Hebrew College of the City of New York, and the Hebrew Theological Seminary Association. The school operated from 1877–1885. See Davis, *Emergence*, 57–58; Meyer apud Karff, *Hebrew Union College*, 40–41. There is much valuable background information relevant to our topic in R. Gottheil, *The Life of Gustav Gottheil: Memoir of a Priest in Israel* (Williamsport: Bayard, 1936).

101. On Gottheil the younger see the memorial notice by J. Bloch, "Richard James Horatio Gottheil 1862–1936," in *JAOS* 56 (1936), 480–489. Gottheil's original appointment at Columbia was to a Chair of Rabbinical literature endowed initially (1887–1892) by Temple Emanuel. Subsequently under Gottheil the chair developed into a Division of Oriental Languages. (See Gottheil, *Memoir*, 196–216). During his years at Columbia, Gottheil taught in most areas of Semitic, including Bible. He served as president of The Society of Biblical Literature in 1903. The bulk of his publication however, was devoted to Syriac rather than to Bible proper. See the bibliography by I. Pratt, *JAOS* ibid, 480–489.

102. On Szold see Davis, *Emergence*, 360–362. On Szold's work see further, Orlinsky, "Scholarship," 296–297.

103. *Sefer Iyyob Mebu'ar Mehadash-Das Buch Hiob nebst einem neuen Commentar* (Baltimore, 1886).

104. ibid, 22.

105. See Orlinsky, "Scholarship," 297–299; idem, "Prolegomenon" to A. Ehrlich, *Mikrâ ki-Pheschutô (Die Schrift nach ihrem Wortlaut;* Berlin, 1903; Reprint, New York: Ktav, 1969), ix–xxxiii; Gottheil, *Memoir*, 75–81. For Ehrlich's given name, a photograph of him, his second wife and his American family as well as additional biographical details, see J. Kabakoff, "New Light on Arnold Bogomil Ehrlich," *American Jewish Archives* 36, No. 2, (Nov., 1984), 202–224.

106. Orlinsky, Prologomenon to reprint of *Mikrâ*, ix.

107. Ginzberg, *Keeper*, 64.

108. The quotation that indicates that Ehrlich's conversion to Christianity was opportunistic is taken from the "Minute" recorded by Gustav Gottheil on behalf of the ecclesiastical court which received Ehrlich back into Judaism. In Ehrlich's own German language letter to the Jewish ecclesiastical court dated March 7, 1876, he attributes his conversion to Christianity to mental instability ("von einem mir selbst nicht Recht bewusten Wahne bethört.") For both documents see Gottheil, *Memoir*, 76–77.

109. Ehrlich claimed that for the most part the translation was of his doing. See Gottheil, *Memoir*, 76.

110. Ehrlich subsequently served as tutor in Bible, Mishnah, Talmud and Modern Hebrew to the young Richard Gottheil. He also taught in the preparatory school of Temple Emanuel. See Gottheil, *Memoir*, 77.

111. De Sola Pool, apud Orlinsky, *Mikrâ* repr., x–xi.

112. The dedication reads: "Den Manen seines unvergesslichen väterlichen Freundes Franz Delitzsch widmet dieses Werk der Verfasser."

113. *Mikrâ*, xxxvi.

114. ibid.
115. ibid, xxxvii.
116. Prolegomenon to *Mikrâ*, xviii.
117. Ehrlich had taught himself Arabic by "working throughout the day and a good part of the night with his feet in cold water as a means of remaining awake." See Gottheil, *Memoir*, 79.
118. ibid, xxiv.
119. *The Holy Scriptures according to the Masoretic Text a New Translation* (Philadelphia: Jewish Publication Society, 1917), vii.
120. A major work of Tur-Sinai's follows the pattern of *Mikrâ* and *Randglossen* and is entitled *Peshutô shel Mikrâ* (Jerusalem: Qiryath-Sefer, 1962–68).
121. See the numerous references to Ehrlich in the index to H. M. Orlinsky, *Notes on the New Translation of the Torah*. (Philadelphia, 1969), 273.
122. See Orlinsky, "Scholarship," 300–302; C. H. Gordon, *The Pennsylvania Tradition of Semitics* (Atlanta: Scholars, 1986), 13–32.
123. The elder Jastrow was also responsible for preparing the Job translation. See *Holy Scriptures*, v.
124. For bibliography see *JAOS* 41 (1921), 337–344.
125. See below.
126. See M. Jastrow Jr., "Constructive Elements in the Critical Study of the Old Testament," *JBL* 36 (1917), 4.
127. ibid, 7.
128. ibid, 23. It may be noted that this approach has become newly popular, particularly in the writings of John van Seters. See e.g. his *Abraham in History and Tradition* (New Haven: Yale, 1975).
129. Philadelphia: Lippincott, 1919.
130. For biographical details see L. Greenspoon, *Max Leopold Margolis A Scholar's Scholar* (Atlanta: Scholars, 1987). A brief account of Margolis' life and essays on various aspects of Margolis' scholarship may be found in R. Gordis (ed.), *Max Leopold Margolis Scholar and Teacher* (Philadelphia: Alumni Association of Dropsie College, 1952). The annotated bibliography of Margolis' publications compiled by J. Reider, originally published in Gordis, *Margolis*, 61–124 has been republished with corrections in Greenspoon, *Margolis*, 135–186. For some interesting personal anecdotes about Margolis see Gordon, *Pennsylvania*, 49–52.
131. M. Margolis, "Commentarius Isaacidis Quatenus ad Textum Talmudis Investigandum Adhiberi Possit, Tractatu 'Erubhin Ostenditur," (New York, 1891). Margolis' doctorate was the first awarded by Columbia's Oriental Department. See Greenspoon, *Margolis*, 5.
132. In a letter to Kaufmann Kohler (Greenspoon, *Margolis*, 15), Margolis spoke of "my love for Judaism" . . . and the unbounded confidence in yourself" as decisive in his return to HUC. According to Gordon (*Pennsylvania*, 50), a higher salary was another factor. Indeed, in 1906 Margolis' salary of $3,600 was the highest paid by HUC to any faculty member (See Meyer apud Karff, *Hebrew Union College*, 66). Twenty years after his depar-

ture from California, Margolis told Gordon that returning to HUC was the greatest mistake he had ever made.

133. See Meyer apud Karff, *HUC,* 63.

134. According to the report of the Proceedings, the fifth plank of the Pittsburgh Platform read in part: "We consider ourselves no longer a nation but a religious community, and therefore expect neither a return to Palestine, nor a sacrificial worship under the sons of Aaron, nor the restoration of any the laws concerning the Jewish state." See Jacob, *Pittsburgh Platform,* 108. It must be noted that several Reform rabbis demurred and espoused Zionism in the 1880's. See D. Polish, "The Changing and the Constant in the Reform Rabbinate," in *American Jewish Archives* 35, 275–276.

135. See Polish, "Reform Rabbinate," 280–281.

136. Margolis' Zionist colleagues on the faculty, Henry Malter and Max Schloessinger, also resigned during that academic year. See Meyer apud Karff, *Hebrew Union College,* 63–64. Malter, a talmudist, would once again be a colleague of Margolis, at Dropsie.

137. Kaufmann Kohler and the Sephardic rabbi Frederick de Sola Mendes served with Jastrow on the editorial Committee. Jastrow had prepared the Job translation, Kohler the Psalms translation and de Sola Mendes the translation of Deuteronomy. It is of interest that there was no Orthodox representation on this committee. Kohler, as we have seen, was a radical reformer; Jastrow was in the left wing of the historical school; and Mendes, one of the original members of the Jewish Theological Seminary Association, was solidly in the Reform camp by the end of his career.

138. See Orlinsky, *Essays,* 354.

139. See the account in the "Preface" to *The Holy Scriptures.* Cf. Orlinsky, *Essays,* 354.

140. The RV actually served as the basic text for the JPS revision. Indeed, Orlinsky has characterized the final product of 1917 as "an extremely modest revision of the English Revised Version of 1885, a revision that probably did not exceed more than a very few percent of the whole." See H. Orlinsky, "The New Jewish Version of the Torah: Toward a New Philosophy of Bible Translation," in idem, *Essays,* 399–400; Cf. L. Greenspoon, "Biblical Translators in Antiquity and the Modern World: A Comparative Study," *HUCA* 60 (1989), 91–113. The RV, like its predecessor KJV, had too Christian a slant to serve the Anglophone Jewish communities. See idem, *Margolis,* 65–66, and Sarna apud Greenspoon ibid, 73.

141. Gordis, *Margolis,* 9.

142. For his speed he earned a bonus. The early completion also facilitated Margolis' appointment to the Dropsie faculty. See Greenspoon, *Margolis,* 63.

143. The non-sectarianism applied to the admission of students. Although in later years such non-Jewish scholars as Morton Enslin and Morton Smith served as faculty members, Dropsie's will had stipulated that the college appoint to the faculty, "only persons who are Jews in faith." See, A. Neumann, "The Dropsie College for Hebrew and Cognate Learning: Basic Principles and Objectives," in A. Neuman and S. Zeitlin (eds.), *The Seventy-*

Fifth Anniversary Volume of the Jewish Quarterly Review (Philadelphia: Jewish Quarterly Review, 1967), 22. For his own part, Moses A. Dropsie was vehemently opposed to Reform Judaism, which he caricatured as "Deform". See Davis, *Emergence*, 338.

144. See A. Katsh and L. Nemoy (eds.) in *Essays on the Occasion of the Seventieth Anniversary of the Dropsie University (1909–1979)*, (Philadelphia: Dropsie University, 1979), ix–xi. The school officially became Dropsie University in 1969, after it had ceased to be an important institution. After a long period of moribundity, Dropsie was enabled by the philanthropy of Walter Annenberg to become, in 1986, the Annenberg Research Institute for Judaic and Near Eastern Studies, predominantly a postdoctoral research center. See B. Lewis and D. Goldenberg, "Annenberg Research Institute for Judaic and Near Eastern Studies Statement of Purpose," *Jewish Quarterly Review* 72 (1986), 1–4. Dropsie's demise was largely due to the widespread availability of Judaica courses of study at major American universities.

145. Israel Friedlaender had also been a candidate for the presidency of Dropsie and for a professorship there in Semitics. See H. Parzen, "New Data on the Formation of Dropsie College," *Jewish Social Studies* 28 (1966), 131–147; Cf. Shargel, *Dreamer*, 10.

146. One early plan had envisioned Dropsie, JTS and Graetz College in Philadelphia as branches of a single university. See Shargel, *Dreamer*, ibid.

147. An English title would be: *The Bible with a Critical Commentary*. Kahana's project began in 1902–03. Although the series was not completed, a number of important commentaries were produced by such luminaries as Samuel Kraus, H. P. Chajes, Felix Perles and M. H. Segal. Margolis was the only American scholar to contribute. Published in 1930 in Tel-Aviv, Margolis' commentaries were probably written about 1910. See F. Zimmerman, in Gordis, *Margolis,* 21 and J. Reider, ibid., 76.

148. M. Margolis and A. Marx, *A History of the Jewish People* (Philadelphia: Jewish Publication Society, 1927).

149. For biographical information see W. Fischel (ed.), *Semitic and Oriental Studies: A Volume Presented to William Popper on the Occasion of his Seventieth Birthday October 25, 1949* (Berkeley and Los Angeles: University of California, 1951), v–x; idem, "Popper, William," *EncJud* 13, 864. For bibliography see idem, *JAOS* 84 (1964), 213–220.

150. See W. Popper, "Parallelism in Isaiah, Chapters 1–10." The monograph is Part II of *SemiCentennial Publications of the University of California 1868–1918: Studies in Biblical Parallelism*; idem, "A Suggestion as to the Sequence of Some Prophecies in the First Isaiah," *HUCA* 1 (1924), 79–96; idem, "Notes on Parallelism," ibid 2 (1925), 63–85. Incidentally, this last piece directly addresses itself to questions of theory and method in a manner rare in early twentieth century Jewish Bible scholarship.

151. Blank, "Bible," 295.

152. Ibid, 296.

153. Morgenstern contributed to every issue of *HUCA* from 1924–1970. For bibliographical information see Blank, "Bible," 296, 313, n.5; See further, I. Berger, *Analytical Subject Index to the Hebrew Union College Annual Volumes 1–37 (1924–1966)*, 127–128.

154. "Amos Studies (Part Four)," appeared in *HUCA* 32 (1961), 295–350.
155. *JBL* 61 (1941), 1.
156. Doubtless influenced by the "Social Gospel" movement within Protestantism, the Pittsburgh Platform of 1885 had set the tone for the involvement of Reform Judaism in social issues outside of the Jewish community. See Polish, "Reform Rabbinate," 303–307.
157. For bibliography see B. Bamberger, *EncJud* 4, 1542. For an assessment of Buttenwieser's contribution to Psalms scholarship, see N. Sarna's introduction to the Ktav reissue of *Psalms, Chronologically Treated* (New York, 1969).
158. Blank, "Bible," 294.
159. See for example, M. Buttenwieser, "The Importance of the Tenses for the Interpretation of the Psalms," *HUCA Jubilee Volume* (Cincinnati, 1925), 89–111.
160. *The Jewish Encyclopedia* (New York: Funk and Wagnalls, 1901–1906).
161. See Ginzberg, *Keeper,* 65–68.
162. *JE* was especially strong in the rabbinics department, thanks in the main to the labors of Louis Ginzberg.
163. Richard Gottheil, who also served on the editorial board, was responsible for "History from Era to 1492." He left "Hebrew Philology" to Crawford H. Toy.

CHAPTER THREE
Between the Wars

The first talented Jewish Bible scholar to emerge in America after the First World War was Israel Eitan, a largely forgotten figure.[1] Eitan (1885–1935), born in Warsaw, did not earn his doctorate until 1924. Unlike some other European-born scholars in our survey, Eitan's traditional East European Jewish education was quite limited. He attended *heder* until the age of eleven, but rather than continuing in a *yeshivah*, he studied in a Jewish gymnasium, in the hope of gaining entrance into a state-sponsored Russian gymnasium. Unable to accomplish that goal, the youngster somehow found his way to Paris where the Alliance Israelite Universelle conducted its École Normale, and studied Jewish texts, classical languages and philosophy. Eitan's primary interest at that point in his life however, was pedagogy. In 1904 he went to Palestine and became a public school principal in Rishon-le Zion but did not remain there. Instead, Eitan returned to Paris where he studied science from 1909-1911. He then returned once more to Palestine and taught science, Latin and Bible at the Jerusalem gymnasium. It was in Jerusalem that Eitan became friends with Eliezer ben Yehudah, generally considered the founder of Modern Hebrew, and David Yellin, the Hebrew grammarian, both of whom encouraged him to study comparative philology.

Having spent the war years in Damascus, where he honed his skills in Arabic, in 1921 Eitan came to Columbia University and studied Egyptian, Coptic, Sumerian, Akkadian and Ethiopic, earning the Ph.D., as Margolis had done thirty years earlier, under Richard Gottheil. Eitan's dissertation, published as *A Contribution to Biblical Lexicography*[2] is a brilliant piece of work despite one glaring theoretical omission. Specifically, Eitan makes disparaging reference to Wellhausen, but never confronts the higher-critical issues raised by the great German scholar. Instead, the monograph deals exclusively with philological problems, as do Eitan's later publications. Eitan is quite conservative with regard to emendations, referring to the "exaggerated talk of corruption" (ibid, 6) in biblical texts. Although by no means committed to the doctrine of inerrancy of the Masoretic texts, Eitan argues that many seemingly corrupt verses can be explained without emendation, by "philological exegesis." In practice, Eitan meant that it was necessary to enlist Arabic, Mishnaic Hebrew, Ethiopic, Akkadian and inscriptional material, to derive contextually appropriate meanings for difficult Masoretic readings. Eitan found a congenial mentor in Gottheil, to whom the book is dedicated, who wrote in his preface to the publication: "Anything that aids us in staying the hand of the blind destroyer of our text called 'The Emendator' and that appeals to our sense of exegetic propriety and philologic exactness must be welcome." In *Contribution* as well as in his articles, Eitan applied this method of "philological exegesis." In agreement with Ehrlich, Eitan considered Arabic a more useful tool than "Assyrian" because of its conservative grammar and phonology as well as its "stupendous richness of vocabulary."[3] It goes without saying that the advantage of Arabic in this regard is a disadvantage when the method is arbitrarily applied, and that at times Eitan is quite arbitrary. Nonetheless, his observations remain a largely unexploited resource for the contemporary biblical philologist.[4] Indeed, Eitan's superb philological sense enabled him to offer some interpretations that were later confirmed by discoveries in Phoenician and Ugaritic.[5]

Unfortunately, Eitan had arrived on the American scene just a little too late to make his mark. The JPS Bible, published in 1917, singles out for special mention Margolis' recourse to such conservatives as Malbim and Luzzato. Eitan's high regard for the traditional Hebrew text would surely have made his work an important resource had it been available a decade earlier. Professionally, Eitan was limited by the lack of openings for Jewish scholars who specialized in Bible and closely related fields. In 1924 Richard Gottheil was still at Columbia. At the University of Pennsylvania, where Morris Jastrow had taught until his death in 1922, George Barton had been named as replacement and James Montgomery was already on the faculty.[6] Max Margolis was at Dropsie where he was to teach until his death in 1932. As for the situation in Jewish seminaries, we have seen that Moses Buttenwieser and his junior colleague Julian Morgenstern were at HUC in Cincinnati. Jacob Hoschander, Assyriologist at Dropsie, had assumed the additional position of Bible Professor at Jewish Theological Seminary upon the untimely death of Israel Friedlaender in 1920.[7] The new Jewish Institute of Religion, founded in 1922, had begun Bible instruction with Felix Perles of

Königsberg as visiting professor.[8] By 1923 the Orientalist Julian Obermann had joined the faculty where he remained until 1931 when he left JIR for Yale.[9] Eitan, compelled to eke out a living as a Hebrew School teacher, never had the opportunity to train successors. This probably explains the unmerited obscurity into which Eitan's work has fallen.[10] Not only was he too late for the original JPS translation. He was apparently ignored as well by the JPS translators who produced the NJV. Eitan's name appears nowhere in the index of notes to NJV's Torah translation. Indeed, although Orlinsky's necrology praises Eitan's work, there is no article on him in *Encyclopaedia Judaica*.

Another of the first Jewish Bible scholars to receive his training in Semitics and Bible the United States was the far more famous Ephraim Avigdor Speiser (1902–1965).[11] Born in Galicia, Speiser graduated from the Gymnasium of Lemberg and came to the United States at the age of eighteen. Studying under Max Margolis and James Montgomery, he earned an M.A. at the University of Pennsylvania in 1923. Speiser wrote his Ph.D. thesis at Dropsie in 1924 under Max Margolis on "The Pronunciation of Hebrew according to the Transliterations in the Hexapla." Speiser emulated his teacher in at least one respect, by marrying into an extremely prominent American Jewish family. His wife was Suzanne Gimbel Dannenbaum, granddaughter of Charles Gimbel, youngest of the Gimbel brothers of retailing fame. With regard to Speiser's scholarly interests, Jacob Finkelstein, the prominent Assyriologist trained by Speiser, wrote that Speiser's

"scholarly career illustrated a kind of grand dialectic. Beginning in the field of Semitic philology and concentrating on biblical text criticism, he very soon branched out into Ancient Near Eastern history, Assyriology, archeology, even Hittitology—in short, everything that came within the purview of the ancient civilizations of Western Asia—but never losing sight of his point of departure."[12]

After completing his doctorate, Speiser turned to advanced studies in Semitics and archaeology. By the age of twenty-nine, Speiser had become a full professor at Pennsylvania and concurrently a professor at Dropsie. Much of his scholarly work during the next two decades was devoted to Mesopotamian culture, although his biblical studies were not entirely neglected. Speiser pioneered in various aspects of Assyriology, making major contributions to the elucidation of the

Akkadian dialect of Nuzi and to the recovery of Nuzi's Hurro-Akkadian culture. Speiser's *Introduction to Hurrian*[13] made that language accessible to modern scholarship. As a professor at the University of Pennsylvania, Speiser was extremely influential in the training of the leading biblical and Near Eastern scholars of the present generation. During the last decade of his life Speiser devoted most of his scholarly activity to the Bible, especially the Pentateuch. He was a member of the JPS Bible translation committee that produced *The Torah* in 1962. He also contributed to and edited the first volume of the authoritative *World History of the Jewish People*[14] Speiser's final book was *Genesis,* the first volume in the Anchor Bible series.[15] Written in Speiser's enviable felicitous style, *Genesis* consists of an introduction, translation and commentary to the biblical book. Speiser's student, Moshe Greenberg, who later succeeded to his mentor's chair at Pennsylvania, describes *Genesis* as "the fruition of . . . lifelong interest."[16] To these three major productions, Speiser brought his broad interest in the languages, history, and the legal and cultural institutions of the ancient Near East. Speiser was not as much a "biblical archaeologist" as were Albright and his followers. Nonetheless, he believed that modern scholars could employ the data supplied by archaeology, especially historical and legal documents, to solve problems uncovered by literary analysis of the Bible. Archaeology could thus serve as a supplement or an alternative to source criticism. Although he demonstrated sensitivity to literary style and diction, Speiser, in direct contrast to his mentor Margolis, did not attach primary importance to the actual preserved text(s) of the Bible. Lifelong study of the ancient Near East had convinced him that the Bible would be best understood when the ancient reality reflected or refracted in the text was recovered. This was especially true with regard to the "patriarchal" traditions preserved in the Pentateuch. Modern scholars, argued Speiser, have access to information that was unavailable to Israelite scribes and compilers of the early first millennium B.C., who often no longer understood the second-millennium Mesopotamian milieu in which many biblical narratives had originated. Accordingly, Speiser maintained, obscurity, repetition and contradiction in the sources of the Pentateuch could often be accounted for by the great antiquity and remoteness of the original underlying traditions.[17] Although Speiser himself "was not a religious man in any conventional sense,"[18] his biblical studies in this vein[19] were received warmly in quasi-orthodox circles where the antiquity of a religious tradition was equated with its historicity and its historicity with its religious truth.[20] The last decade has seen much of his synthesis of biblical and ancient Near Eastern data aggressively challenged.[21] Nonetheless, we do well to remember Speiser's statement: "Sooner or later, the intellectual fortunes that we amass in peripheral fields get to be wisely invested in the Bible."[22]

The University of Pennsylvania was the training ground for Cyrus Herzl Gordon.[23] The Bible, if not his actual focus, has been a constant point of reference in Gordon's work. Born in Philadelphia in 1908, Gordon has an educational background similar to Speiser's[24] and even broader comparative interests, embracing not only western Asia but the Aegean as well. He earned the B.A. and M.A. at the University of Pennsylvania and received his Ph.D. there as a student of James Montgomery. From 1931–1935, Gordon acquired experience in field archaeology at the American Schools of Oriental Research in Jerusalem and Baghdad, excavating at Tell Beit Mirsim, Tell Billa and Tepe Gawra. He also accompanied Nelson Glueck on his work in Moab and Edom. Gordon has trained several generations of students, including B. Levine, a contributor to the present volume. Gordon has taught at Johns Hopkins, Smith, Princeton, Dropsie and Brandeis and is, at present, teaching at New York University. One realizes Gordon's linguistic breadth when it is recalled that he held the professorship in Assyriology and Egyptology at Dropsie.[25] Gordon has contributed significantly to several areas of Semitics. Like his mentor Montgomery before him, Gordon has advanced the understanding of Aramaic incantation literature. Gordon has also done important work on the Nuzi tablets and other cuneiform collections including most recently, material from Ebla. He is best known however, for his work in Ugaritic. *Gordon's Ugaritic Textbook,*[26] based on the pioneering researches of the author and others in the language, is the standard pedagogical tool.[27] Gordon's biblical researches emphasize cultural comparisons more than historical continuity. He has attempted, not without opposition, to establish the academic respectability of "Mediterranean Studies," in his teaching and in such monographs as "Homer and the Bible: The Origin and Character of East Mediterranean Literature,"[28] *Before the Bible,*[29] and *Ugarit and Minoan Crete*[30]. Gordon, as did Speiser, tends to minimize the importance of literary criticism, which he considers too mechanistic. Instead, his biblical studies attempt to reconstruct the actual events or forgotten practices which might have given rise to a particular biblical narrative.[31]

Sheldon Blank[32] (1896–1989) an older contemporary of Gordon, was born in Mount Carmel, Illinois. He received his B.A. and M.A. at the University of Cincinnati and was ordained at Hebrew Union College. Julian Morgenstern, by then president of the College, verbally and financially encouraged Blank and his classmate Nelson Glueck to pursue graduate studies in Germany. Blank completed his doctorate at Jena in 1925 with a thesis on "Das Wort torah im Alten Testament," and joined the HUC faculty in 1928, where throughout his long lifetime he enjoyed a well-deserved reputation for dignity and kindness. Blank's articles show an acute sense of textual nuances.[33] Much of his writing was been on prophetic literature. Blank acknowledged Buttenwieser and Morgenstern as significant influences on his work. Perhaps Blank's greatest contributions to biblical scholarship stem from his editorship of the *Hebrew Union College Annual,* in which he remained actively involved until his death at age ninety-two.

Blank's classmate Nelson Glueck (1900–1971) was born in Cincinnati into a poor family of Lithuanian immigrants. Having decided as a rabbinic student that the pulpit would not suit him, he accepted Morgenstern's offer of support for foreign study. After studying with H. Gressmann in Berlin and W. Staerk in Jena, Glueck received the Ph.D. at Jena in 1925 for his still-authoritative study on *hesed* in the Bible.[34] But as Meyer[35] notes, "linguistic and conceptual study of the Bible was not to be a permanent interest." In 1927, Glueck left Germany for Palestine and became the disciple of W. F. Albright, then director of the American School of Oriental Research in Jerusalem. His major scholarly work in subsequent years was in archaeology. Throughout some thirty years Glueck carried on extensive surveys of the Negeb and Transjordan. Much of this work[36] was extensively employed by others, notably Glueck's own mentor in archaeology, Albright, as a basis for reconstructing early biblical history. As president of HUC (1947–1971), Glueck was responsible for transforming its institutional structure and building its graduate programs. Under Glueck's leadership, HUC merged with the Jewish Institute of Religion in New York.

Mention must also be made of Julius Lewy (1896–1963). A native of Berlin, Lewy was primarily an Assyriologist, with a particular interest in the dialect and institutions of the Old Assyrian period (ca.

1950–1750 B.C.).[37] A professor at the University of Jena, Lewy was dismissed by the Nazis in 1933 and came to the United States in 1934. Lewy was the first of the refugee scholars brought to America through the efforts of Julian Morgenstern, to come to HUC and remain on its faculty.[38] After a year in New York at Jewish Theological Seminary, Lewy was appointed to HUC in 1935 as lecturer in history of the ancient Near East. At HUC his interests in Bible deepened and he subsequently was named professor of Bible and Semitic languages.[39] A number of Lewy's publications[40] on history and institutions are significant for biblical studies. The writings of the leading Assyriologist, Hildegarde Lewy,[41] wife of Julius, also contain much that is valuable for biblical studies.

The Jewish Theological Seminary remained insignificant in biblical Studies until the nineteen-thirties. Upon the untimely death of Israel Friedlaender in 1920, Cyrus Adler, then serving as president of both JTS and Dropsie College, appointed Jacob Hoschander (1874–1933) to the seminary's Bible position, without consulting the faculty.[42] A native of Teschen, Silesia, Hoschander, a talented Assyriologist,[43] had earned the Ph.D. at Marburg. Unlike Friedlaender, Hoschander devoted himself completely to scholarship. He wrote a regular "Survey of Recent Biblical Literature" for *Jewish Quarterly Review*. In his own writings on Bible, Hoschander was an odd combination of "defender of the faith"[44] and radical critic. These contradictory tendencies may best be seen in his curious work, *The Book of Esther in the Light of History*,[45] which attempts to demonstrate that the Purim festival is historical rather than mythical in origin, by rewriting the narrative of Esther to prove that Haman was a Zoroastrian zealot!

In retrospect, it is clear that Hoschander's death marked a monumental change in the direction of biblical studies at JTS. As part of American Jewish attempts to aid refugee European scholars who had been forced out by the Nazis, Julius Lewy and Alexander Sperber were brought temporarily to JTS in 1934 as visiting professors. With the appointment in 1936 of Harold Louis (or as he preferred to sign: H. L.) Ginsberg (1903–1990) in 1936, JTS brought to its faculty a Bible scholar of the highest stature.[46]

H. L. Ginsberg, born in Montreal, Canada had initially considered a career in medicine. He changed his mind however, and instead studied Semitics at the University of London, where he earned the Ph.D., after which he spent several years in Palestine. Shortly after the discovery of the Ugaritic tablets, Ginsberg began to produce studies and translations of Ugaritic, which fifty years later can still be read with benefit. Indeed, it was Ginsberg who, at age thirty-three, first demonstrated the extent of the cultural continuity between Ugaritic literature and the Bible.[47] Ginsberg's early studies on Aramaic dialect problems likewise remain fundamental.[48] In a sense, Ginsberg's appointment to the JTS faculty might have seemed to some a continuation of the seminary's policy of seeking Semiticists whose scholarly focus and research were primarily extra-biblical. Indeed, although the writings of his Palestine period contain numerous biblical references, it was only with Ginsberg's arrival in the United States and his appointment to the JTS faculty that he began to concentrate on the Bible, while continuing to contribute significantly to the understanding of Ugaritic, Aramaic and Phoenician.

Most of Ginsberg's publications have a philological orientation, but at the same time often contribute to our understanding of Israelite history and culture. Indeed, Ginsberg employed his *Sprachgefühl* for biblical diction as a tool in demonstrating inner-biblical literary and ideological influences. Moshe Held once noted that "Ginsberg's work is characterized by an abundance of emendations."[49] If current scholarly fashion tends to frown on the freer emendatory tendency of an earlier period, it nonetheless concedes that Ginsberg's emendations always demonstrated the depth of their author's penetration of biblical diction. One is constantly struck by the common sense of Ginsberg's observations. To cite just one example, he accounted for the Aramaisms in Job by the insight that the book's protagonists are "Easterners" and as we (and Job's author) know from Genesis, "Easterners" speak Aramaic.[50] It is sometimes difficult to read Ginsberg's work because of his extremely terse writing style, which can border on the mathematical. Nonetheless, the student who wishes to understand Isaiah, Hosea, Daniel, Job, or Ecclesiastes must study Ginsberg's numerous articles and monographs devoted to these works. The results of many of Ginsberg's researches have come before the larger public thanks to his role in editing and translating the Torah, the Megillot and especially, the Prophets sections of the new Jewish Publication Society translation (NJV). It may be further noted that Ginsberg's articles in *Encyclopaedia Judaica*, of which he served as Bible Editor, contain original scholarship and detail to a far greater degree than one expects in contemporary encyclopedia entries.[51]

Ginsberg's earlier scholarship was generally not directed to Torah-literature, possibly owing in some measure to Schechter's baleful post-mortem influence on the JTS curriculum. In his later years however, Ginsberg's researches on Hosea and Isaiah led him back to the Pentateuch. On the basis of his studies of biblical diction, Ginsberg has offered provocative and original reconstructions of the ancient Israelite calendar and festivals.[52]

Ginsberg had little opportunity to train graduate students directly, but as will be seen in the next chapter, many graduates of JTS, where talmudic studies were emphasized at the expense of Bible, and which had no Ph.D. program until the 1960's, were inspired by Ginsberg to continue their studies in Bible and Semitics at universities. Ginsberg was not famed as a pedagogue and indeed, struck many students as alternately nervous and intimidating. What drew those who attempted to follow in the footsteps of the master was a brilliance accompanied by an uncompromising sense of scholarly integrity. Once, in a seminar in Daniel, Ginsberg remarked that the word ʿillâ "pretext" did not have a positive sense in Aramaic. A student replied that in a talmudic passage he had, by coincidence, studied earlier that day it appeared that ʿillâ might indeed have a positive connotation. But, the student added, one of the medieval talmudic commentaries had given the talmudic passage an alternative explanation. Accordingly, concluded said student, Ginsberg's statement required no retraction or qualification. Ginsberg replied that his own correctness or incorrectness was of no concern. "What we are after," he said, "is the truth."

Ginsberg's concern with the pursuit of truth often brought him to reconsider his earlier opinions, specifically his own relative dating of the sources of the Pentateuch. For a long time, Ginsberg had been an enthusiastic proponent of the Israeli scholar Yehezkel Kaufmann (1889–1963), who attempted, against Wellhausen, to demonstrate that the Priestly Code was older than Deuteronomy.[53] Indeed, it had been due to Ginsberg that Kaufmann's writings attained wide currency in Jewish Bible scholarship in the United States. Nonetheless, by the end of his life, Ginsberg's views had moved much closer to Wellhausen's.[54]

Robert Gordis (b. 1908) joined the Department of Bible at JTS, initially as an annual lecturer, in 1937. Gordis had been graduated from City College of New York, had earned the doctorate at Dropsie at the beginning of the Great Depression and then come as a rabbinic student to JTS, which ordained him in 1932. It must be noted that as the recipient of the Ph.D. from Dropsie College in 1929 for his dissertation on the masoretic traditions of *qere* and *ketib,* written under the tutelage of Margolis, Gordis has the distinction of being the first native born American Jewish Bible scholar educated completely in the United States through the Ph.D.[55] Despite his busy career as a congregational rabbi and community leader, Gordis has found time to write prolifically on a wide variety of subjects.[56] His biblical interests have included masoretic problems, biblical poetry and literary technique. He has contributed book-length studies on Ecclesiastes, Canticles and Job. Gordis's strengths lie in his ability to concentrate on literary themes and sizable conceptual units. Thoroughly at home in talmud and midrash, Gordis has made good use of rabbinic sources as tools in biblical lexicography.[57] Gordis was the first Jewish scholar to teach Bible at New York's Union Theological Seminary. He has also taught at Columbia, Dropsie and Temple University.

Harry M. Orlinsky was born 1908 in Owen Sound, Ontario and grew up in Toronto. Orlinsky has been in the forefront of American biblical scholarship and easily the most visible Jewish Bible scholar, for over four decades.[58] He has been aptly credited as the one who "inaugurated the new breed of working presidents"[59] of the Society of Biblical Literature (1970) in reference to his role in reshaping the SBL. Orlinsky's entry in the 1931 yearbook of University College of the University of Toronto singles out "humour" and "independent thinking" as characteristic attributes. Encouraged by his teacher Theophile Meek, Orlinsky went to Dropsie, where he received the Ph.D. in 1935. Although he had the benefit of Margolis' teaching for only a short while, Orlinsky's contributions as a text-critic and his researches in Septuagint and Masorah testify to Margolis' lasting influence. Orlinsky, like other Dropsie students, also benefitted from the cross-registration agreement between Dropsie and the University of Pennsylvania, which enabled him to study with Montgomery, Speiser and Enslin.[60] Upon completion of his Ph.D. in 1935, Orlinsky's first teaching position brought him to Baltimore Hebrew College. Orlinsky had worked briefly as a post-doctoral fellow with Albright in Palestine. Once in Baltimore, he began to attend Albright's seminars at Johns Hopkins. Albright quickly became aware of the young scholar's potential and wished to bring him to Hopkins. But Albright's plans were thwarted by the outbreak of the war in

1941, which made it impossible to increase the size of the JHU faculty. Fortunately for Orlinsky and for Bible scholarship, a position opened at the Jewish Institute of Religion in New York City.

The Jewish Institute of Religion had been founded by Stephen S. Wise in opposition to Hebrew Union College. Stephen Wise (1874–1949),[61] unrelated to I. M. Wise, was a Reform rabbi but not a product of HUC.[62] Born in Hungary, Wise did not share HUC's preference for the Germanic style of Judaism. In addition, Wise was a committed Zionist at a time when the HUC administration was strongly anti-Zionist. A founder of the American Civil Liberties Union and the National Association for the Advancement of Colored People, Wise was also a champion of organized labor. Wise's strong commitments to social action and political Zionism coupled to a "driving quest for power and influence"[63] convinced him of the inadequacy of HUC. In his own words:

"The only things to be changed at the College are the Faculty, the Board of Governors, the students and the course of studies—to say nothing of the Spirit of the place."[64]

Although Wise had scholarly interests and held a Ph.D. in Semitics earned under Richard Gottheil,[65] he preferred activism to scholarship. In 1922, Wise founded the Jewish Institute of Religion and throughout its independent existence remained the driving force behind the school. Wise was committed to the idea of *"kelal Yisrael,"*[66] an all-inclusive definition of Judaism, which, in contrast to the clearly delineated Reform ideology of HUC, would make possible the training of rabbis of all shades of ideology and practice. Wise always claimed that JIR was a school in which a student of any Jewish religious orientation could feel at home. Yet as Meyer observes, "few fully observant Jews chose to study there."[67] Despite the occasional presence of ritually observant Jews on the faculty, the school was committed to critical scholarship, held nontraditional chapel services and was tolerant of radical theology. In the final analysis, the difference between HUC and JIR was one of style rather than substance. In contrast to the situation prevailing at HUC in those days, a student could be ritually observant at JIR without coming under suspicion of heresy.[68] Nevertheless, as a liberal institution JIR tended to produce rabbis who were best suited to serve in Reform congregations. Over the years, the differences between HUC and JIR became overshadowed by their common interests.

Changing Jewish demographics, the rise of Zionism within the Reform movement, and simple economics pointed in the direction of merger. Wise participated in the negotiations that brought about the official merger of the two schools in 1950, shortly after his death.

It was Wise who, at Albright's recommendation, brought Orlinsky to JIR in 1943, where he continues as an active member of the HUC-JIR faculty. As his fellow undergraduates realized in 1931, Orlinsky was, and remains, an independent thinker, as witness for example his work on the figure of "the suffering servant" in Deutero-Isaiah.[69] Repeatedly, Orlinsky has compelled the world of biblical scholarship to re-examine such notions as "universalism" in the prophets,[70] which had attained the virtual status of dogma. It was Orlinsky who demonstrated the textual unrelability of the St. Mark's Isaiah scroll at a time when most scholars were hailing it as an important source of valuable variants to the received Hebrew texts of Isaiah.[71] In like manner, he has chastised would-be text critics for their reluctance to examine the Versions seriously and their concommitant reliance on the apparatus of Kittel's *Biblia Hebraica*.[72] Orlinsky's independent manner also made him one of the few scholars to mount an early challenge to the Alt-Noth hypothesis of an amphictyony in pre-monarchic Israel.[73] Orlinsky has been a historian of modern Jewish Bible scholarship and its champion, as well as a staunch supporter of the Israel Exploration Society. Much of Orlinsky's work has been made available to non-specialists, Christian as well as Jewish, in such serious yet readable works as the widely distributed college textbook, *Ancient Israel*.[74] Albright's recognition of his talent was largely responsible for Orlinsky's unique status as the only Jewish scholar to serve on the RSV translation committee.[75] Following in the footsteps of Margolis, and ultimately of Leeser, Orlinsky played a leading role in the work of the Jewish Publication Society. Working alongside his fellow Canadian by birth, H. L. Ginsberg, Orlinsky served as editor in chief of the JPS Torah translation (1962, revised 1965) and as co-editor of the JPS Prophets translation (1978).

A scholarly individualist contemporary with Orlinsky is Theodor H. Gaster, born in England in 1906. In the manner of Ehrlich, Gaster has depicted himself as a solitary laborer. The following statement from the preface to Gaster's *Myth, Legend, and Custom in the Old Testament* is characteristic:

"I have had no help from colleagues in preparing this book, and have been constrained, over these long years, to plow a lonely furrow. The field is not yet sufficiently cultivated, and the ground is still very hard."[76]

During his active academic career, Gaster taught at Fairleigh Dickinson, Dropsie, Columbia and most recently at Florida State University. Not primarily a Bible scholar, Gaster has nonetheless, contributed significantly to modern biblical scholarship.[77] Gaster has identified his specialization as "the field of Religion". Indeed, "comparative material of encyclopedic proportions"[78] has been said to comprise the body of his writings. His numerous publications include studies on Bible, Ugaritic, Hittite, ancient Near Eastern religion, Judaics, Classics, and Samaritan as well as on method in the study of religion in general. Although Gaster has often decried the narrowness of philologists, he himself has made numerous significant contributions to philology. The earliest scholarly influence on Gaster was his father Moses Gaster, a leader of the English Sephardic community and a scholar of comparative folklore. Other significant influences were the pioneering anthropologist Sir James Frazer and the classicist Gilbert Murray. Gaster does not seem, however, to share the historical orientation of these mentors. Indeed, Gaster has been somewhat inaccurately identified with the "myth and ritual" school of comparative religion.[79] To be sure, his classic, *Thespis*[80] demonstrates Gaster's emphasis on the study of the relationship between myth and ritual, and especially their joint impact on the development of literary genres and stylistic elements. But unlike the "myth and ritual" scholars, Gaster does not see myth as an outgrowth of ritual or vice-versa. What especially differentiates Gaster from both the British and Scandinavian "myth and ritual" schools is that he allows for the inner dynamics of literature. Accordingly, the demonstration that say, a biblical psalm employs the motifs known from the seasonal pantomime of a New Year festival "in no way implies that the seasonal pantomime actually obtained in the Israelite cultus."[81] Instead, Gaster employs the grammatical model of the "punctual" versus the "durative" to argue that ritual and myth represent parallel expressions through two concurrent media. Whereas ritual takes place at specific times and places, its parallel, myth, describes events that transcend the confines of time and space. Of immeasurable value to biblicists is Gaster's monumental *Myth, Legend*.[82] The author describes *Myth, Legend* succinctly as "an attempt to gather into one place all that can be derived from Comparative Folklore and mythology for the interpretation of the Old Testament."

Frank Zimmermann was graduated from City College of New York. He then pursued graduate studies at Dropsie where he earned his doctorate in 1935. In the course of writing his dissertation, Zimmermann studied for the rabbinate at Jewish Theological Seminary which ordained him in 1936. Zimmermann has divided his professional career between the Jewish community and the academy. He served many years as a congregational rabbi and as a *mohel* (ritual circumciser). From 1959–1968, Zimmermann was Professor of Bible at Dropsie. Among his important contributions to biblical scholarship, Zimmermann was the first serious proponent of the theory that the Book of Ecclesiastes is a translation from a lost Aramaic original.[83] The translation theory enabled Zimmermann to propose solutions to numerous problems in the extant Hebrew.[84] Zimmermann's reasoning was accepted by C. C. Torrey and found its most powerful advocate in H. L. Ginsberg.[85] Interestingly, Zimmermann's hypothesis was repeatedly opposed by one of Zimmermann's oldest friends and colleagues from student days at Dropsie, Robert Gordis.[85] A similar translation theory had long been a hypothesis to account for the Hebrew sections of Daniel but Zimmermann was the first to demonstrate its cogency in detail.[87]

It may be seen from this chapter how greatly North American Jewish Bible scholarship had matured between the two world wars. Jewish Bible scholars, along with their gentile colleagues, had benefitted immeasurably from the continuing progress in Middle Eastern archaeology. Primary sources from ancient Ugarit, Mari, Nuzi and Kanish were becoming increasingly available to biblicists prepared to utilize them in reconstructing the real world in which ancient Israelite writers had produced the Bible. Of special significance to Jewish scholarship was the change in composition and character of the American Jewish community which had grown larger, more prosperous and better educated. Such change would become even more pronounced in the aftermath of World War II once the Nazi anninhilation of the most vital Jewish communities of Europe had brought about a shift in the center of gravity of Jewish intellectual activity to the United States and to the new State of Israel.

Notes to Chapter Three

1. For a biographical sketch of Eitan, see S. Feigin, *Men of Letters, Scholars and Writers*, (New York: Ohel, 1950) 40–55 (in Hebrew). Cf. J. Reider, "*Biqqoret ha-Miqrâ beyn Bĕnĕ-bĕrit be 'Artsot ha-Bĕrît*," *Gilyonot*

31 (1954), 137–138. For bibliographical references see Feigin, op. cit; Orlinsky, "Scholarship," 320.

2. I. Eitan, *A Contribution to Biblical Lexicography* (Contributions to Oriental History and Philology No. 1; New York: Columbia University, 1924).

3. See *Contribution*, 15–17.

4. See for example I. Eitan, "An Unknown Meaning of Rahamim," *JBL* 53 (1934), 269–271. Note further his interesting suggestion ("Contribution," 16–17) to derive the problematic *wayyiqaḥ Qôraḥ* in Num 16:1 from Arabic *waqiḥa* "be impudent." See further idem, "Two Onomatological Studies," *JAOS* 49 (1929), 3–33; idem, "Three ʾ*im* Particles in Hebrew," ibid, 54 (1935), 295–297.

5. Thus, in *Contribution* (8), Eitan correctly explains *štʿ* (/ / *yrʾ*) in Isa 41:10, 23 as "agitated" on the basis of Arabic *satiʿa*, an explanation corroborated by the parallelism *yrʾ* / / *ttʿ* in Ugaritic. (The difference between the Arabic and Ugaritic forms is due to dissimilation.) Further proof is furnished by *štʿ* "fear" attested in Ammonite and Phoenician. Similarly, his explanation of ʿ*āzĕrû* in Zech 1:15 on the basis of Arabic ʾ*gazura* "be copious" can now claim additional support from Ugaritic, and is clearly reflected in the translations of Zech 1:15 of NJV and NEB respectively. See further, Orlinsky, *Essays*, 358.

6. See Gordon, *Pennsylvania*, 33–56.

7. See below.

8. See below.

9. See Meyer apud Karff, *Hebrew Union College*, 153.

10. On December 17, 1989, at the annual meeting of the Association for Jewish Studies, S. D. Sperling delivered a paper entitled, "Israel Eitan: A Forgotten Jewish Bible Scholar," in which some of Eitan's contributions were discussed in detail. In a room filled with professional biblicists, only two or three scholars had heard of Eitan. The title of the paper had proved all too apt.

11. For biographical information, see M. Greenberg, "In Memory of E.A. Speiser," *JAOS* 88 (1968), 1–2. For the less flattering aspects of Speiser's character see Gordon, *Pennsylvania*, 70–72. According to Gordon, Speiser "had more than a touch of a Napoleonic complex." For a bibliography see J. Finkelstein and M. Greenberg (eds.), *Oriental and Biblical Studies Collected Writings of E. A. Speiser* (Philadelphia, 1967), 587–603.

12. *Oriental and Biblical*, 606.

13. The book apeared as Annual of the American Schools of Oriental Research vol 20 (1941).

14. The first volume is entitled *At the Dawn of Civilization: A Background of Biblical History* (Tel-Aviv: Massadah, 1964).

15. (Garden City, 1964).

16. *JAOS* 38, 2; The *Register* published by Dropsie shows that as early as 1935–36, Speiser offered "The Book of Genesis in Light of the Ancient Orient." The class was devoted to "selected readings from Genesis with careful analysis of the archaeological and epigraphical material bearing on the period preceding the Exodus."

17. Note Speiser's statement: "Away from their native environment . . . borrowed customs may be cut off in due time from their original import. Tradition may reserve or recall the usage, but not always the purpose. . . . But if the tradition continues faithful, and if its witnesses are blessed with the genius of a J or an E, posterity remains in a position to recover, or at least glimpse the underlying processes." (*Oriental and Biblical*, 93). Source criticism had generally been held to undermine the credibility of biblical tradition. Speiser's formulation, in contrast, enabled quasi-orthodox students of the Bible to employ source criticism as a buttress to claims made for the reliability of biblical tradition. Instead of talking simply about the history of traditions, in the manner of Alt and Noth for example, one could speak of a historical and social reality behind the traditions.

18. Finkelstein, *Oriental and Biblical*, 606.

19. See for example, E. Speiser, "The Wife-Sister Motif in the Patriarchal Narratives," *Oriental and Biblical*, 62–88; idem, "I Know Not the Day of My Death," ibid, 96; idem, "Leviticus and the Critics," ibid, 123–142; and the treatment of Genesis 14 in the Anchor Bible *Genesis*.

20. For two good examples of this tendency in works by important scholars, which manifest a quasi-orthodox bent, see the semi-popular N. Sarna, *Understanding Genesis* (New York: McGraw-Hill, 1966), and the even more conservative work by K. Kitchen, *Ancient Orient and Old Testament* (Chicago: Inter-Varsity, 1966).

21. See e.g. S. Greengus, "Sisterhood Adoption at Nuzi and the 'Wife-Sister' in Genesis," *HUCA* 46 (1975), 5–31; and especially J. van Seters, *Abraham in History and Tradition*. (New Haven: Yale, 1975); T. Thompson, *The Historicity of the Patriarchal Narratives* (Berlin: De Gruyter, 1974).

22. *Oriental and Biblical*, 606.

23. For biographical and bibliographical information see R. Adler, M. Arfa, G. Rendsburg and N. Winter (eds.), *The Bible World Essays in Honor of Cyrus H. Gordon* (New York: Ktav and Institute of Hebrew Culture and Education at New York University, 1980), vii–viii, 293–312. For some of his personal recollections see Gordon, *Pennsylvania*.

24. Gordon studied biblical philology with Margolis at Dropsie concurrently with his undergraduate work at Pennsylvania (*Pennsylvania*, 35), and was briefly a student of Speiser, who introduced him to Nuzi Akkadian (ibid, 70–71).

25. A department of Egyptology had been added to Dropsie in 1925 with the appointment of Nathaniel Reich (1882–1943) to the faculty. Gordon's appointment in 1946 added the assyriological component. A year earlier the great Assyriologist A. Leo Oppenheim had served as visiting professor of Assyriology and Egyptology.

26. (Rome, 1965). Earlier editions were C. Gordon, *Ugaritic Grammar* (Rome: Pontifical Biblical Institute, 1940); idem, *Ugaritic Manual* (Rome: Pontifical Biblical Institute, 1955).

27. There is a new English introduction to Ugaritic by S. Segert entitled *A Basic Grammar of the Ugaritic Language* (Berkeley: University of California, 1984). Segert (ibid, viii) specifically acknowledges his indebtedness to Gordon and stresses that his grammar is intended to supplement, rather than to replace, Gordon.

28. *HUCA* 26 (1955), 43-108.
29. (New York: Harper and Row, 1962).
30. (New York: Norton, 1966).
31. See e.g., C. Gordon, "Biblical Customs and the Nuzu Tablets," reprinted *BAR*, 2, 21-33; idem, "Abraham of Ur," in D. Winton Thomas and W.D. McHardy (eds.), *Hebrew and Semitic Studies Presented to Godfrey Rolles Driver* (Oxford: Clarendon, 1963), 77-84.
32. For biographical and bibliographic details see Blank, "Bible," 298-300; R. Ahroni, "Professor Sheldon H. Blank, Rabbi," *Hebrew Annual Review* 8 (1984), 1-2.
33. See e.g. his interpretation of Ps 118:26: *bārûk habbāʾ bĕšem YHWH*, in *HUCA* 32 (1961), 75-79.
34. The dissertation was published in 1927 as *Das Wort ḥesed im alttestamentlichen Sprachgebrauche als menschliche und göttliche gemeinschaftsgemässe Verhaltungsweise*. The translation by A. Gottschalk, Glueck's successor as president at HUC-JIR, is entitled *Hesed in the Bible* (Cincinnati: Hebrew Union College, 1967).
35. "With Vision and Boldness," in Karff (ed.), *Hebrew Union College*, 173.
36. For Glueck's publications see E. K. Vogel, "Bibliography of Nelson Glueck," in J. Sanders (ed.), *Archaeology in the Twentieth Century* (Garden City: Doubleday, 1970), 382-394. For recent assessments of Glueck's work see e.g., G. Pratico, "Nelson Glueck's 1938-1940 Excavations at Tell el-Kheleifeh: A Reappraisal," *BASOR* 254 (Summer, August, 1985), 1-32.
37. See H. Tadmor, *EncJud* 11, 182.
38. See Meyer apud Karff, *Hebrew Union College*," 125-128.
39. See Blank, "Bible," 301-302.
40. e.g. J. Lewy, "The Biblical Institution of Deror in the Light of Akkadian Documents," *Eretz Israel* 5 (1958), 21-31; H. and J. Lewy, "The Origin of the Week and the Oldest Asiatic Calendar," *HUCA* 17 (1942-43), 1-155; "Les textes paléo-assyriennes et l'Ancient Testament," *Revue de l'histoire des religions* 110 (1934), 29-65; "The Feast of the Fourteenth Day of Adar," *HUCA 14* (1939); "A New parallel between Hâbiru and Hebrews," *HUCA* 15 (194), 47-58.
41. e.g. H. Lewy, "Origin and Significance of the Mâgēn Dâwîd," *Archiv Orientální* 18 (1950), 330-365; "Assyro-Babylonian and Israelite Measures of Capacity and Rates of Seeding," *Journal of the American Oriental Society* 64 (1944), 65-73; "Nitokris-Naqîa," *Journal of Near Eastern Studies* 11 (1952), 264-286. H. Lewy taught Assyriology at HUC as a visiting professor after her husband's death.
42. See Ginzberg, *Keeper*, 136-137.
43. See e.g., his review of A.T. Clay, *Amurru* (Philadelphia, 1909), in *Jewish Quarterly Review* (N.S.) 10 (1910), 139-150; and his review of H. Hilprecht, *The Earliest Version of the Babylonian Deluge Story* (Philadelphia, 1910), ibid, 419-424.
44. So, Orlinsky, "Scholarship," 325. In the foreword to the posthumous J. Hoschander, *The Priests and the Prophets* (New York: Jewish Theological Seminary, 1938), xvi, Cyrus Adler wrote: "He [Hoschander] felt it almost a sacred duty to engage in polemics against the modern biblical criticism."

45. (Philadelphia, 1923).
46. For some biographical details see A.S. Halkin, "H.L. Ginsberg—An Appreciation," in *Eretz Israel* 14 (H.L. Ginsberg Volume; 1978), ix–xii.; For bibliography see J. Tigay, ibid, 13–27 (in Hebrew section); for a descriptive appreciation of Ginsberg's contributions see M. Held, "H.L. Ginsberg: An Appreciation," *Conservative Judaism* 30 (1976), 3–9.
47. In his pioneering *Kithve Ugarit* (Jerusalem: Bialik, 1936).
48. See e.g. H.L. Ginsberg, "Aramaic Dialect Problems," *American Journal of Semitic Languages* L (1933), 1–9; idem, "Aramaic Dialect Problems. II," *AJSL* LII (1936), 95–103. During this period he also wrote an important study on talmudic Hebrew. See idem, "Zu den Dialekten des Talmudisch-Hebräischen," *Monatsschrift für die Geschichte und Wissenschaft des Judentums* 77 (1933), 413–429.
49. Held, "Appreciation," 8.
50. See Ginsberg, "Job, The book of," *EncJud* 10, 120.
51. In addition to "Job" see especially "Hosea, Book of," 8, 1010–1023; and the section s.v. "First Isaiah," within the article "Isaiah," ibid, 9, 49–60.
52. See H. L. Ginsberg, "The Grain Harvest Laws of Leviticus 23:9–22 and Numbers 28:26–31," *Proceedings of the American Academy for Jewish Research* 46–47 (1980–81), 141–153.
53. See Y. Kaufmann, *The Religion of Israel* (Chicago: University of Chicago, 1960). Abridgment and translation by M. Greenberg of Hebrew original, 1938–1956.
54. See H.L. Ginsberg, *The Israelian Heritage of Judaism*. (New York: Jewish Theological Seminary, 1982).
55. The dissertation was published as R. Gordis, *The Biblical Text in the Making* (Philadelphia: Dropsie College, 1937).
56. For bibliography of Gordis, see *Hebrew Annual Review* 7 (1983), 3–13. For a collection of representative scholarly articles, see R. Gordis, *The Word and the Book: Studies in Biblical Language and Literature* (New York: Ktav, 1976).
57. See e.g. R. Gordis, "Studies in the Relationship of Biblical and Rabbinic Hebrew," in *Louis Ginzberg Jubilee Volume* (New York: Jewish Theological Seminary, 1945), 173–199.
58. See, A Gottschalk, "Harry M. Orlinsky- An Appreciation," in *Eretz Israel* 16 (*Harry M. Orlinsky Volume;* 1982), ix–xi. For bibliography, see P. Miller, "A Selective Bibliography of the Writings of Harry M. Orlinsky," ibid, xii–xxviii.
59. Saunders, *Searching*, 61.
60. All students enrolled at Dropsie received fellowships. For these students, a cross-registration agreement waived Pennsylvania's tuition, which Orlinsky could not afford.
61. For a detailed biographical sketch see C. Voss, "Wise, Stephen Samuel," in *EncJud* 16, 566–568. For Wise's role at JIR see Meyer apud Karff, *HUC*, 137–169.
62. Wise had studied privately with his father, Aaron Wise, a member of the "historical school." (On the elder Wise, see Davis, *Emergence*, 365–366). Two other teahers were Alexander Kohut, a rabbi of similar orientation

and the Reform Gustav Gottheil. Wise was accepted to HUC, but decided instead to obtain private ordination from Adolph Jellinek of Vienna.

63. So, Meyer apud Karff, *Hebrew Union College,* 141.

64. Quoted ibid, 144.

65. Wise wrote his Ph.D. dissertation on an Arabic treatise by Solomon ibn Gabirol. He had also prepared the translation of Judges for the editorial board of the Jewish Publication Society during the tenure of Marcus Jastrow. See the "Preface" to *The Holy Scriptures.* See further, Greenspoon, *Margolis,* 65.

66. The sense of the term is not easily conveyed by its usual translations: "All Israel" or "the Jewish People in its entirety." "Christendom" suggests itself as an analog.

67. Meyer apud Karff, *HUC,* 159.

68. It was difficult to observe the Jewish dietary laws at HUC. Students lived in the dormitory and took their meals in its non-kosher dining hall. Because JIR had no dormitory, students could easily observe or ignore the dietary laws in their residences as they wished.

69. Orlinsky, *Studies on the Second Part of the Book of Isaiah. The So-Called 'Servant of the Lord' and 'Suffering Servant' in Second Isaiah.* (Leiden: Brill, 1968; Reprinted with additions and corrections, 1977).

70. See Orlinsky, "Nationalism-Universalism and Internationalism in Ancient Israel," in H. Frank and W. Reed (eds.), *Translating and Understanding the Old Testament: Essays in Honor of Herbert Gordon May* (Nashville: Abingdon, 1970), 206–236.

71. See P. Miller, "Bibliography," items 63, 69, 78, 79, 91, 92, 93.

72. See Orlinsky, "The Textual Criticism of the Old Testament," in G.E. Wright (ed.), *The Bible and the Ancient Near East. Essays in Honor of William Foxwell Albright* (Garden City: Anchor, 1965), 113–132; idem, "Whither Biblical Research?," *JBL 90* (SBL Presidential Address; 1971), 1–14.

73. Orlinsky, "The Tribal System of Israel and Related Groups in the Period of the Judges," (originally published in 1962) reprinted in *Essays,* 66–77.

74. Ithaca, 1954, revised, 1960. See further, H. Orlinsky, *Understanding the Bible through History and Archaeology* (New York: Ktav, 1972).

75. He was a member of the committee that prepared the RSV revision, the New Revised Standard Version.

76. T. H. Gaster, *Myth, Legend, and Custom in the Old Testament,* (New York: Harper and Row, 1969), I, xxiii.

77. For bibliography to 1973, see D. Marcus, (ed.), *The Gaster Festschrift* (New York: ANE Society, 1974), 446–453.

78. So, M. Lichtenstein, "Theodor H. Gaster: An Appreciation," *Gaster Festschrift,* 9.

79. See e.g., A Goetze in his review of *Thespis in Journal of Cuneiform Studies* 6 (1952), 99–103. Contrast Gaster in "Myth and Story," *Numen* 1 (1954), 184–212 and especially, 210–212. Note that the recent survey by W. Harrelson, "Myth and Ritual School," *Encyclopedia of Religion* 10, 282–285, accurately omits Gaster from the list of "myth and ritual" scholars.

80. T. H. Gaster, *Thespis: Ritual, Myth and Drama in the Ancient Near East*. New York, 1950 (Revised; New York, Harper and Row, 1964).

81. T. Gaster, "Psalm 29," *Jewish Quarterly Review* 37 (1946/47), 64.

82. *Myth* was originally intended to update the classic J. Frazer, *Folklore in the Old Testament* (London, 1918), but outgrew its original purpose. Gaster had previously published *The New Golden Bough* (New York: Criterion, 1959), an updated abridgment of another Frazer classic.

83. F. Zimmermann, "The Aramaic Provenance of Qoheleth," *Jewish Quarterly Review* 36 (1945), 17–45; idem, "The Question of Hebrew in Qoheleth," *JQR* 40 (1949), 79–102; idem, *Biblical Books Translated from The Aramaic* (New York: Ktav, 1975). Zimmermann has also argued, along with many NT scholars, that the Gospels were originally composed in Aramaic. See idem, *The Aramaic Origin of the Four Gospels* (New York: Ktav, 1979).

84. E.g. Qoh 1:5, 7:5, 12, 10:17; 12:1, 13.

85. The Aramaic translation theory is central to H. L. Ginsberg, *Studies in Koheleth* (New York: Jewish Theological Seminary, 1950; idem, *A New Commentary on the Torah, The Prophets, and The Holy Writings Koheleth* (Hebrew; Tel Aviv and Jerusalem: M. Newman, 1961); idem, "Ecclesiastes," *EncJud* 6, 350–355.

86. See R. Gordis, "The Original Language of Qoheleth," *JQR* 37 (1946), 67–84; idem, "The Translation-Theory of Qoheleth Re-examined," *JQR* 40 (1949), 103–116; idem, "Koheleth-Hebrew or Aramaic," *JBL* 71 (1952), 93–109; idem, *Koheleth-The Man and His World* (New York: Jewish Theological Seminary, 1951).

87. See F. Zimmerman, "The Aramaic Origin of Daniel 8–12," *JBL* 57 (1938), 258–272; idem, "Some Verses in Daniel in the Light of a Translation Hypothesis," *JBL* 58 (1939), 349–354; cf. H.L. Ginsberg, *Studies in Daniel* (New York: Jewish Theological Seminary, 1948), 41–62.

CHAPTER FOUR
The Second Wave

The scholars whose work is chronicled here completed their doctorates between 1942–1965 and may be considered the Second Wave of American Jewish Bible scholarship. In all, our survey includes only fourteen scholars. To some extent the small number is due to university admissions policies following the Second World War. As had happened in Europe during the nineteenth century, prestigious universities became increasingly receptive to Jewish students. No sooner were the university doors opened wider, that many a bright Jewish youth who might have become a rabbi or teacher of Judaica, chose a career in law, medicine, general academics or the like. What the figures obscure is a qualitative maturity of North American Jewish biblical scholarship in the period in question. Scholars of the Second Wave, like their Gentile colleagues, greatly refined the pioneering methods of their predecessors. This is especially true with regard to the use made of the written and unwritten data unearthed by archaelogy. So greatly does comparatism characterize the Second Wave that some of the people whose work is surveyed in this chapter are better known for their accomplishments in allied fields, rather than in Bible. We must also emphasize that several of the academicians whose work is described in this chapter were famed for their teaching abilities. There can be no doubt that the quality of instruction provided by these teachers played a great part in attracting the next generation, whose numbers would be much larger.

The senior member of the Second Wave is Mattitiahu Tsevat.[1] Both in Germany in 1913, he exemplifies the best of the Judeo-German academic tradition. As a youth in Germany, Tsevat was active in the Zionist movement Hechalutz ("Pioneers"). He studied at the Jüdisch-Theologisches Seminar in Breslau from 1934–1938 and then under increased pressure from the Nazis, immigrated to Palestine. From 1938 until 1949, when he came to the United States, Tsevat studied at the David Yellin Hebrew Teachers' College and at the Hebrew University of Jerusalem, where he received the M.A. degree in 1948. Tsevat continued his graduate studies in America, spending 1949 at Dropsie. In 1950, he came to the Hebrew Union College, Cincinnati, which awarded him the Ph.D. in 1953. Julius Lewy, the noted Assyriologist and likewise a refugee from Nazi Germany,[2] was one of Tsevat's teachers and a significant academic influence.

Tsevat joined the faculty of HUC in 1959. In 1979, he was named Julian Morgenstern Professor of Bible, a position he held until becoming Emeritus in 1984. In a sense, Tsevat has lived two intellectual lives, determined in great measure by the tragic events which preceded the Second World War. He more than once expressed his indebtedness to Martin Buber,[3] with whom he studied in an intimate group in Germany during the years 1935–1938, a time in which some of Buber's own seminal ideas were taking shape. Undoubtedly, this formative experience largely accounts for Tsevat's later interest in theology, some of which emerged in his work on Job.[4]

Tsevat's work exhibits a firm commitment to the study of language and diction, as well as to lexicography, exegesis and literary structure. A polymath, Tsevat epitomizes the scholar of the classical mode. He has mastered many languages, including Hittite,[5] and is always very close to the source. Tsevat's studies are carefully rooted in textual analysis, even when the discussion is conceptual or philosophical, and he does not ignore the art-historical evidence.[6] In 1955 he published *A Study of the Language of the Biblical Psalms*[7] and between 1961–1965, a series of important articles entitled, "Studies in the Book of Samuel," appeared in volumes of the *Hebrew Union College Annual*.[8] Tsevat has also contributed significantly to our understanding of the Alalakh tablets and of Ugaritic.[9]

The unifying factor in all of Tsevat's scholarship has been an interest in the phenomenon of language. At the same time, Tsevat has never neglected the conceptual element of biblical studies. Indeed, among the biblicists of his generation, Tsevat's keen philosophical interest stands out.[10] Accordingly, one is not surprised by his particular attraction to biblical Wisdom literature.

In terms of his personal history, Tsevat represents a scholar who was already highly educated in Bible and Semitics when he arrived at these shores. Both European and Israeli scholarship are evident in his earlier training. In the United States, where he completed his graduate studies, Tsevat has pursued a distinguished career in American scholarship.

William W. Hallo, the other scholar of the Second Wave with roots in the Judeo-German tradition was born into a prominent Jewish family in Kassel in 1928. His father, the art historian Rudolf Hallo, was one of the founders of the discipline of Jewish art history. Both Rudolf's mother and his wife had been very close to Franz Rosenzweig, and it was Rudolf Hallo who succeeded the incapacitated Rosenzweig as head of the Freies Jüdisches Lehrhaus in Frankfurt.[11] William Hallo was one of a small group of Jewish children saved from the Nazis and brought to the United States just before the outbreak of the Second World War. He graduated Harvard in 1950 and received the Ph.D. from the Oriental Institute of the University of Chicago in 1955 after studying with several masters, most notably with Ignacz Gelb. Hallo also spent a year of study in Leiden, the Netherlands. His first academic appointment was at HUC-JIR in Cincinnati where he taught for six years, until 1962, when he left for Yale. Hallo is currently Laffan Professor of Assyriology and Babylonian Literature at Yale as well as curator of the university's Babylonian Collection.

Hallo is primarily known as a leading scholar of Mesopotamian literature and culture, with a special emphasis on its Sumerian component.[12] He has, nonetheless, shown a cultivated interest in biblical studies. Some of his biblical work has reached a wide audience, thanks to his participation in a Torah commentary sponsored by Reform Judaism's Union of American Hebrew Congregations. To this commentary Hallo contributed a series of background essays dealing with the ancient Near Eastern context of Torah literature, and with issues intrinsic to the text of the Torah itself.[13]

In more technical work, Hallo has pioneered what he calls a "contextual" approach to biblical literature, a method aimed at highlighting what is distinctive to biblical Israel, not only that which may be compared to other ancient Near Eastern civilizations. In brief, Hallo argues that in bringing cuneiform and biblical texts to illuminate each other, we must be prepared to test the evidence "for a whole spectrum of relationships . . . because a comparative approach that is truly objective must be broad enough to embrace the possibility of . . . contrast. And contrast can be every bit as illuminating as [positive] comparison."[14]

Hallo authored a history of the ancient Near East, together with the noted Egyptologist, William Kelly Simpson.[15] In general, Hallo's historical studies have considerable bearing on biblical history and culture.[16] Hallo is sensitive to the comparative implications of all ancient Near Eastern evidence, whatever its precise provenance.[17] This sensitivity has frequently induced him to shed light on aspects of biblical law, and to comment on epigraphic finds from the land of Israel.[18]

Another distinguished alumnus of the University of Chicago and likewise a protege of Gelb was Stanley Gevirtz (1929–1988). After receiving his B.A. from Brooklyn College, Gevirtz earned the Ph.D. at Chicago in 1959 and remained to serve on the faculty of Chicago's Oriental Institute until 1972. At that point, he left to become a professor of Bible at the Los Angeles campus of HUC-JIR, where he taught until his untimely death. As a young man, Gevirtz had studied drama in the dream of becoming an actor. He also had a great love of world literature. These two avocations contributed to making Stanley Gevirtz an outstanding classroom teacher and a brilliant public lecturer.

Gevirtz's monograph, *Patterns in the Early Poetry of Israel*,[19] demonstrates its author's developed interest in poetry as a subject for study, and his great competence in engaging crucial biblical passages, some of which have resisted definitive explanation since antiquity. To the resolution of difficult textual problems Gevirtz applied his literary acumen, and as well, his extensive knowledge of the ancient Semitic languages: Phoenician, Aramaic, Ugaritic and Akkadian. Numerous additional studies complement *Patterns*. In these, Gevirtz demonstrates a special talent in recovering the West-Semitic (and often biblical) poetic style, grammar and syntax that had been hidden under the cuneiform garb of the Amarna letters.[20] In other work, Gevirtz showed an interest in ancient Near Eastern law.[21]

Methodologically, Gevirtz was not adverse to emending the biblical text when it was warranted. He usually sought comparative evidence to support suggested emendations, some of which were ingenious. His penetrating insight into poetic diction and literary plays may be seen in his various studies on Jacob's "blessings" in Genesis 49,[22] as well as on other texts.[23]

Four scholars of the Second Wave were trained by E. A. Speiser. Among these the best known is Moshe Greenberg, born in Philadelphia in 1928. Son of a prominent Conservative rabbi, in the single year 1954 Greenberg managed to receive rabbinic ordination from JTS and a Ph.D. from University of Pennsylvania. Greenberg's primary teacher at Pennsylvania was E. A. Speiser, to whose chair he eventually succeeded. Greenberg remained at Pennsylvania until 1970, when he accepted a professorship in Bible at the Hebrew University in Jerusalem, where has served ever since.

As might have been expected of a student of Speiser, Greenberg's early interests were primarily of a comparative character. His doctoral dissertation was published as a monograph under the title: *The Hab/piru*.[24] The work is a comparative inquiry into the evidence bearing on that elusive ancient group, whose name had suggested a possible connection with ʿibrî, "Hebrew" of biblical sources. Other early work by Greenberg related to biblical law, again in comparative perspective. In the article, "Some Postulates of Biblical Criminal Law,"[25] he explored the underlying postulates of the biblical legal system and how these contrasted with the assumptions of cuneiform law. In his study of the *terapîm,* which play a significant role in the narrative of Genesis 31, Greenberg sought parallels in Roman society to the role played by the gods of family and household.[26]

Greenberg has been deeply influenced by the writings of Yehezkel Kaufmann. In order to make that Israeli scholar's work available to a wide audience, Greenberg produced an English abridgment in one volume of the eight-volume classic *Toledot Ha'emunah Ha-yisre'elit,* under the title: *The Religion of Israel*.[27] Not only was Greenberg's translation extremely lucid, but his scholarly selectivity preserved the main thrust of Kaufmann's provocative thesis, unencumbered by the excessive verbiage and gratuitous polemic of the original. Greenberg also produced *Introduction to Hebrew,* an extremely well-written grammar of biblical Hebrew, intended primarily as a college textbook.[28]

The above contributions demonstrate Greenberg's vital interest in the educational relevance of biblical scholarship and his willingness to devote considerable energy to the dissemination of learning. An outstanding pedagogue in his own right, Greenberg in 1969 published the semi-popular *Understanding Exodus*[29] for the Melton Foundation's project in Jewish education. Since settling in Israel, Greenberg has continued to be a force in educational activities, serving for a time as consultant to the Israel Ministry of Education in curricular development. More recently, he has embarked on a major Hebrew Bible commentary suitable for use in Israeli schools and colleges, to be entitled, *Or La ʿam (A Light to the People).* Greenberg, along with

J. C. Greenfield and N. M. Sarna, was a member of the scholarly committee which produced the Jewish Publication Society's new translation of the Hagiographa entitled *Kethubim*.[30]

When one compares Greenberg's earlier work with his more recent efforts in biblical scholarship, one notes a significant shift of method and emphasis. To be sure, the basic apparatus and the philological and comparative skills are still evident. Nonetheless, the appearance of Greenberg's long- anticipated volume on Ezekiel 1–20 in the Anchor Bible series[31] demonstrates how far the author has come in "holistic interpretation," a method in which Greenberg pioneered, and which has become very influential.[32] By "holistic," Greenberg means that a biblical commentator should proceed on the working assumption that a book under study is "the product of art and intelligent design. . . . Details of this . . . design disclose themselves to the patient and receptive reader who divests himself of preconceptions regarding what an ancient prophet should have said and how he should have said it."[33]

Of interest as well as Greenberg's collection of studies on biblical prayer.[34] It may be underlined that even compared with the scholars of his generation, who are well-schooled in rabbinics, Greenberg makes extensive use of classical rabbinic sources and of medieval Jewish commentators. Conspicuous in Greenberg's writings are references to the French rationalists, Eliezer of Beaugency, Rashbam, Joseph Kara, Joseph Bekhor Shor and the fifteenth century Spanish scholar Isaac Abravanel.

Yochanan Muffs was born in New York City in 1932. He was ordained at JTS in 1956 and received the Ph.D. from the University of Pennsylvania in 1964. His two most significant mentors were Ginsberg at JTS and E. A. Speiser at Pennsylvania. Muffs began teaching at JTS while still a student, and remains there as a professor of Bible.

Muffs is a scholar with a broad range of interests and with significant strengths in several areas. He is primarily a Semiticist with excellent training in Assyriology and a thorough knowledge of classical Arabic. He is also exceptionally well-grounded in rabbinic literature.

Despite being plagued by illness for many years, Muffs has made extremely valuable contributions to scholarship. His most significant work is the monograph, *Studies in the Aramaic Legal Papyri from Elephantine*,[35] which traces the formulary employed in these legal documents from their earliest attestations in the Old Babylonian period in the early second millennium B. C., through the peripheral cultures of the West Semitic sphere, down to Achaemenid times. Indeed, in many instances, Muffs demonstrates the continuity of this ancient formulary into talmudic, gaonic and Islamic legal sources. *Studies* demonstrates how Muffs' extensive grasp of the ancient Near Eastern languages has enabled him to perfect a method for identifying semantic equivalents and terms of reference having the same function in related (and sometimes unrelated) languages. In effect, Muffs has adapted the "interdialectal distribution" method associated with Albright, Landsberger and Held to the legal field.[36]

In the biblical field, as it is more strictly defined, Muffs has produced a number of in depth studies of biblical narrative, and has proposed a new interpretation of the prophetic role as that of the intercessor for, rather than the castigator of, Israel.[37] He writes in both Hebrew and English. In one two-part study, he explores the rhetoric of "joy and love" in biblical and post-biblical Jewish literature.[38] Muffs is able to shed light on some of the major themes of biblical concepts of God and biblical perceptions of reality. He writes in a richly textured, allusive style, and his works abound in interpretative insights.

Shalom (Seymour) Paul was born in Philadelphia in 1936. He acquired the fundamentals of Judaic training at Gratz College and earned the B.A. in classics at Temple University. In 1962, he was awarded rabbinic ordination at JTS. Encouraged by H. L. Ginsberg, Paul did graduate work at Pennsylvania and in 1964 received the Ph.D. after studying with E. A. Speiser and Moshe Greenberg. While still a graduate student, he began teaching Bible at JTS, where he remained until moving to Israel in 1971. There he taught first at Tel-Aviv University (1971–1976), and then at Hebrew University, Jerusalem, where he continues to serve. Paul publishes his scholarship in both Hebrew and English.

Paul's early work focused on biblical law in its ancient Near Eastern context, a subject represented by his monograph on the Book of the Covenant (Exodus 21–23),[39] and several further studies. Paul deals with the relationship of biblical law to the Mesopotamian legal traditions,[40] a subject encouraged to a great extent by his teacher E. A. Speiser.

Subsequently, Paul demonstrated a keen interest in biblical prophecy, both in comparative perspective and in terms of the transmission of prophetic themes within biblical literature itself.⁴¹ In his work, diction comes in for considerable discussion as a means of tracing literary transmission,⁴² a method well-utilized by H. L. Ginsberg. In several articles Paul addresses historical as well as philological problems.

Paul's work shows the clear influences of Ginsberg, Speiser, and Held as well as that of the Israeli Assyriologist, Hayim Tadmor. All in all, Paul has produced some thirty- odd journal articles as well as substantial entries in *Encyclopaedia Judaica,* including the article "Prophecy." He is currently preparing a commentary on Amos for the Hermeneia series.

Herbert Chanan Brichto was born in mandatory Palestine in 1925, and brought to the United States as a youngster. After graduation from the College of the City of New York (CCNY) in 1948, Brichto pursued rabbinic studies at Jewish Institute of Religion in New York, which ordained him in 1950. For several years Brichto served as a congregational rabbi. He then began to pursue graduate studies at University of Pennsylvania, where he received the Ph.D. in 1962 under the sponsorship of E. A. Speiser. He returned to the faculty of what had become in the interim, Hebrew Union College-Jewish Institute of Religion HUC-JIR), to become a professor of Bible at the Cincinnati campus.

Brichto's doctoral dissertation was published in 1963 under the title: *The Problem of "Curse" in the Hebrew Bible*.⁴³ This oft-quoted monograph focuses on Numbers 5 and the ordeal of the suspected wife (Hebrew: *Sotah*).⁴⁴ Here, Brichto demonstrates his grasp of extra-biblical legal traditions of the ancient Near East, and of cultic studies, themes he would return to again. Brichto tends to de-emphasize the purely "magical" component of the *Sotah's* ordeal, stressing rather its legal efficacy and its prayerful aspect. Some other important studies by Brichto appeared in *Hebrew Union College Annual (HUCA):* "Kin, Cult, Land and Afterlife: A Biblical Complex,"⁴⁵ and "On Slaughter and Sacrifice, Blood and Atonement."⁴⁶ In these studies Brichto brings into bold relief the function of ritual in expressing ancient Israelite communality, and in determining the social fabric of the Israelite family and clan.

Three scholars of the Second Wave were trained by Cyrus Gordon, one at Dropsie and two at Brandeis. Nahum M. Sarna was born in London, England in 1923. He graduated Jews' College, London in 1947 and shortly thereafter immigrated to the United States. Sarna pursued graduate studies at Dropsie, where, under Gordon's tutelage, he received the Ph.D. in 1955. Between 1957-1963, he served as Librarian at JTS and as a member of its Bible faculty. Sarna accepted an appointment at Brandeis in 1965. In 1967, he was named Doris Golding professor of Biblical Studies at Brandeis, a position he held until his retirement.

Sarna has published a number of scholarly articles on biblical philology and exegesis, and has shown considerable interest in literary analysis, and *Sitz im Leben*, most notably in the Psalms.[47] Sarna has also written about medieval traditions of Jewish biblical exegesis, an interest reflected in his monographic study on the Spanish schools of biblical interpretation.[48]

The better part of Sarna's energies has been devoted to major projects of a scholarly and educational character. He has written two companion volumes, one entitled: *Understanding Genesis,* and the second, *Exploring Exodus.*[49] On the one hand, these could be regarded as textbooks for the use of teachers and advanced students. On the other hand, both are replete with comparative information of ancient Near Eastern relevance, as well as discussions of major themes suggested by these books of the Pentateuch. Sarna shows particular sensitivity to the structure of biblical narrative.

Sarna served as a member of the committee which translated *Kethuvim* (Hagiographa) for JPS. Sarna's interest in the biblical canon and ancient versions is exemplified by his contribution to Brittanica III, in which he discusses ancient versions, translations- ancient and more recent- and the manuscripts of the Hebrew Bible.[50] Among his other accomplishments, Sarna initiated the JPS Torah Commentary project and served as its general editor. He wrote the Commentaries to Genesis and Exodus.[51]

Sarna places great emphasis on philology and exegesis and discusses comparative evidence at length. He also freely utilizes rabbinic and medieval exegetical writings, especially for the thematic insights afforded by the traditional interpreters. Sarna seems less interested in source criticism than in form criticism. He shows more concern in clarifying the historical background reflected in the biblical text than in the literary history of the text, or the date of its composition.

Baruch A. Levine was born in Cleveland, Ohio in 1930. He graduated Case Western Reserve University in 1951 with a concentration in Romance languages. Having as a boy acquired a strong background in talmudic studies at Cleveland's famed Telshe Yeshivah, Levine came to JTS. He was ordained there in 1955 and served several years as a pulpit rabbi in the Boston area. Realizing that his heart was not in the rabbinate but in academics, Levine pursued graduate studies at Brandeis. Upon earning the Ph.D. under Cyrus Gordon in 1962, Levine was named to the Brandeis faculty, where he remained until 1969. At that time, he joined the faculty of New York University as Professor of Hebrew and Near Eastern Languages, a post he has held ever since. In his JTS days, Levine was greatly influenced by H. L. Ginsberg, with whom he sustained a lasting relationship as a disciple. He has also spent considerable time in Israel, both for purposes of research and as a university instructor.

Levine's numerous articles have dealt with two principal areas: biblical studies proper, with a strong emphasis on cult and ritual; and Semitic epigraphy—Ugaritic and Aramaic principally, with some involvement in Phoenician-Punic and in Assyriological texts. Levine writes both in Hebrew and English.

In the biblical field, Levine has contributed a monograph on sacrifice, exploring the terms for various offerings in conjunction with ritual phenomenology.[52] More recently, in 1989, Levine's commentary on the book of Leviticus appeared as part of the JPS Torah Commentary.[53] The Leviticus commentary and Levine's individual studies on which it is ultimately founded, seek the historical *Sitz im Leben* of the priestly writings of the Torah (the "P" source) in post-exilic priestly activity.[54] These same studies demonstrate Levine's deep interest in the institutions of religion as well as in such socio-religious concepts as "purity" and "holiness."[55]

The link between Levine's biblical studies and his epigraphic investigations is often reflected by his focus on religious manifestations as well as on the phenomenon of magic in the comparative cultures. Thus, he has produced works on Ugaritic ritual and magic and on Aramaic magical texts.[56] On occasion, Levine has also written on ancient Near Eastern and biblical law.[57] Recently, he has written studies on the "Balaam Texts" from Deir Allâ in Transjordan.[58] Levine has also investigated aspects of Qumran literature.[59]

First and foremost, Levine is an exegete who first investigates a text in philological and contextual terms. From that point, he may proceed to a consideration of historical and phenomenological issues based on the understanding derived from study of the text.

Anson Rainey was born in Dallas, Texas in 1930. He earned his first B.A., in Religious Education, at John Brown University in Siloam Springs, Arkansas in 1949. For two years thereafter, he served as a social worker in the County Welfare Department in San Bernadino, California. He then enrolled at California Baptist Theological Seminary in Covina, California where he earned an M.A. in Old Testament, a B.D. in Biblical Theology and an M.Th. in Old Testament. In 1954, he joined the faculty of the seminary. Between 1955–1956, Rainey earned a second B.A., in ancient history, at UCLA. Having decided to pursue further graduate study, Rainey came to Brandeis in 1957. By 1962, Rainey had spent over a year in Israel, had mastered Modern Hebrew, and had completed the Ph. D. under Cyrus Gordon.

Upon completing the doctorate, Rainey returned to Israel to settle in 1962. Since that time, he has taught at Tel-Aviv University continuously, becoming a Full Professor in 1981. Throughout his years in Israel, Rainey has been engaged in archaeological activity in the field. Under the tutelage of the late Yohanan Aharoni, Rainey worked at Arad, Beersheba, and more recently at Tell Michal and Tel-Gerisa (1981–1983, 1986).

Originally, Rainey had been affiliated with a Christian community in Israel known as Nes Ammim. In 1980 however, he converted to Judaism, which accounts for his inclusion in this volume, and which certainly makes Rainey distinctive in the Second Wave. On the one hand, he is one of four members of this group to have settled in Israel. On the other hand, Rainey's experience as a Christian seminarian parallels that of any number of the present group who had attended Jewish seminaries.

Rainey writes both in Hebrew and in English. He has contributed major studies in the field of Ugaritic, beginning with his monograph on the social structure of Ugarit,[60] which was followed by a series of articles on linguistic and textual questions.[61] In 1970, he produced an edition of those Amarna tablets which had been unavailable to Knudtzon, the original primary editor.[62] Thanks to a grant from Tel-Aviv University's Research for Peace Project, Rainey was able to visit Cairo in the early eighties and to collate all the El Amarna Tablets in the Cairo Museum. Indeed, Rainey has contributed significantly to our understanding of Amarna Canaanite, and its reflexes in biblical Hebrew.[63] He has also employed his knowledge of Canaan in the Amarna age to elucidate biblical history and institutions.[64]

In the biblical field, strictly defined, Rainey has contributed a number of important articles,[65] including a study of sacrifice, in which he established the difference between the administrative order of listing sacrifices and the functional operative order within the cult.[66] Hebrew epigraphy has also accounted for a number of studies by Rainey.[67]

It would distort matters however, to apply a strictly topical criterion to Rainey's scholarly effort, which has produced several volumes, and more than eighty articles, many of which are of considerable interest to biblical studies. Rainey, like several other scholars of the Second Wave, exemplifies the student of ancient Near Eastern Cultures whose work in linguistics, philology, exegesis, historical geography and archaeology nourish the field of biblical studies and provide both information and insight into the life and culture of biblical Israel.

Another American-born scholar of the Second Wave who has settled in Israel is Jonas C. Greenfield. Born in New York City in 1926, he graduated from the College of the City of New York in 1949 with a B.A. in English. Greenfield at first pursued graduate work in the same field, earning the M.A. at Yale in 1952. But his past won out. While acquiring his earlier secular education, Greenfield had spent considerable time studying in Orthodox *yeshivot,* where, as we saw in the second chapter, the primary object of study was the Babylonian Talmud, the largest monument of Jewish Aramaic. Yale provided the opportunity for Greenfield to combine his interests in language with his talmudic learning. Accordingly, he shifted his graduate focus and earned the Ph.D. in Near Eastern languages at Yale in 1956.

After an instructorship at Brandeis University, Greenfield taught at the University of California, Los Angeles (1956–1965) and then at Berkeley, where he was Professor of Semitics until 1971. Thereupon, Greenfield settled in Israel, accepting a position as Professor of Ancient Semitic Languages at the Hebrew University, Jerusalem, where he has served ever since.

Greenfield is primarily a Semiticist, with strong interests in lexicography and semantics. In his numerous studies on ancient Near Eastern epigraphy, he treats biblical Hebrew as an ancient Semitic language, as though the Hebrew Bible represented an actual epigraphic or documentary source, rather than merely a canonical collection of writings. The contents of the Hebrew Bible thus qualify as original linguistic evidence.

Greenfield has authored about one hundred articles, ranging in their subject matter and textual references from pre-biblical to Medieval times, and in their language orientation from Akkadian and Ugaritic through Phoenician and early Aramaic to Persian, and several phases of post-biblical Hebrew. Greenfield has written most of his pieces in English, with a few having been published in Hebrew as well.

Undoubtedly, Aramaic has been a major focus of Greenfield's work. He has edited and published important texts in that language, including the Bisitun Inscription of Darius the Great.[68] In various publications, he has elucidated the Elephantine and other Egyptian papyri of the Achaemenid period, discussing not only their subject matter, but problems of language and formulation pertaining to them.[69] Actually, Greenfield has contributed notably to Early Aramaic studies as well.[70]

Greenfield's first scholarly works were lexicographical. In them, he demonstrated the relevance of post-biblical Jewish sources for our understanding of biblical Hebrew, while at the same time bringing to bear evidence from contemporary extra-biblical literature. He was able to resolve some long standing problems of biblical Hebrew philology.[71]

Greenfield's most obvious connection with biblical studies has been as a member of the scholarly committee that produced the new Bible translation of *Kethubim* for the Jewish Publication Society, along with Greenberg and Sarna.

The work of Jonas Greenfield illustrates quite incisively how biblical studies are nourished by comparative investigation. His specific pieces are usually very detailed and precisely focused on discrete textual units or definite linguistic problems, and yet are broad in their cultural and methodological implications.[72] Good examples of Bible-related studies are to be found in some of Greenfield's articles on Ugaritic and Phoenician.[73]

As was true of Tsevat, Moshe Held reversed the pattern of movement from America to Israel. Born in Poland in 1924,[74] Held was brought to Palestine at the age of eleven and raised in Tel Aviv. (Among his fellow students at Tel Aviv's Balfour secondary school was Abraham Malamat.) Held's studies at the Hebrew University in Jerusalem were interrupted by two periods of military service, first in the British Army during the Second World War, then in the Haganah during the Israeli War of Independence. Nonetheless, he managed to study with most of the great professors of that generation in Hebrew, Arabic, Semitics, and even Rabbinics. Held's initial primary concentration at Hebrew University was in medieval Hebrew and Arabic, and indeed his M.A. was in Hebrew Literature. Thanks to U.M. D. Cassuto, a pioneer in comparative biblical and Ugaritic studies, Held decided to shift his interests. In 1953, an exchange fellowship brought Held to the United States, his *zisn golus,* (Yiddish for "sweet exile"). In the United States he pursued graduate studies in Bible and ancient Near Eastern Languages under W. F. Albright at Johns Hopkins University.

Recognizing Held's extraordinary aptitude for language, Albright sent him to the Oriental Institute at Chicago where his primary studies were in Akkadian with Benno Landsberger (1890–1968), "one of the greatest Assyriologists of all time."[75] After four years at the Oriental Institute, Held returned to Johns Hopkins where he was awarded the Ph.D. in 1957.

In that same year, Held came to Dropsie to replace Cyrus Gordon, who had moved to Brandeis. In 1959, while still at Dropsie, Held began what was to become a twenty-five year association with JTS as an adjunct faculty member.[76] The JTS position also brought Held under the close tutelage of H. L. Ginsberg. Held remained at Dropsie until 1966, when he was brought to the Department of Middle East Languages and Cultures at Columbia to fill the vacancy created by the death of Isaac Mendelsohn.

As a writer, Held preferred footnotes to text.[77] Where other scholars might have expanded a note into an article, Held, whether writing in Hebrew or English, emulated his post-doctoral mentor, Ginsberg, in regularly condensing an article into a note.[78] In consequence, his twenty-one published articles contain a far greater wealth of material than might ever be imagined.

Beginning in Ugaritic studies, Held's interests seemed to shift in the 1960's, turning to Assyriology, more particularly to Old Babylonian Akkadian.[79] Held remained a comparatist however, and seldom walked into an Akkadian class without a Hebrew Bible at hand. Fully fourteen of his articles are inter-linguistic, comparing features of Ugaritic with Hebrew and Akkadian with Hebrew. This represents the relevance of Held's work for biblical studies. In the areas of lexicography and syntax, Held regularly sheds light on, and contributes to, the resolution of crucial lexemes and passages in the Hebrew Bible.[80] He persisted throughout his life in utilizing his thorough knowledge of classical Arabic in the investigation of ancient Semitic materials, and consequently in his recourse to the medieval Jewish lexicographers and commentators such as Saadia and ibn Janah who wrote in Arabic.

Held's work reveals the man's exceptional talent in lexicography, in which he synthesized method derived from his teachers, both immediate and removed, and made it his own.[81] From Albright and Landsberger he learned to stress usage over etymology in comparative lexicography. Second, he followed Cassuto's insistence that comparisons take account of diction so as to distinguish among everyday language, technical language such as one finds in economic or ritual texts, and the language of poetry. Third, Held, with many scholars, relied heavily on parallelism in delineating the semantic range of lexemes. These three principles were steps towards plotting the "interdialectal distribution." This last, which Cohen has most aptly characterized as the "hallmark"[82] of the Held method may be summarized quite simply: Held taught that one learned little of importance from comparing, for example, Hebrew *melek*, "king" with Akkadian *malku* "prince" or by comparing Akkadian *ṭābu* "sweet" with Hebrew *ṭôb* "good." Far more significant comparison resulted from establishing how a native speaker would have said "king" or "prince" or "sweet" or "good" in Hebrew, Akkadian, Ugaritic, Arabic, Phoenician and whatever other languages one was comparing.

Jacob Milgrom was born in Brooklyn, New York in 1923 and graduated from Brooklyn College in 1943. He was ordained as a rabbi in 1946 by JTS, where he also received a Doctor of Hebrew Letters under H. L. Ginsberg. For some years, Milgrom served as a congregational rabbi before devoting himself to academic life. In 1965 he began teaching in the Department of Near Eastern Languages at Berekeley, where he now is Professor of Bible. Milgrom writes both in Hebrew and in English.

Milgrom is a major exponent of cultic studies. He utilizes comparative evidence extensively in an attempt to place biblical religion in its proper ancient Near Eastern context. Milgrom's method is philological and exegetical in its initial phases, but he proceeds to engage broad questions of phenomenology and ritual system.

Milgrom's early work studied terminology relevant to the Levites, in which focused on the levitical assignments as projected in the tabernacle traditions.[83] He has gone on to write more than forty articles on sacrifice, purification and literary-historical questions, most of which have now been collected in two companion volumes.[84] From these it is clear that Milgrom has, over the years, elaborated an internally consistent approach to biblical religion. Along with showing the interrelatedness of biblical and other ancient Near Eastern religious systems, Milgrom stresses the distinctiveness of biblical attitudes. One senses a marked indebtedness to Yehezkel Kaufmann in Milgrom's work. More recently, Milgrom has contributed the commentary on Numbers to the JPS Torah Commentary.[85]

Robert Alter is a comparatist of a different kind. Whereas the other scholars of the Second Wave read the Bible in light of documentation from the ancient near East, Alter came to the Bible from the literature of the modern Western world. Born in New York City in 1935, Alter was graduated from Columbia College with a B.A. in English in 1957. He then went on to Harvard to earn an M.A. (1958) and Ph.D. (1960) in comparative literature. While a student at Columbia, Alter attended classes at the affiliated schools at JTS[86]. He also spent 1959–60 as a special student in Modern Hebrew Literature at the Hebrew University in Jerusalem. After receiving his doctorate, Alter returned to Columbia's English Department where he taught from 1962–1966. Since 1967, he has taught Hebrew and comparative literature at the University of California at Berkeley.

Alter's engagement of biblical literature developed in two stages. As a student of general literature, he exhibited interest in modern Hebrew Literature. As a student of modern Hebrew literature, Alter sought further to apply literary methods of analysis to biblical literature, qua literature.[87] Alter is a scion of a recent movement among Israeli scholars of literature, most notably Benjamin Hrushovsky (Harshav), who give their attention to the literary features of Biblical writing, poetic and prosaic. The organ of this movement is the journal *Ha-Sifrut,* founded and edited for an extended period by Harshav himself.

As a student of world literature, Alter's primary focus has been the novel as a literary genre. Beginning with *Rogue's Progress: Studies in the Picaresque Novel*[88], Alter has over the years published volumes on Fielding and Stendahl, as well as individual studies on the novel.[89] This dimension of Alter's work has made of him a noted authority on the novel, and in addition, a major exponent of the literary investigation of biblical literature.[90]

In this last area, Alter has written two volumes, one may say companion volumes: *The Art of Biblical Narrative*[91] and *The Art of Biblical Poetry*.[92] Some of the subjects and contents of these volumes first appeared in *Commentary,* a popular journal Alter has used extensively to expound his approach to biblical literature. Alter, like Greenberg, emphasizes the final products of biblical literary creativity, such as entire narratives and poems. He seeks to trace, first how such writings were composed, and then what lends them coherence. He is especially interested in the intertextual connections between narratives. In his investigation of biblical poetry, Alter, as expected, discusses the character and functions of poetic parallelism, shows an interest in semantics, and deals with poetic structures. His work has added to our appreciation of the literary processes reflected in biblical literary creativity. Tacitly, and at times vocally, Alter questions the sufficiency of the more accepted modes of modern critical Bible scholarship, including exegesis, philology and source and form-criticism.

It behooves us at this point to offers some generalizations for the benefit of the reader. The first noteworthy observation is that fully nine out of the fourteen members of the Second Wave underwent formative academic training in a rabbinical seminary or its affiliated schools. Five are graduates of Jewish Theological Seminary (JTS): M. Greenberg, B. A. Levine, J. Milgrom, Y. Muffs and S. Paul. Although R. Alter never trained for the rabbinate, he studied at the Seminary College of JTS and worked in the Ramah Summer Camp System of the JTS Teachers' Institute.

One member of the group, Brichto, is a rabbinic graduate of Hebrew Union College-Jewish Institute of Religion (HUC-JIR). Mattiahu Tsevat spent four years at Breslau's Jüdisch-Theologisches Seminar and would have been ordained there had the Nazis not made that impossible. Nahum Sarna graduated from Jews' College in London with a Minister's Diploma, a degree essentially equivalent to rabbinic ordination from non-Orthodox American Jewish seminaries.[93] To add a tenth scholar with a seminary background, we have noted that Anson Rainey graduated from a Christian seminary before converting to Judaism later in his life. In interesting respects, Rainey's experience parallels the careers of Jewish scholars of the second wave and their Christian counterparts, who possess a seminary education, and who went on to work in the field of biblical studies. For Jewish scholars, the seminary education contributed a general grounding in Hebraic studies, and a conversance with sources deriving from later periods of Judaic creativity. Some younger Jewish Bible scholars who would not attend seminaries or their affiliated schools will be seen to lack this kind of general background, which affords access to classical rabbinic and medieval Jewish exegesis, as well as to Israeli scholarship published in scientific Hebrew.

Of the fourteen, only S. Gevirtz, J. Greenfield, W. Hallo and M. Held never experienced a seminary education, but to stop at that would be misleading. Jonas Greenfield had studied within the *yeshivah* context at an earlier stage of his life. As regards the remaining three, Gevirtz, Hallo and Held each spent a considerable amount of their teaching careers at seminaries. In other words, every member of the Second Wave has or had a seminary affiliation.

A further observation to be made about the scholars of the second wave is that four of them ultimately settled in Israel, and currently hold academic posts in Israeli institutions of higher learning: M. Greenberg, J. Greenfield and S. Paul at Hebrew University, and A. Rainey at Tel-Aviv University. We shall see that a number of younger Bible scholars continued this trend into the 1970's and 1980's. In contrast, two of the group, M. Held and M. Tsevat, began their graduate training in Israel, and only subsequently came to the United States, where they completed their doctoral studies and remained to pursue academic careers. These biographical facts indicate the high degree of interaction between Israel and North America in the area of Bible.

We have already explained that the Jewish Bible scholars of the second wave have competence in post-biblical Judaic literature. Indeed, the work of some of these scholars relies more heavily on the utilization of the Judaic tradition in understanding the Bible than does the work of the scholars who trained them.

The survey presented above brings us to the mid-1960's and indicates just how restricted Jewish Bible scholarship was in North America until recently. The number of Jewish scholars whose center of gravity could be identified as "biblical" rather than Semitic or Assyriological was not large. In the discussion of the next period, from 1965–1980, we shall encounter a greater degree of focus on biblical studies, as more strictly defined. This trend is, however, more recent than we had tended to assume.

It must also be remembered that the approach taken in this study is to date individual scholars by the time of their entry into the field.

As a practical matter however, a scholar who received the Ph.D. in 1962, for example, would not have begun to make an impact on the field until well after 1965, perhaps in the early 1970's or even later. The chronological gap between entry into the field and impact effectively pushes the development of Jewish scholarship in North America ahead in time and makes of it an even more recent phenomenon.

Yet, by 1965, it was clear that the participation of Jewish scholars in biblical and related studies in North America was firmly rooted. Students were pursuing doctoral studies in the field, publication was increasing, and significant contributions by Jewish scholars were helping to set the course of North American Bible scholarship in all of its aspects.

Notes to Chapter Four

1. The name, Hebrew for "tongs," is a Hebrew rendition of Tsevat's European family name, Pinczower.
2. On Lewy see our previous chapter.
3. Note his reference to Buber and Rosenzweig's employ of "Leitwörter," in *HUCA* 203 (1961), n. 76; See also M. Tsevat, "The Foundation of the Monarchy," in idem, *The Meaning of the Book of Job and Other Essays* (New York: Ktav, 1980), 84, n. 19.
4. See ibid, 1-37; note further idem, "Theology of the Old Testament: A Jewish View," in *Horizons in Biblical Theology* 8 (1986), 33-50.
5. See e.g. M. Tsevat, "Traces of Hittite at the Beginning of the Ugaritic Epic of Aqhat," *Ugarit Forschungen* 3 (1971), 351-352.
6. See e.g. idem, "The Skin of His Face was Radiant, (Ex. 34:19)," *Eretz Israel* 16 (1982), 163-167 (in Hebrew).
7. M. Tsevat, *A Study of the Language of the Biblical Psalms* (Philadelphia: SBL, 1955).
8. idem, "Studies in the Book of Samuel," *HUCA* Pts. 1-5, 32-46 (1961-1975); See further idem, "Samuel, I and II," *IDBSup*, 777-781.
9. See e.g. M. Tsevat, "Alalakhiana," *HUCA* 29 (1958), 109-134; idem, "Comments on the Ugaritic Text UT 52," *Eretz Israel* 14 (1978), 24*-27*; idem, "Eating and Drinking, Hosting and Sacrificing in the Epic of Aqhat," *Ugarit Forschungen* 18 (1987), 345-350.
10. Note his offhand reference to Kant's rarely read "Conflict of the Faculties," in Tsevat, "Leeser's Biblical Work," 311, n. 41.
11. See J. Kraemer, "Hallo, Rudolf," *EncJud* 7, 1201-1202. The family connection to Rosenzweig led Hallo to translate the latter's most famous work of Jewish theology. See F. Rosenzweig, *The Star of Redemption* translated from the Second Edition of 1930 by William W. Hallo (New York: Holt, Rinehart and Winston, 1971).
12. From his numerous significant contributions in this area we cite W.

Hallo, *Early Mesopotamian Royal Titles: A Philologic and Historical Analysis* (American Oriental Series, 43, New Haven: American Oriental Society, 1957); idem, (with J. van Dijk), *The Exaltation of Inanna* (New Haven: Yale University, 1968); idem. "Toward a History of Sumerian Literature," in S. Lieberman (ed.), *Sumerological Studies in Honor of Thorkild Jacobsen* (Assyriological Studies 20; Chicago: University of Chicago, 1975), 181–203.

13. W. G. Plaut (ed.), *The Torah: A Modern Commentary* Commentaries by W. G. Plaut and B. Bamberger; Essays on Near Eastern Literature by W. Hallo (New York: Union of American Hebrew Congregations, 1981).

14. See W. Hallo, "New Moons and Sabbaths: A Case-study in the Contrastive Approach," *HUCA* 48 (1977), 1–18. The quotation is from ibid, 2.

15. W. Hallo and W. K. Simpson, *The Ancient Near East: A History* (New York: Harcourt Brace Jovanovich, 1971).

16. See e.g. W. Hallo, "From Qarqar to Carchemish: Assyria and Israel in the Light of New Discoveries," *Biblical Archaeologist* 23 (1950), 33–62; idem, "Biblical Abominations and Sumerian Taboos," *JQR* 76 (1985), 21–40.

17. See e.g. idem, " 'As the Seal upon Thine Arm': Glyptic Metaphors in the Biblical World," in L. Gorelick and E. Williams-Forte (eds.), *Ancient Seals and the Bible* (Malibu: Undena, 1983), 7–17.

18. See e.g. idem, "A Letter Fragment from Tell Aphek," *Tel-Aviv* 8 (1981), 18–24; idem (with H. Tadmor), "A Lawsuit from Hazor," *Israel Exploration Journal* 27 (1977), 1–11.

19. S. Gevirtz, *Patterns in the Early Poetry of Israel* (2nd edition; Chicago: University of Chicago, 1973).

20. See e.g. idem, "Evidence of Conjugational Variation in the Parallelization of Sefsame Verbs in the Amarna Letters," *Journal of Near Eastern Studies* 32 (1973), 99–104; idem, "On Canaanite Rhetoric—The Evidence of the Amarna Letters From Tyre," *Orientalia* 42 (1973), 162–177; idem, "Of Syntax and Style in the 'Late Biblical Hebrew'-'Old Canaanite' Connection," *Journal of the Ancient Near Eastern Society* 18 (1986), 25–29.

21. idem, "West Semitic Curses and the Problem of the Origins of Hebrew Law," *Vetus Testamentum* 11 (1961), 137–158.

22. See e.g. idem, "Naphtali in the Blessing of Jacob," *JBL* 103 (1984), 513–521; idem, "The Issachar Oracle in the Testament of Jacob," *Eretz Israel* 12 (1975), *104–*112; idem, "Asher in the Blessing of Jacob, (Genesis xlix 29)," *Vetus Testamentum* 37 (1987), 154–163; idem, "Adumbrations of Dan in Jacob's Blessing on Judah," *Zeitschrift für die alttestamentliche Wissenschaft* 93 (1981), 21–37; idem, "Simeon and Levi in the Blessing of Jacob, Gen. 49:5–7)," *HUCA* 52 (1981), 93–128.

23. See idem, "Of Patriarchs and Puns: Joseph at the Fountain, Jacob at the Ford," *HUCA 46* (1975), 33–54; idem, "Abraham's 318," *Israel Exploration Journal* 19 (1969), 110–13.

24. M. Greenberg, *The Hab/piru* (New Haven: American Oriental Series 39, 1965).

25. idem, "Some Postulates of Biblical Criminal Law," in M. Haran (ed.), *Yehezkel Kaufmann Jubilee Volume* (Jerusalem: Magnes, 1960), 5–28;

cf. more recently, idem, "More Reflections on Biblical Criminal Law," *Scripta Hierosolymitana* 31 (1986), 1-17).
26. idem, "Another Look at Rachel's Theft of the Teraphim," *JBL* 81 (1962), 239-48.
27. Y. Kaufmann, *The Religion of Israel From Its Beginnings to the Babylonian Exile* (translated and abridged by Moshe Greenberg; Chicago: University of Chicago, 1960). The material of Volume 8 was not included in Greenberg's version.
28. M. Greenberg, *Introduction to Hebrew* (Englewood Cliffs: Prentice-Hall, 1965).
29. idem, *Understanding Exodus* Part I (New York: Melton Research Center Jewish Theological Seminary, 1969).
30. See our chapter on "Compendia," below.
31. M. Greenberg, *Ezekiel 1-20* (Anchor Bible 22; Garden City: Doubleday, 1986).
32. See our "Introduction," as well as the chapter on "The Current Scene."
33. See Greenberg, *Ezekiel*, 26.
34. M. Greenberg, *Biblical Prose Prayer* (Berkeley: University of California, 1983).
35. Y. Muffs, *Studies in the Aramaic Legal Papyri from Elephantine* (Leiden: Brill, 1969).
36. On the method see below. Cf. the review of *Studies*, by D. Boyarin, *JANES* 3 (1971), 57-62.
37. Y. Muffs, "Reflections on Prophetic Prayer in the Bible," *Eretz Israel* 14 (1978), 48-54 (in Hebrew).
38. idem, "Joy and Love as Metaphorical Examples of Willingness and Spontaneity in Cuneiform, Ancient Hebrew, and Related Literatures," in J. Neusner (ed.), *Christianity, Judaism and Other Greco-Roman Cults Studies . . . Morton Smith III* (Leiden: Brill, 1975), 1-36; idem, "The Joy of Giving (Love and Joy as Metaphors of Volition in Hebrew and Related Literatures, Part II)," *JANES* 11 (1979), 91-111; Note also idem, "Two Comparative Lexical Studies," *JANES* 5 (1973), 287-98.
39. S. Paul, *Studies in the Book of the Covenant in the Light of Cuneiform and Biblical Law* (Leiden: Brill, 1975). The book had its origin in Paul's 1964 dissertation, "Studies in the Book of the Covenant."
40. See S. Paul, "Unrecognized Biblical Legal Idioms in the Light of Comparative Akkadian Expressions," *Revue biblique* 86 (1979), 231-39; idem, "Adoption Formulae: A Study of Cuneiform and Biblical Legal Clauses," *MAARAV* 2/2 (1979-1980), 173-85.
41. See e.g. S. Paul, "Deutero-Isaiah and cuneiform Royal Inscriptions," *JAOS* 88 (1968), 180-86; idem, "Literary and Ideological Echoes of Jeremiah in Deutero-Isaiah," *Fifth World Congress of Jewish Studies* (1972), 102-20.
42. See e.g. idem, "Jerusalem- A City of Gold," *Israel Exploration Journal* 17 (1967), 259-63; idem, "Sargon's Administrative Diction in II Kings 17:27," *JBL* 88 (1969), 73-74.
43. H. C. Brichto, *The Problem of "Curse" in the Hebrew Bible* (JBL

Monograph Series 13; Philadelphia, 1963).

44. See further idem, "The Case of the Sota and a Reconsideration of Biblical Law," *HUCA* 46 (1975), 55-70.

45. *HUCA* 44 (1973), 1-54.

46. *HUCA* 47 (1976), 1-17; See also, H. Brichto, "The Worship of the Golden Calf: A Literary Analysis of a Fable on Idolatry," *HUCA* 54 (1983), 1-44.

47. See e.g., N. Sarna, "Psalm 89: A Study in Inner Biblical Exegesis," in A. Altmann (ed.), *Biblical and Other Studies* (Cambridge: Harvard, 1963), 29-46; idem, "The Psalm for the Sabbath Day, (Psalm 92)," *JBL* 81 (1962), 155-68; idem "The Psalms Superscriptions and the Guilds," in S. Stein and B. Loewe (eds.), *Studies in Jewish Religious and Intellectual History* (University AL: University of Alabama, 1979), 281-300; idem, "Psalms, Book of," *EncJud* 13, 1303-22.

48. N. Sarna, "Hebrew and Bible Studies in Medieval Spain," in R. Barnett (ed.), *The Sephardi Heritage* (New York: Valentine Mitchell, 1971), 323-66.

49. idem, *Understanding Genesis* (New York: Melton Research Center JTS, 1966); idem, *Exploring Exodus* (New York: Schocken, 1986).

50. idem, "Old Testament Canon, Texts and Versions," *New Encyclopaedia Brittanica Macropaedia*, (Chicago: Benton, 1973) Vol 2, 881-95.

51. *The JPS Torah Commentary Genesis the Traditional Hebrew Text with the New JPS Translation* Commentary by Nahum M. Sarna (Philadelphia: Jewish Publication Society, 1989); idem, *Exodus* (1991).

52. B. Levine, *In the Presence of the Lord* (Leiden: Brill, 1974).

53. *The JPS Torah Commentary Leviticus. The Traditional Hebrew Text with the New JPS Translation.* Commentary by Baruch A. Levine. (Jewish Publication Society: Philadelphia, 1989). Cf. our chapter on "Compendia," below.

54. See e.g. B. Levine, "Research in the Priestly Source: The Linguistic Factor," *Eretz Israel* 16 (1982), 124-131 (in Hebrew); idem, "The Epilogue to the Holiness Code: A Priestly Statement on the Destiny of Israel," in J. Neusner, B. Levine and E. Frerichs (ed.), *Judaic Perspectives on Ancient Israel* (Philadelphia: Fortress, 1987), 9-34.

55. See e.g. idem, "The Language of Holiness: Perceptions of the Sacred in the Hebrew Bible," in M. O'Connor and D. N. Freedman (eds.), *Backgrounds for the Bible* (Winona Lake: Eisenbrauns, 1987), 241-55.

56. See e.g. B. Levine, "Ugaritic Descriptive Rituals," *JCS* 17 (1963), 105-11; idem, "The Descriptive Ritual Texts from Ugarit: Some Formal and Functional Features of the Genre," in C. Meyers and M. O'Connor (eds.), *The Word of the Lord Shall Go Forth Essays . . . Freedman* (Winona Lake: Eisenbrauns, 1983), 467-75; idem (with J-M de Taragon), " 'Shapshu Cries Out in Heaven': Dealing with Snake Bites at Ugarit," *Revue biblique* 95 (1988), 481-518; idem, "the Language of the Magical Bowls," apud J. Neusner, *A History of the Jews in Babylonia* V (Leiden: Brill, 1969), 345-73.

57. See B. Levine, "In Praise of the Israelite *Mišpâḥâ*: Legal Themes in the Book of Ruth," in H. Huffmon, F. Spina and A. R. Green (eds.), *The*

Quest for the Kingdom of God: Studies . . . Mendenhall (Winona Lake: Eisenbrauns, 1983), 95-106.

58. See e.g., B. Levine, "The Deir Allâ Plaster Inscriptions," *JAOS* 101 (1981), 195-205.

59. e. g. idem, "The Temple Scroll: Aspects of its Historical Provenance and Literary Characteristics," *BASOR* 232 (1979), 4-25.

60. A. Rainey, *The Social Structure of Ugarit* (Jerusalem: Bialik, 1967 [in Hebrew]); see further idem, "The Scribe at Ugarit, His Position and Influence," *Proceedings of the Israel Academy of Science and Humanities* 3 (1968), 126-47; idem, "Business Agents at Ugarit," *Israel Exploration Journal* 13 (1963), 313-21.

61. e.g. idem, "Gleanings from Ugarit," *Israel Oriental Studies* 3 (1973), 34-62; idem, "Observations on Ugaritic Grammar," *Ugarit Forschungen* 3 (1971), 151-72.

62. idem, *El Amarna Tablets 359-379* (Kevalaer and Neukirchen-Vluyn: Butzon & Bercker and Neukirchener, 1970; Revised, 1978).

63. e.g. idem, "Reflections on the Suffix Conjugation in West Semitized Amarna Tablets," *Ugarit Forschungen* 5 (1973), 235-62.

64. See e.g., Rainey's critical review of N. Gottwald, *The Tribes of Yahweh* in *JAOS* 107 (1987), 541-43.

65. See e.g. idem, "Compulsory Labor Gangs in Ancient Israel," *Israel Exploration Journal* 20 (1970), 191-202.

66. idem, "The Order of Sacrifices in Old Testament Ritual Texts," *Biblica* 51 (1970), 485-98.

67. e.g. idem, "A Hebrew 'Receipt' from Arad," *Bulletin of the American Schools of Oriental Research* 202 (April, 1971), 23-30; idem, "Semantic Parallels to the Samaria Ostraca," *Palestine Exploration Quarterly* 102 (1970), 45-51.

68. See J. Greenfield and B. Porten, *The Bisitun Inscription of Darius the Great Aramaic Version* (London: Lund Humphries for Corpus Inscriptionum Iranicarum, 1982).

69. Note the following: J. Greenfield and B. Porten, *Jews of Elephantine and Aramaeans of Syene (Fifth Century B.C. E). Fifty Aramaic Texts with Hebrew and English Translations* (Jerusalem: Hebrew University, 1974); idem (also with Porten), "The Aramaic Papyri from Hermopolis," *ZAW* 80 (1968), 216-31; idem (with J. Naveh), "Hebrew and Aramaic in the Persian Period," in W. D. Davies and L. Finkelstein (eds.), *The Cambridge History of Judaism I* (Cambridge: Cambridge University, 1984), 115-29. 70. Several of his articles deal with the Sefire Aramaic inscriptions of the eighth century B.C. We note J. Greenfield, "Stylistic Aspects of the Sefire Treaty Inscriptions," *Acta Orientalia* 11 (1966), 1-18; idem, "Three Notes on the Sefire Inscriptions," *Journal of Semitic Studies* 11 (1966), 98-105. More recently, Greenfield has studied the biblingual inscription from Tel-Fekherye. See idem (with A. Shaffer), "Notes on the Akkadian-Aramaic Bilingual Statue from Tell Fekhereye," *Iraq* 45 (1983), 109-16; idem (also with Shaffer), "Notes on the Curse Formulae of the Tell Fekherye Inscription," *Revue biblique* 92 (1985), 47-59.

71. See e.g. J. Greenfield, "Lexicographical Notes I," *HUCA* 29 (1958),

203–28; idem, "Lexicographical Notes II," Ibid 30 (1959), 141–51). More recently, note idem, "Baal's Throne and Isa. 6:1," in A. Caquot, S. Legasse and M. Tardieu (eds.), *Mélanges bibliques et orientaux en l'honneur de M. Mathias Delcor* (AOAT 25; Kevalaer and Neukirchen-Vluyn: Butzon & Bercker and Neukirchener, 1985), 193–98. For a study in a similar vein see the Hebrew article, J. Greenfield, "Two Biblical Passages in the Light of their Near Eastern Background-Ezekiel 16:30 and Malachi 3:17," *Eretz Israel* 16 (1982), 56–61.

72. See e.g. idem, "The Seven Pillars of Wisdom (Prov. 9:1)—A Mistranslation," *Jewish Quarterly Review* 76 (1985), 13–20. 73. See e.g. idem, "Some Glosses on the Keret Epic," *Eretz Israel* 9 (1969), 60–65; idem, "Notes on the Asitawada (Karatepe) Inscription," (Hebrew) *Eretz Israel* 14 (1978), 74–77.

74. For biographical information see S. Lieberman, "Moshe Held (1924–1984)," in *JQR* 76 (1985), 1–3; E. Greenstein and D. Marcus, "Professor Moshe Held: Our Teacher," *JANES* 19 (1989), 1–2. For Held's bibliography see ibid, vii–viii.

75. So, Thorkild Jacobsen, *Monographs on the Ancient Near East* Volume 1, fasc. 4 (Malibu: Undena, 1976), 3.

76. For Held and the Seminary-Columbia connection as an influence on the next generation, see our chapter on "The Current Scene," below.

77. For a particularly good example, see M. Held, "The Action-Result (Factitive-Passive) Sequence of Identical Verbs in Biblical Hebrew and Ugaritic," *JBL* 84 (1965), 272–82. Indeed, the plethora of notes compelled *JBL* to publish them as endnotes in departure from its usual practice. See ibid, 272.

78. See e.g. *JAOS* 79 (1959), 173, n. 79; *Journal of Cuneiform Studies* 15 (1961), 11–12 (note to I:7 of the text); *JANES* 6 (1974), 107, n. 8.

79. See e.g. M. Held, "A Faithful Lover in an Old Babylonian Dialogue," *JCS* 15 (1961), 1–26; idem, "On Terms for Deportation in the Old Babylonian Royal Inscriptions with Special Reference to Yahdunlim," *JANES* 11 (1979), 53–62. Note however, that this last article, despite its title, makes constant biblical and West-Semitic comparisons.

80. See e.g. M. Held, "The Root *zbl/sbl* in Akkadian, Ugaritic and Biblical Hebrew," *JAOS* 88 (1968), 90–96; idem, "Pits and Pitfalls in Akkadian and Biblical Hebrew," *JANES* 5 (1973), 173–90.

81. Cf. C. Cohen, "The 'Held Method' for Comparative Semitic Philology," *JANES* 19 (1989), 9–23.

82. ibid, 13.

83. J. Milgrom, *Studies in Levitical Terminology I* (Berkeley: University of California, 1970 [2nd edition]).

84. J. Milgrom, *Cult and Conscience: The Asham and the Priestly Doctrine of Repentance* (Leiden: Brill, 1976); idem, *Studies in Cultic Theology and Terminology* (Leiden: Brill, 1983).

85. See our chapter on "Compendia," below.

86. It should be emphasized that Judaic studies were available to undergraduates at very few colleges and universities until the late-1960's and early 1970's. Accordingly, college students who wished to study Hebraica and

Judaica apart from their regular studies attended classes at various Hebrew Teachers' Colleges which were to be found in the larger cities. In addition to JTS, mention should be made of Boston Hebrew Teachers' College, Baltimore Hebrew College, Gratz College in Philadelphia, and College of Jewish Studies in Chicago.

87. Among Alter's works on modern Hebrew literature are R. Alter, *Modern Hebrew Literature* (New York: Behrman House, 1975); and several articles on S. Y. Agnon, some written in Hebrew. His article, "The Israeli Novel," appeared in *Daedalus* (Fall, 1966). During the 1960's Alter contributed no fewer than fourteen pieces to *Commentary* magazine pertaining to modern and contemporary Hebrew literature.

88. (Cambridge: Harvard, 1964).

89. R. Alter, *Fielding and the Nature of the Novel* (Cambridge: Harvard, 1968); idem, *A Lion in Love: A Critical Biography of Stendahl* (New York: Basic Books, 1979). Other works on the novel include: *Partial Magic: The Novel as a Self-Conscious Genre* (Los Angeles: UCLA, 1975); *Motives: On Fiction* (Cambridge: Harvard, 1984).

90. The first signal of Alter's interest in biblical literature was his article, "A Literary Approach to the Bible," (*Commentary*, December, 1975). It was followed shortly thereafter by "Biblical Narrative," (ibid, May, 1976).

91. R. Alter, *The Art of Biblical Narrative* (New York: Basic Books, 1981).

92. idem, *The Art of Biblical Poetry* (New York: Basic Books, 1985).

93. On Jews' College see V. D. Lipman, "Jews College," *EncJud* 10, 98–99. Jews' College includes a modernist rabbinic program in its curriculum. Ministerial graduates are trained to serve in the pulpit but are required to undertake additional schooling in the law codes if they desire the title "rabbi," which is reserved for those with traditional Orthodox rabbinic ordination. See above Chapter Two, especially, n. 9.

CHAPTER FIVE
The Current Scene

Our survey of Jewish biblical scholarship in North America turns now to the field as it exists today, represented by scholars who earned the doctorate between 1965–1980, a period in which significant trends and changes may be identified. First, it may be observed that thanks in part to such scholars as Levine, Milgrom and Sarna in the period immediately preceding, the Jewish quasi-taboo against higher critical study of the Pentateuch had been shattered. Despite the fact that these scholars were themselves divided over such issues as the respective priority of "P" and "D", the historical reliability of the Bible, the question of whether the biblical cult was "magical" or whether Israelite monotheism had originated early or late, they agreed in directly confronting the questions central to modern biblical study. As a result, such formerly sensitive issues as Mosaic authorship of the Pentateuch were rendered as neutral as the questions of Solomonic authorship of Ecclesiastes and the unity of Isaiah. In addition, the agenda of Pentateuchal studies, and biblical studies in general, had shifted from the confrontation between a "traditional" and a "historical" approach to more strictly academic questions of method, such as "literary" or "philological" versus "historical," "archaeological," or "anthropological." In sum, the scholars who came to maturity after 1965 were heir to the rich diversity in the work of the immediately preceding generation. Perhaps the greatest factor in the increasing refinement of method after 1965 was played by the radical change in the population of Jewish biblicists.

First and foremost was the swelling of the ranks. The number of Ph.D. degrees awarded in Bible and related areas increased as the general graduate school population grew in the 1960's. As in previous generations, most of the members of this group, especially the older ones, had initially come to graduate school motivated by an interest in Bible. Because Bible proper was studied primarily in departments of Religion in denominational settings and in divinity schools, Jewish students of this generation were as likely as their predecessors to enroll in departments of Middle East languages and Semitics. To judge from dissertations, subsequent publication and personal communications, initial interest in Bible was often diverted into neighboring areas, primarily Northwest Semitic, Assyriology and archaeology. The academic retrenchments of the 1970's following on the overproduction of Ph.D.'s made employment opportunities scarce, especially in esoteric fields. At the same time however, enrollments in college Bible classes began to increase, thanks in part to the resurgence of religion in America and to the related increased availability of religious studies in such non-confessional settings as state universities. The net result was to rekindle an interest in Bible in many a scholar who had become involved in other areas of ancient Near Eastern studies.

But the increase in numbers is only part of the story. The second obvious change in North American Jewish Bible scholarship is the presence of women scholars.[1] It would be difficult to overstate the significance of the feminist movement for our field. Two results of feminism may be emphasized here. First, feminism has encouraged women to make their mark in Bible and ancient Near Eastern studies just as they have been doing in other areas of academic and professional life. Second, feminism has raised scholarly issues that had usually been overlooked before women entered the field. In consequence, both female and male Jewish scholars, have with their gentile colleagues, begun to examine the depiction of women by the biblical writers and to seek the recovery of the social location of women in ancient Israel.[2]

Most significant for Jewish biblical scholarship in the period under survey however, was the legitimation of ethic studies, including Jewish or Judaic studies programs, on college campuses, and the related increase in American and Canadian Jewish participation in study-programs in Israel.[3] The effects of these developments may be seen by comparing the educational profile of the post-1965 scholars with that of the scholars described in the preceding chapter. Most of the Jewish Bible scholars of the earlier generation had acquired the fundamentals required for graduate study while in rabbinical school, and especially the Conservative movement's Jewish Theological Seminary.[4] In contrast, by the mid-1970's it had become increasingly possible for would-be biblicists to receive undergraduate training in Hebrew and Judaica and to attend graduate school after the award of the B.A. just as in most other disciplines. Whereas in the past, college Bible courses had usually been taught by Christians, Jewish studies programs were most often staffed by Jews. To be sure, in such programs Modern Hebraists often taught Bible and biblicists often taught modern Hebrew. Although mixed blessings resulted from these academic unions, they served the needs of professors who wanted jobs, students whose inchoate interests in Judaics ranged through Bible, holocaust and Israeli demographics, and administrators who had to count bodies and balance budgets. The net result was that more Jewish students took Bible courses in college. It may also be observed that increased ethnic awareness among Jewish students in Judaics programs has had an impact on the presentation of Jewish biblical scholarship. The scholars of the 1965–1980 generation (and perhaps more so, those of the present decade) have tended more than their predecessors to attempt to delineate the distinctive features of Jewish Bible scholarship in contrast to Christian.[5] We may also detect an increasing deference to the earlier Jewish exegetical tradition.[6] As an ancillary development, whose results have yet to be fully evaluated, Jewish scholars who chose academic careers in fields such as English or comparative literature, often acquired sufficient background as students to encourage them to make observations on the Bible.[7]

An important characteristic of much current Bible scholarship, Jewish as well as Gentile, is the search for new theoretical models. Because of the perception that many of "the sense making paradigms have ceased to make full sense,"[8] Bible scholars now bring to their work an impressive variety of approaches imported from other disciplines. It will further be observed that scholars trained between 1965–1980 have made a point of articulating their theories and methods to a far greater degree than did their predecessors.[9] Nowhere is this truer than in the literary interpretation of the Bible, which has moved its practitioners much more into the academic mainstream. The appeal of the literary approach is obvious to anyone who has taught OT or NT in translation: It is easier for example, to draw undergraduate students into the narrative flow of the Joseph story than into the analysis of its sources. By adapting to biblical studies the analytical tools borrowed from contemporary literary theory; notably structuralism, semiotics and deconstruction, scholars, Jewish and Gentile, have divested themselves of the unwarranted and undesired stereotype of the biblicist as a combination of covert missionary and student of arcana. Simply stated, approaching the Bible as literature provides a potentially wider audience.[20] Because the literary interpretation of the Bible has attained the status of a sub-field within biblical studies of the late twentieth century, it will be useful to make some, necessarily sketchy, remarks on the literary approach, with particular reference to Jewish participation in the endeavor.

Literary interpretation of the Bible was anticipated in the work of Jewish scholars outside of North America whose writings were somewhat adverse to the methods and conclusions of mainstream biblical studies.[11] In their different ways, U. M. D. Cassuto (1883–1957),[12] M. H. Segal (1876–1968),[13] Martin Buber (1878–1965), Franz Rosenzweig (1886–1929),[14] and Benno Jacob (1862–1945)[15] de-emphasized or rejected the analytical dissection of the text as practiced in classical source-criticism, concentrating instead on the search for elements of textual unity and thematic coherence. Although these men were hardly fundamentalists, their post-critical stance was perceived, with some justification, as an ideological agenda imposed on the biblical texts. Accordingly, their work was not very influential during their own lifetimes. In addition, although all of these scholars were attentive to literary features within the Bible that had generally been ignored in classical criticism, they did not have recourse to the theoretical terminology[16] employed in the contemporary study of literature. More recently however, the emphasis placed by these writers on the books of the Bible as completed works,[17] has gained ground. The study of the final form of literary units became particularly attractive to contemporary Jewish scholars once it was realized that the entire process by which a tradition passed from its earliest stages through final redaction might now be appreciated as an example of Israelite and Jewish literary creativity, rather than demeaned as the pasting together of jumbled fragments by small-minded post-exilic priests.[18] It may also be observed that concentration on the received textual entity has brought about a corresponding positive re-evaluation of midrash and of pre-critical Jewish Bible commentary both of which, in the manner of literary interpretation, draw conclusions on the presumption of conscious unity of authorship.

Useful as these developments are, important caveats have been raised. Michael Fishbane has characterized some tendencies in the literary approach as advocating the principle: "What the text has joined together let no critic rend asunder."[19] Obviously, unchecked "holistic" or "synchronic" readings can easily degenerate into neofundamentalism.[20] A related danger is that "absorption in innertextual interplay will reduce literary meanings to a garden of mentalistic delights and so sponsor a new narcissism."[21]

Unfortunately, two formerly popular approaches to the Bible, both of which could obviate Fishbane's objections and place literary interpretation on a solid footing, are on the wane. The first is text-criticism. Serious literary interpretation of the Bible requires reliable Hebrew texts and these have not been forthcoming.[22] Equally serious has been the decline of interest in the study of the Bible in the light of ancient Near Eastern sources. Some factors contributing to this second development may be identified. Most obvious, archaeology has demonstrated both the complexity and diversity of the civilizations of the ancient Near East and the relative unimportance of the political and cultural contributions of the minor kingdoms Israel and Judah to their contemporary world. Accordingly, Assyriologists, Egyptologists, Hittitologists and others whose focus is on the great cultures and major political powers of Near Eastern antiquity need not study Hebrew or read the Bible any more than students of modern English or French literature need study Czech. Second, misuse of the comparative method, particularly in lexicography, has led to a "radical purism"[23] in certain circles of ancient Near Easterrn studies, where anything having to do with the Bible is viewed with suspicion. Third, some scholars have become disillusioned by the failure of "biblical archaeology" to fulfill some of its more extravagant claims.[24] In some respects then, literary interpretation, which treats the text as a "self-regulating universe of discourse"[25] is a return to the Wellhausenian preoccupation with the text to the exclusion of data drawn from the ancient Near East. There is no little irony in this development because ultimately, only if such terms as "authorship," "editing," "redaction," "prose," "poetry," "literature," "framing," "Leitwörter," "codes," "point of view," "voice," "thematic organization," "symmetry" and "envelope structure" can be shown to have heuristic value in the study of writings produced by the contemporaries of ancient Israel, are they likely to be valid for biblical studies.

In addition to the influences of literary theory, it will be seen presently that scholars trained between 1965–1980 have been aided by advances in the fields of linguistics, cultural anthropology, sociology, and comparative folklore.[26]

Understandably, this chapter differs from the earlier ones in some respects. Because of the larger numbers, and more important, because the individual surveyed will continue working, *deo volente,* less space is devoted to each individual scholar. Nonetheless, we have attempted, as in the previous chapters, to identify the significant contributions and distinctive characteristics in each writer's publications. As in the preceding chapter, the post-1965 scholars have been grouped according to the institution where they earned the doctorate.

Brandeis University[27] contributed significantly to Jewish biblical scholarship in the period under discussion. Brandeis, the first nonsectarian liberal arts institution in America under Jewish auspices, enrolled its first class in 1948.[28] Although the university chose at first to develop its offerings in later periods of Judaica rather than in Bible, the appointment of Nahum Glatzer, a disciple of Franz Rosenzweig, as Chair of Near Eastern and Judaic Studies (NEJS) assured that the method developed by Rosenzweig and Buber would be given broad currency. In 1957, Cyrus Gordon was brought from Dropsie to the NEJS department. Frictions with Glatzer soon led to Gordon's relocation to the new department of Mediterranean Studies where the curriculum was designed to reflect Gordon's broad cross-cultural perspective. In 1965, Nahum Sarna, who had earlier written his Ph.D. under Gordon at Dropsie, left JTS to join NEJS, to remain there for the rest of his teaching career. Subsequent faculty appointments in Bible and Semitics over the years have served to make Brandeis a natural choice for students wishing to pursue graduate work in biblical studies.

Jack Sasson born in Aleppo, Syria, received his Ph.D. in the Department of Mediterranean Studies at Brandeis after studying under Michael Astour and Cyrus Gordon. Sasson's broad interests range from ancient Near East[29] to Arabic.[30] His numerous publications on Mari,[31] including those texts with alleged connections to biblical prophecy, have made Sasson especially sensitive to the proper use of ancient Near Eastern materials to illuminate the Bible.[32] Of special interest to biblicists is his book, *Ruth: A New Translation with a Philological Commentary and a Formalist Interpretation.*[33] The Russian formalist Vladimir Propp in his *Morphology of the Folk Tale* had analyzed all folktales as consisting of seven "spheres of action" and thirty-one fixed elements or "functions". Sasson applies the Proppian analysis[34] to the Book of Ruth and concludes that the biblical story was composed on a folktale model.[35] More recently,

Anchor Bible has published Sasson's commentary to Jonah.[36] Sasson is a professor of religion at University of North Carolina and adjunct professor at Duke.

Carol Meyers graduated Wellesley and earned her Ph.D. in the Near Eastern and Judaics department at Brandeis with a dissertation on the tabernacle *menorâ*.[37] Trained in philology by Nahum Sarna and Baruch Levine, Meyers is one of the few current American Jewish field archaeologists[38] who is also a biblicist. Her work combines close attention to text and data drawn first hand from archaeology with the insights of the social sciences. Of particular value to biblicists are Meyers' clear descriptions of biblical cultic objects and their symbolism within the Bible and against the larger Near Eastern background.[39] Together with her husband Eric Meyers, likewise an archaeologist, Meyers is co-author of the commentary to Haggai and Zechariah[40] for the Anchor Bible series. A professor of religion at Duke, some of Meyers' scholarly work has been directed to the study of women in ancient Israel and their treatment by biblical authors.[41] Whereas most studies on the subject are confined to the biblical texts, Meyers draws attention to the fact that those texts are primarily the product of a male-oriented urban culture in which ancient Israelite woman participated minimally at best. As Meyers demonstrates in *Discovering Eve: Ancient Israelite Women in Context*,[42] biblical accounts of women and their location within Israelite society tell us very little unless they are read against the background of the hard data of archaeology augmented by social-science models.

Michael Fishbane earned his doctorate under Nahum Sarna at Brandeis with a thesis on biblical magic.[43] Fishbane's scholarly interests extend well beyond Bible.[44] At an early stage,[45] Fishbane's work followed Sarna's lead in examining the use made by later biblical writers of the work of earlier authors; what is now generally referred to as "inner-biblical exegesis."[46] More recent writing shows an intensification of this interest[47], and in the continuation of early exegetical patterns in the development of later midrash.[48] Fishbane also has an eye for biblical religious phenomena[49]. His synchronic reading and attention to *Leitwörter* in tracing the inner dynamics of biblical narrative show the influence of the Rosenzweig-Buber approach.[50] Fishbane served as an associate editor of *Harper's Bible Dictionary*.[51] After teaching at Brandeis for many years, Fishbane moved to the Divinity School of the University of Chicago in 1990.

Frederick Greenspahn earned the B.A. at University of California,

Santa Cruz, was ordained at HUC-JIR in Cincinnati and wrote his Ph.D. thesis at Brandeis under Nahum Sarna. Greenspahn is an avid student of the history of medieval Jewish Bible exegesis.[52] Especially noteworthy is Greenspahn's work on hapaxlegomena, which traces the history of the study of hapax legomena from earliest to modern times. The monograph brings contemporary statistical-linguistic theory, which has been employed in the study of hapax legomena in other corpora, to bear on the biblical occurrences of the phenomnon.[53] Hapax Legomena are by dictionary definition "those words which occur only once and seem unrelated to otherwise attested roots."[54] Yet this seemingly clear definition depends on delimiting the corpus studied and on determining the precise sense of "occur only once." Indeed, modern scholars have differed considerably on these very points. Accordingly, Greenspahn concentrates on "absolute hapaxlegomena", defined to include "any word other than a proper noun which is the only exemplification of its root within the Hebrew sections of the received text."[55] Two significant conclusions reached by the writer are that the Hebrew Bible is surprisingly low in hapax legomena, containing only 289 examples meeting the above definition; and that the occurrence of hapax legomena is more frequent in poetry than in prose. Greenspahn is currently a professor in the Center of Judaic Studies at University of Denver.

Everett Fox was educated at Brandeis from the B.A. through the Ph.D. Fox's interests are mainly in the structural and thematic analysis of narrative texts. In keeping with the current tendencies of literary interpretation, Fox concentrates less on source-analysis than on the final or canonical form of the biblical text. Fox wrote his dissertation on "Technical Aspects of the Translation of Genesis of Martin Buber and Franz Rosenzweig." The German Bible of Buber and Rosenzweig was a "Germanization" ("Verdeutschung"), that is, a closely-literal rendition of the Hebrew into German, which attempted to retain the original foreign flavor of the Hebrew, often at the expense of German idiomacity. Fox continues this tradition in English with his "New English Rendition" of the first two books of the Pentateuch[56] which attempts "to reflect the particular rhetoric of the Hebrew whenever possible, preserving such devices as repetition, allusion, alliteration and wordplay."[57] Currently, Fox teaches at Clark University where he directs the program in Jewish Studies.

The proximity of Columbia and Jewish Theological Seminary to each other on New York's Morningside Heights, proved especially significant during the period under discussion.[58] Although Bible was secondary to Talmud in the curriculum of the JTS Graduate Rabbinical School, the opposite was true in its Teachers' Institute[59] and its Seminary College of Jewish Studies, where many undergraduates from Columbia, Barnard and other New York City colleges were introduced to serious biblical scholarship, primarily by H. L. Ginsberg, Moshe Held and Yochanan Muffs. Both Held and Muffs were in different ways, extremely charismatic teachers. Muffs' impassioned reading of Jeremiah could make undergraduate students believe they were hearing the prophet himself at first-hand. Held, with equal vigor, convinced some of the same students that the survival of civilization depended on the rigorous and disciplined application of comparative Semitic philology. Held's adjunct position at JTS for twenty-five years served to attract graduate students to him in the Department of Middle East Languages and Cultures at Columbia,[60] so that something of a Ginsberg-Held-Muffs[61] school developed, which also includes, at least peripherally, academics who began in the Columbia-Seminary network and went elsewhere for the doctorate.[62]

David Marcus, native of Ireland, studied at Dublin's Trinity College and received an M.A. at Cambridge. Beginning his doctoral studies with Held and the grammarian Meir Bravmann[63] at Dropsie, Marcus followed Held to Columbia where he received his Ph.D. for a dissertation on Ugaritic grammar.[64] At Columbia he founded the *Journal of the Ancient Near Eastern Society (JANES)*, which continues as a significant scholarly forum.[65] Marcus devoted his early scholarly publication to grammar[66] and philology.[67] As a professor of Bible at JTS, his interests have broadened to include biblical law and institutions[68] as well as literary style. A good example is Marcus' study of the story of Jephthah and his daughter[69] in which Marcus makes a strong case in favor of the minority exegetical position that the tale does not actually describe a human sacrifice.

Edward Greenstein earned the B.A. at Columbia while studying at the same time at Seminary College of JTS. He wrote his thesis, "Phonological Studies in Akkadian" under Held.[70] Currently, Greenstein teaches Bible at JTS. His early interest in the ancient Near East is maintained in the editorship of *JANES*.[71] Nonetheless, Greenstein's more recent work shows a shift of foci into linguistics and into literary interpretation of the Bible. Under Held, Greenstein had developed an interest in the study of parallelism. Whereas Held had limited his researches to lexical parallelism, Greenstein's studies, like those of most of his contemporaries, are much more grounded in modern linguistic theory.[72] Specifically, Greenstein explains parallelism as the repetition of a syntactic pattern. On this analysis, lexical and semantic parallelism on which earlier generations of biblicists concentrated, is a secondary feature of grammatical parallelism, so that it is grammatical parallelism that brings about semantic parallelism. Grammatical and semantic parallelism tend to occur together because of the psycholinguistic nexus between structure and meaning.[73] Another important aspect of Greenstein's scholarship may be seen in his work on the literary aspects of the Bible and in his advocacy of the need for theoretical models.[74] Greenstein has been an associate editor of *Prooftexts: A Journal of Jewish Literary History* since its inception in 1979.

Hayim (Harold) Cohen, a graduate of Columbia and the Teachers' Institute of JTS, wrote his doctorate under Held on biblical hapaxlegomena.[75] The work examines the contribution of Akkadian and Ugaritic to the elucidation of the of hapaxlegomena in the Bible. Cohen, in contrast to Greenspahn,[76] follows Zelson in defining a hapax legomenon as "any biblical word whose root occurs in but one context," thus including "words which occur more than once in parallel verse [and] . . . more than once in the same single context."[77] Whereas Greenspahn's emphasis is on the historical treatment of the phenomenon and the contributions of contemporary linguistic theory, Cohen's emphasis is on deriving philological solutions from Ugaritic and Akkadian. Rather than relying solely on cognates, Cohen attempts to control etymological comparisons by attending to the principle of interdialectal distribution associated with Held[78] and his teachers, W. F. Albright and the Assyriologist Benno Landsberger.[79] Scholars would do well to regard the work of Cohen and Greenspahn as complementary. Other interesting work by Cohen involves the comparison of the biblical treatment of Assyria in the light of neo-Assyrian parallels.[80] Cohen settled in Israel and now teaches at Ben-Gurion University in Beersheba.

Another Held Ph.D. currently teaching at Ben-Gurion is Mayer Gruber, a rabbinic graduate of JTS whose major work, *Aspects of Nonverbal Communication in the Ancient Near East*[81] examines gestures and body-idioms in biblical and extra-biblical sources.[82] In *Communication,* Gruber supplements his own philological studies with the results of contemporary research in kinesics. Some of

Gruber's publications exemplify the ways in which feminism has impelled male scholars to raise previously unasked questions in biblical research. Of special interest in this regard are Gruber's studies "The Motherhood of God in Second Isaiah,"[83] and "Feminine Similes Applied to God in Deutero-Isaiah."[84]

S. David Sperling, co-author of this volume, is a rabbinic graduate of JTS, where he was very much influenced by H. L. Ginsberg and the talmudist Saul Lieberman. He then received the Ph.D. at Columbia under Held's tutelage, with a dissertation entitled, "Studies in Late Hebrew Lexicography in the Light of Akkadian." Sperling, whose philological method is closely patterned on Held's,[85] concentrated in his early studies on Akkadian and Late Hebrew comparisons.[86] Under the influence of Theodor Gaster, his senior colleague while teaching at Barnard, Sperling's work has increasingly broadened its scope to examine religious and historical questions as well.[87] He has taught at SUNY, Stony Brook and is currently a professor of Bible at the New York School of HUC-JIR.

Murray H. Lichtenstein, who earned the Ph.D. under Held, has taught at SUNY, Stony Brook and currently teaches at Hunter College. Lichtenstein's work on the effect of ritual on the evolution of poetic form[88] demonstrates the additional influence of Gaster's teaching.[89] Lichtenstein's interests are primarily in biblical poetry and its ancient Near Eastern counterparts.[90] Especially noteworthy is the attention Lichtenstein pays to conceptual and imagerial parallelism[91] alongside of lexical pairing.

A number of current Bible scholars earned the doctorate at Yale between 1965–1980. Jeffrey Tigay began his Bible studies at JTS while still an undergraduate at Columbia. His graduate work at Pennsylvania, while enrolled in JTS rabbinic school, was interrupted by Speiser's untimely death. After ordination, Tigay completed his doctorate at Yale, working primarily with Speiser's student J. J. Finkelstein, and with William Hallo and the biblicist Brevard Childs, the foremost representative of canon criticism. Highly significant for current biblical research is Tigay's book, *The Evolution of the Gilgamesh Epic* (Philadelphia, 1982). An outgrowth of his dissertation,[92] the book was motivated by Tigay's desire to show that biblical source-criticism has an empirical basis.[93] Noteworthy as well, is Tigay's recent study of ancient Hebrew proper names in epigraphic sources.[94] Based on an exhaustive evaluation of the onomasticon, Tigay argues that Yehezkel Kaufmann was essentially correct in characterizing the religion of Israel as montheistic. At present, Tigay teaches at the University of Pennsylvania as occupant of the Ellis Chair once held by Speiser.

Peter Machinist, studied as an undergraduate at Harvard under Frank Cross, and earned the Ph.D. at Yale under Hallo. In Machinist's cultural-history approach to the Bible, we may discern the influences of Hallo, J. J. Finkelstein, and the Israeli Assyriologist, Hayim Tadmor. Machinist's forte is the ability to employ Assyriology as circumstantial evidence bearing on the text of the Bible and Israelite history. In an early essay, "Literature as Politics: The Tukulti-Ninurta Epic and the Bible"[95], Machinist demonstrated how King Tukulti-Ninurta I (1242–1206) encouraged the creation of literature and new literary forms, employing them as propaganda to blunt opposition to his political reorientation of Assyria. Machinist then proceeded to show how David and Solomon similarly employed literature to justify the radical break they had made with Israel's political past. In a more recent essay, "Assyria and its Image in the First Isaiah,"[96] Machinist demonstrated the effectiveness of later Assyrian public relations: "At least in the First Isaiah, the empire was seen very much within the frame . . . that it itself had set through its own propaganda."[97] Machinist has taught at Case-Western Reserve, University of Arizona, University of Michigan, and currently teaches at Harvard.

Stephen Kaufman, currently a professor of Bible at HUC-JIR in Cincinnati, also earned the doctorate at Yale, under Franz Rosenthal.[98] Before coming to HUC-JIR, Kaufman taught at Chicago and then spent two years at the University of Haifa. Kaufman has made significant contributions to Aramaic[99] and is now engaged along with Joseph Fitzmyer and Delbert Hillers in editing the historic undertaking, the *Comprehensive Aramaic Lexicon*. In his biblical studies, Kaufman directs his attention to law and institutions[100] as well as to literary criticism.[101]

Alan Cooper, a professor of Bible at HUC-JIR in Cincinnati,[102] was first introduced to Bible as a Columbia undergraduate by Moshe Held. Although, as we have seen, Jewish Bible scholars of this generation and earlier have earned the Ph.D. in the Near Eastern Studies department at Yale, as of this writing, Cooper is the only Jewish scholar ever to complete the Ph.D. at Yale in Religious Studies/Old Testament. At Yale, Cooper studied primarily with Franz Rosenthal, Brevard Childs and Marvin Pope.[103] Pope's influence is especially manifest in Cooper's use of comparative mythology to illuminate biblical texts and concepts.[104] Cooper's work combines critical philological scholarship with attention to earlier Jewish and Christian commentary. An advocate of "holistic biblical interpretation" in the manner of Moshe Greenberg, Cooper also has a predilection for literary theory.[105]

Tikva Frymer-Kensky was introduced to serious biblical study via undergraduate courses at JTS with Muffs, Ginsberg and Held. A student of William Hallo and Jacob Finkelstein, Frymer-Kensky received her doctorate at Yale in 1976 with a dissertation entitled "Studies on Trial by River Ordeal."[106] Subsequent work has concentrated on biblical and ancient Near Eastern religious institutions and on rituals affecting pollution and purification.[107] Her studies of Sumerian and Akkadian have enabled Frymer-Kensky to make good use of Near Eastern myth in illuminating biblical traditions.[108] She pays close attention to literary structure and physical realia and, in the manner of many others of the current generation, emphasizes the importance of a holistic approach to the extant biblical texts.[109] Frymer-Kensky has recently become a professor of Bible at the Reconstructionist Rabbinical College in Philadelphia.

In contrast to the earlier periods surveyed, the years 1965–1980, saw Harvard produce a number of Jewish Bible scholars. We begin with Susan Niditch, who studied under Frank Cross. Her work has combined Cross' training in philology and text-criticism with the rigorous approach to folklore and oral and traditional literature taught by Albert Lord.[110] Of special significance is her work on symbolic visions in the Bible.[111] Niditch's diachronic approach "discourages the creation of synchronic categories which do not account for changes which occur in the form through time."[112] Instead, Niditch traces the form of the symbolic vision from its simplest examples in the pre-exilic prophets, beginning with Amos, through the more elaborate narratives in Zechariah, Daniel and the apocryphal works. Following the lead of Cross,[113] Niditch argues that the symbolic vision became increasingly "baroque" in keeping with the increasingly transcendent view of God espoused by the writers of the exilic and post-exilic periods. Readers of *Symbolic Vision* will quickly discern the influences of Cross and Freedman and ultimately, of Albright, in Niditch's treatment of Israelite poetry. Of interest as well is Niditch's *Chaos to Cosmos*[114] in which the author subjects Genesis 1–11 to an analysis informed by Lévi-

Strauss' concepts of "overrating", "underrating"[115] and "intermediary"; and the concepts of "communitas" and "liminality" associated with the anthropologists Arnold van Gennep and Victor Turner.[116] She finds that "two major movements emerge in Genesis 1-11, the movement from chaos to order and from ideal order to reality, and each of these movements is expressed in a thematic chain."[117] Niditch's areas of interest include hellenistic Jewish and rabbinic literature in addition to Bible.[118]

Stephen Geller came to JTS from Cornell with a strong background in German literature. While still a rabbinic student, he began to study Semitic languages at Columbia, where he was one of the last students of Isaac Mendelsohn. He completed the Ph.D. under Cross at Harvard. Geller's scholarly interests are primarily in biblical poetry[119] and narrative literary structure.[120] As a proponent of the literary interpretation of the Bible, he has attempted to avoid what he considers the over-subjectivity and anachronistic readings of other practitioners by concentrating in Formalist fashion,[121] on "literary devices", which he argues, enable us to distinguish an author's "primarily conscious intention . . . from primarily unintended levels of meaning, psychological in nature."[122] Indeed, he maintains[123] that of the literary devices found in the Bible, "parallelism . . . offers the surest insight into poetic intention." An outgrowth of his dissertation, Geller's book, *Parallelism in Early Biblical Poetry* was one of the earliest[124] in the new wave of interest in the phenomena involved in biblical parallelism.[125] Geller has taught at JTS and the Reconstructionist Rabbinical College in Philadelphia. He has the historic distinction of having served as the last professor of Bible at Dropsie before its transformation into the Annenberg Research Institute. Geller is currently teaching at JTS.

Jon Levenson who also earned his Ph.D. at Harvard under Cross, taught in the Divinity School of the University of Chicago before returning to Harvard for a chair at Harvard Divinity School. He entered biblical studies with a strong background in literature and in Jewish religious thought. Indeed, Levenson's concern with theology and hermeneutics is rare among semiticists and rarer still among Jewish students of the Bible. In some particularly provocative essays, Levenson continues the polemical tradition of Yehezkel Kaufmann in examining the christological assumptions, stated and unstated, that have led many prominent Christian scholars to "to use historico-critical methods to validate the literary context that is the

Christian Bible."[126] Of particular interest is his book *Sinai and Zion: An Entry into the Jewish Bible*[127] in which Levenson attempts what might be called a "Jewish biblical theology."

Richard Friedman, another Jewish student of Frank Cross, studied for a time at Jewish Theological Seminary and earned his Th.D. at Harvard Divinity School.[128] Friedman exemplifies the current interest of Jewish scholarship in torah-literature. A practitioner of source and redaction criticism, Friedman accepts the theory of a double redaction of the Deuteronomistic history, the first Josianic, the second exilic. Particularly interesting is Friedman's argument that the second edition (Dtr2), in its final form, depicts Israelite history as a horrifying circle; Israel begins its life enslaved in Egypt awaiting redemption by Yahweh, and ends it back in Egypt, once again enslaved in consequence of failure to keep Yahweh's covenant.[129] Of significance as well is Friedman's thesis that P, a late pre-exilic document, was composed by a writer who wished to present an ideological alternative to JE.[130] Friedman's major scholarly interests are in the meeting of the literary and historical study of the Hebrew Bible.[131] In his study of literary technique in biblical writers Friedman acknowledges his indebtedness to the hermeneuticist E. D. Hirsch, whose criticism distinguishes between the "meaning" of a literary work assigned by the author and the "significances" assigned by readers.[132] At present teaching in the Department of Literature at University of California, San Diego, Friedman chairs UCSD's program in Judaic Studies, possibly the only such American program with a concentration in Bible. Friedman's best-selling *Who Wrote the Bible*[133] demonstrates the author's exemplary talent for bringing scholarly issues to the attention of a wide audience.

Baruch Halpern, a professor of humanities at York University in Toronto, received his doctorate as a student of Cross and T. Lambdin.[134] Post-doctoral work followed under Hayim Tadmor in Israel and Klaus Baltzer and Manfred Weippert in Germany. In his book, *The Emergence of Israel in Canaan*,[135] Halpern seeks new points of departure for understanding the pre-monarchic period in the wake of the collapse of Noth's "amphictyony" model. The book attempts to account for the emergence of Israel and the shaping of its regional and tribal character and to explain the formation of "its nativist or xenophobic consciousness."[136] Specifically, Halpern challenges those scholars who have elaborated Mendenhall's revolt model of the Israelite settlement. Adherents of the revolt model, notably Gottwald,[137] have accepted Mendenhall's reading of the fourteenth century Amarna letters as depicting "the withdrawal . . . politically and subjectively, of large population groups from any obligation to the existing political regimes,"[138] arguing that Canaan's "intense and consistent anti-royalism"[139] of the Amarna period provides the background for the rise of Israel in succeeding centuries. In contrast, Halpern follows those historians who see "no indication that Egyptian control of Canaan was slipping away to the local vassals."[140] Instead, Halpern attributes the well-documented violence in fourteenth century Canaan to internal power-struggles and to threats posed by Mitanni and Hatti, rather than to anti-monarchic tendencies. Much of Halpern's argumentation is built on the analysis of the lists of Israel's tribes in what are taken to be early Israelite poems. The relative dates of Judges 5, Deuteronomy 33 and Genesis 49 are established by the author in line with the typological method closely associated with Cross.[141] More recently in *The First Historians*[142] Halpern attempts to define biblical history in terms of authorial intention: "Whether a text is history, then depends on what its author meant to do."[143] If the "point of the story is to communicate the reconstruction of events,"[144] and if the "narrator [had] reason to believe what he or she wrote,"[145] then says Halpern, we may consider that narrator a historian. On this analysis Halpern terms the Deuteronomist the "first historian." Although Halpern's criteria for historical writing are not without problems,[146] the book has the great merit of confronting the methodological questions of reading the Bible from a historical as a opposed to a literary perspective.

The next group in our survey received the Ph.D. from schools that did not graduate other Jewish Bible scholars between 1965–1980.

Ziony Zevit received his doctorate from Berkeley[147] as a student of Jonas Greenfield and spent several years teaching at Israeli universities. At present, Zevit is a professor of Bible and Northwest Semitic Languages at University of Judaism, the California affiliate of Jewish Theological Seminary. In his biblical studies, Zevit has concerned himself primarily with problems of orthography, vocabulary, grammar and diction, although historical and religious issues[148] are also considered[149]. Of special significance for the study of the history of the biblical text, although not directed to the Bible *per se*,[150] is Zevit's monograph, *Matres Lectionis in Ancient Hebrew Epigraphs*.[151]

Adele Berlin earned her Ph.D. at Pennsylvania where she studied with E. A. Speiser, Moshe Greenberg and the renowned Sumerologist Samuel Noah Kramer. Berlin's dissertation, although a text-edition of a Sumerian poem,[152] already demonstrated its author's interest in the literary approach[153] to the Bible. Since that time, Berlin's work in Bible has firmly established her as a leading exponent of the literary method.[154] In contrast to Alter who came to biblical poetry and narrative from the works of modern writers, Berlin's work begins with a thorough grounding in ancient Near Eastern literature. In approaching biblical poetry, Berlin seeks repetitions and patterns in the use of individual words and in larger phrases. She is alert to the particular structuring of words and ideas and for rhetorical devices such as chiasm and inclusio.[155] Berlin has also applied modern linguistics as a tool in her study of the phenomenon of biblical parallelism.[156] She is currently teaching in the Department of Hebrew and East Asian Languages and Literatures at the University of Maryland.

Gary Rendsburg continues the long line of students trained by Cyrus Gordon. Rendsburg completed his Ph.D. at New York University and began his teaching career at Canisius College. Currently, Rendsburg teaches at Cornell University. Like Gordon, Rendsburg is opposed to traditional source criticism[157] and relies heavily on extrabiblical data from Ugarit and Nuzi to interpret the Bible and ancient Israelite institutions. In *Redaction of Genesis,* Rendsburg seeks to discover what Sasson had earlier termed the "redactional structuring" within the cycles of Genesis,[158] by specifically building on the Genesis researches of earlier students of Cyrus Gordon, namely Sasson, Sarna and Fishbane as well as on the work of Cassuto. In their respective studies of Genesis narratives, each of these scholars had attempted to demonstrate the existence of matching units, related themes and theme-words within what have been termed "the four great cycles." Rendsburg's book, devoted to the Joseph story, attempts to demonstrate that the units comprising Gen 37:1–50:26 "are also paired, aligned chiastically, with interrelated themewords."[159] The conclusion for Rendsburg is "the realization that all of Genesis is brilliantly constructed, the accomplishment of an ancient Israelite genius who formed the book into a literary whole," and who flourished in the period of David and Solomon.[160] Interestingly, given the Gordon connection, Rendsburg does not completely address the archaeological[161] and linguistic anachronisms in

Genesis that militate against so early a date for the book's final redaction.

Michael Fox, currently a professor of Hebrew at University of Wisconsin and editor of the journal *Hebrew Studies,* studied Bible and ancient Near East through the M.A. at Michigan. After ordination at HUC-JIR in Cincinnati, Fox continued his studies in Israel and earned the Ph.D. under Menahem Haran at the Hebrew University in Jerusalem. Fox taught for several years in Israel before coming to the University of Wisconsin. Noteworthy in his work is a strong interest in rhetoric.[162] Rhetorical criticism as a method in biblical study was first advocated by James Muilenburg who in his 1968 presidential address to the SBL called for biblicists to study not only what the text says, but what means it uses to convey its message. Bible scholars, he argued, should interest themselves in "understanding the nature of Hebrew literary composition, in exhibiting the structural patterns . . . employed for the fashioning of a unit and in discerning the . . . devices by which predications are . . . ordered into a unified whole."[163] Muilenburg's method was synchronic in that it focused on the received text. He was especially interested in formal devices such as parallelism, strophic structure, particles and repetition.

Fox criticizes Muilenburg and his followers by observing that biblicists have employed the term "rhetorical criticism" differently from rhetorical theorists from Aristotle on. Rhetorical criticism on the Bible has concentrated on revealing the formal features of a text. In contrast, says Fox, rhetorical criticism, as generally understood, examines the ways in which discourses attempt to achieve certain effects and responses in listeners and readers. It is in this sense that rhetorical criticism should be applied to the Bible and "should focus on the analysis and evaluation of the suasive force of discourse rather than on its formal literary features or its structure."[164] As such, Fox calls attention to a significant fact often ignored in contemporary study of the Bible: The relative unavailability of books in antiquity meant that the written word was likely to reach most of its audience orally.[165] Other noteworthy features in Fox's work are the comparisons drawn between biblical and Egyptian literature. Unlike most biblicists, whose comparitism is usually directed to Northwest Semitic or Assyriology, Fox is trained in Egyptology.[166] Of special interest in this regard is his recent book, *The Song of Songs and the Ancient Egyptian Love Songs.*[167]

James Kugel studied at Yale and Harvard and holds the Ph.D. from City University of New York. Kugel taught religious studies and comparative literature at Yale before coming to his present position as Starr Professor of Hebrew Literature at Harvard. Kugel combines an interest in modern biblical criticism with a thorough knowledge of the history of biblical exegesis.[168] A scholar with strong literary interests, Kugel was formerly poetry editor for *Harper's Magazine,* and a founder of *Prooftexts A Journal of Jewish Literary History*. His book, *The Idea of Biblical Poetry*[169] has been widely read. *Idea* closely examines the workings and semantic function of biblical parallelism. Two of the book's theses are particularly provocative and merit specific notice. First, Kugel questions the whole notion that one can differentiate prose from poetry in the Bible. Second, Kugel argues against a common understanding of verse-halves in parallelism as synonymous. The underlying principle of parallelism Kugel understands to be "seconding" or "extending." Thus, the relation between members in parallelism is "A, and what's more B."[170] Kugel has also maintained forcefully[171] that the quest in biblical studies for "original meaning" is based on a Protestant model. Jewish biblicists in particular, he argues, should treat modern scholarship as part of a larger history of biblical exegesis.

Joel Rosenberg is a professor of Hebrew Literature and Judaic Studies at Tufts University. Rosenberg, although not trained specifically as a Bible scholar, studied extensively at HUC-JIR and at Graduate Theological Union in Berkeley. He earned the Ph.D. in the History of Consciousness with a specialization in Literature at University at University of California at Santa Cruz.[172] Among the direct influences on his work, Rosenberg identifies James Ackerman, Robert Alter, Michael Fishbane and Edward Greenstein. Rosenberg's training in literature is apparent in his synchronic, rather than diachronic approach to narrative. His biblical studies emphasize the "dynamic relationship"[173] or "intertextuality" among the components of Scripture, in contrast to classical classical source-criticism, which diachronically views "each stage followed upon its predecessor as a separate sedimentation."[174] In Rosenberg's *King and Kin,* the critically-moderated influences of Hermann Gunkel and Benno Jacob are readily apparent.[175] For Rosenberg, the operation of allegory within the Bible has often been overlooked or underemphasized. Thus in 1 and 2 Samuel, "the stories of Israel's and David's maturation are essentially the same story."[176] In a similar vein, Rosenberg argues that Genesis is a "midrash" on the court history of David as recorded in 2 Samuel.

Robert Cohn received his Ph.D. in Religious Studies at Stanford as a student of Edward Good. Cohn has taught at Pennsylvania State and Northwestern. Currently, he is a professor in the Jewish Studies program at Lafayette College. Cohn's biblical studies acknowledge the strong influence of the Israeli scholar Shmaryahu Talmon. In his choice of theoretical models, Cohn relies heavily on anthropology and the history of religions. Biblicists will be particularly interested in Cohn's application of Victor Turner's notion of "liminality" to the pentateuchal traditions of wilderness wandering. Also discernible are the influences of Mircea Eliade.[177]

The above survey demonstrates the varied nature of work being done by current Jewish Bible scholars. It will be useful at this point to make some summary observations. First, the impact of the state of Israel cannot be overstated. All of the members of the 1965–1980 generation grew up after the formation of the state of Israel. Virtually all have spent considerable time in Israel and been influenced by Israeli scholarship. But more influential than the particulars of Israeli scholarship has been the consciousness that the survival of Jews and Judaism is not threatened, as Geiger had feared,[178] by attempts to reconstruct the historical reality of ancient Israel. One obvious result is that although the members of the "class of 1965–1980" differ greatly among themselves in their theological perspectives and in their religious observance, there are no true fundamentalists among them. Radicals, liberals and conservatives and liberals alike in this group accept the validity of critical study of the Torah. Thus for example, Rendsburg's opposition to traditional source-criticism and his advocacy of an early, consciously artistic redaction of Genesis, are not echoes of I. M. Wise's insistence on the Mosaic authorship of the Pentateuch. In like manner, Friedman's pre-exilic date for "P" may sound conservative, but in the manner of Yehezkel Kaufmann who had dedicated much of his energies to dating "P" before the exile, Friedman accepts a documentary hypothesis. When we turn to those biblicists conversant with rabbinics, we find a similar picture. Scholars such as Fishbane, Cooper and Tigay may consult the rabbis more frequently than do Cohen, Lichtenstein or Kaufman, but more for the rabbinic questions than the rabbinic answers. James Kugel, who, perhaps more than any other member of this group, valorizes the Jewish exegetical tradition, hardly considers it infallible.

Some of the scholars surveyed have refined and extended the social and anthropological approaches of their forbears. From this perspective, Cohn and Niditch may be seen as continuators of methods adumbrated by Morgenstern and Gaster. While several scholars, for example, Frymer-Kensky, Gruber, Kaufman, Machinist, Sasson, Sperling, and Zevit, have continued the philological and cultural comparatism practiced by their teachers, others have struck out in different directions. It is fair to say that S. N. Kramer and M. Held had far less interest in theory than their respective students A. Berlin and E. Greenstein. In keeping however, with the principle of *plus sa change* . . . , the theological interests of Jon Levenson are remarkable. While his approach to theological system formation departs from the paradigm of Jewish Bible scholarship of the past century and one-half, the combination of close reading and theology is indebted to such medieval commentators as Gersonides and Nachmanides.

In sum, in the century since the Society of Biblical Literature and Exegesis accepted its first three Jewish members, Jewish biblical study has grown and matured in ways that Marcus Jastrow and Gottheil Sr. and Jr. could never have imagined.

Notes to Chapter Five

1. The reader will note that the only woman scholar mentioned in the previous chapters was Hildegarde Lewy, who was primarily an Assyriologist.

2. To cite just two recent works see A. Yarbro Collins (ed.), *Feminist Perspectives on Biblical Scholarship* (Chico: Scholars, 1985); A Schüssler Fiorenza, *Bread Not Stone: The Challenge of Feminist Biblical Interpretation* (Boston: Beacon, 1985).

3. It is fair to say that a good student would easily master as much Hebrew in a year in Israel as in four or five years at an American rabbinical seminary.

4. Of potential interest to students of Jewish biblical scholarship in North America is the Reconstructionist Rabbinical College (RRC) in Philadelphia. Founded in 1968, RRC is based on the principles of Rabbi Mordecai Kaplan, who was one of the few early champions of biblical higher criticism at Jewish Theological Seminary (See Chapter 2, n., 96). On the RRC curriculum see R. Alpert, "Reconstructionist Rabbis," in *Encyclopaedia Judaica Year Book* 1983-85, 101-105. Tikva Frymer-Kensky joined the RRC faculty in 1988.

5. This may be observed even in such superficial details as the use of

"B. C. E." for "B. C." and "Tanakh" or "Hebrew Bible" for "Old Testament" in books and articles by many contemporary Jewish biblicists, and in works by Christian scholars attuned to the newer consciousness of their Jewish colleagues. For extended discussion, see our "Introduction," above.

6. See e.g. the papers of Jon Levenson, Michael Fishbane and James Kugel given at the symposium, "Biblical Studies and Jewish Studies in the University," in *Association for Jewish Studies Newsletter* 36 (Fall, 1986), 16–24.

7. See the remarks of E. Greenstein, "Robert Alter on Biblical Poetry: A Review Essay," *Hebrew Studies* 27 (1986), 82–91, especially, 88.

8. See L. Silberman, "Listening to the Text," *JBL* 102 (1983), 6. Silberman's paper (ibid, 3–26) was originally delivered as an SBL presidential address. Noteworthy are the numerous references to the Russian formalist Shklovsky, the literary theorist Frank Kermode and the phenomenologist Don Ihde.

9. For a good discussion of the issue, see E. Greenstein. "The Role of Theory in Biblical Criticism," *Proceedings of the Ninth World Congress of Jewish Studies* (Jerusalem, 1986), Division A, 167–174.

10. It is also true that most college and university libraries have much better holdings in general literature and literary criticism than in Semitics and archaeology.

11. This was less so in Christian circles. Thus, literary concerns were addressed in form-criticism and clearly articulated in the writings of such mainstream scholars as Gerhard von Rad and James Muilenburg. See e.g. J. Muilenberg, "Form Criticism and Beyond," *JBL* 88 (1969), 1–18. Note especially Muilenberg's high evaluation of Cassuto (ibid, 8). Not coincidentally, Muilenburg began his teaching career in the field of English literature. See B. Anderson and W. Harrelson (eds.), *Israel's Prophetic Heritage* (New York: Harper, 1962), xi.

12. See e.g. U. Cassuto, *The Documentary Hypothesis and the Composition of the Pentateuch* (Jerusalem: Magnes, 1941).

13. See M. Segal, *The Pentateuch: Its Composition and Its Authorship and Other Biblical Studies* (Jerusalem: Magnes, 1967).

14. Invaluable for understanding the approach to the Bible which Buber and Rosenzweig evolved together is R. Bat-Adam (ed.), *Franz Rosenzweig Sprachdenken Arbeitspapiere zur Verdeutschung der Schrift* (Boston: Martinus Nijhoff, 1984).

15. See e.g. B. Jacob, *Das Erste Buch der Tora: Genesis* (Berlin: Schocken, 1934; reprint, New York: Ktav, 1974). Jacob was in regular contact with Buber and Rosenzweig. See Bat-Adam (ed.), *Rosenzweig,* xxxi.

16. Rosenzweig found it necessary to coin the term "Leitwort" now widely employed in literary interpretation. See Bat-Adam, *Rosenzweig,* xvii. (There is some irony in the fact that Rosenzweig's inspiration for "Leitwort" came from "Leitmotif," coined for music by the virulently anti-Semitic Richard Wagner.); It is easy to forget that a term as popular as "close reading" only came into use in general literary criticism thanks to the work of F. R. Leavis and Q. D. Leavis at Cambridge and the journal *Scrutiny* launched by them in 1932. (See T. Eagleton, *Literary Theory* [Minneapolis:

University of Minnesota, 1983], 30-45.) *Scrutiny* was not required reading for biblicists. Similarly, the "holistic approach" surely characterizes the work of Cassuto and of Moshe Greenberg (See e.g. M. Greenberg, "The Vision of Jerusalem in Ezekiel 8-11: A Holistic Interpretation," J. Crenshaw and S. Sandmel (eds.), *The Divine Helmsman: Studies on God's Control of Human Events, Presented to Lou H. Silberman* [New York: Ktav, 1980], 146-164), but Cassuto did not have the term at hand.

17. See Greenberg, *Understanding Exodus*, 1 and cf. our "Introduction."

18. Greenberg, ibid, 4-5; Cf. our "Introduction."

19. See M. Fishbane, "Recent Work on Biblical Narrative," *Prooftexts* 1 (1981), 100.

20. Cf. D. Berger, "On the Morality of the Patriarchs in Genesis in Jewish Polemic and Exegesis," in C. Thoma and M. Wyschogrod (eds.), *Understanding Scripture* (New York: Paulist, 1987), 62, n. 36.

21. Fishbane, *Prooftexts* 1, 103; Cf. Geller's statement: "Literary critics who renounce history for freedom should consider the spiritual dangers of a hubris that makes the biblical text no more than a mirror of narcissistic self-reflection." See S. Geller, "Through Windows and Mirrors into the Bible. History, Literature, and Language in the Study of Biblical Literature," in *A Sense of Text The Art of Language in the Study of Biblical Literature*. (A Jewish Quarterly Review Supplement; Winona Lake: Eisenbrauns, 1982), 21.

22. It may be noted that among all the contributors to the 1985 survey of contemporary biblical research in Knight and Tucker (eds.), *Hebrew Bible*, only E. Gerstenberger, "The Lyrical Literature," (ibid, 409-444) devotes any space (ibid, 410-412) to text criticism. See further n. 32 of our "Introduction."

See Y. Muffs, "Two Comparative Lexical Studies," *The Gaster Festschrift* (New York: ANE Society, 1974), 296, n. 11.

24. See W. Hallo, "New Moons and Sabbaths: A Case-Study in the Contrastive Approach," *Hebrew Union College Annual* 48 (1977), 1-2; Cf. J. Roberts, "The Ancient Near Eastern Environment," in Knight and Tucker (eds.), *Hebrew Bible*, 96.

25. See Fishbane, *Prooftexts* 1, 100.

26. See the convenient summary in R. Culley, "Exploring New Directions," in Knight and Tucker (eds.), *Hebrew Bible*, 167-200.

27. For a history of the founding of Brandeis and its subsequent growth see A. L. Sachar, *A Host at Last* (Boston: Little, Brown and Company, 1976).

28. Unlike Dropsie, which was founded as a graduate institution devoted to "Hebrew and Cognate learning," Brandeis began as an undergraduate institution devoted to the whole range of liberal arts. In further contrast to Dropsie, non-sectarianism at Brandeis encompassed from the first both the faculty and the student body. Yeshiva University, which dates its foundation to 1886, is an Orthodox Jewish institution that admits non-Jews to its various professional programs, but accepts only observant Jews to its undergraduate single-sex colleges, Yeshiva College and Stern College for Women. (For

details about Yeshiva see below.)

29. See e.g. J. Sasson, "Canaanite Maritime Involvement in the Second Millennium B.C.," *JAOS* 86 (1966), 126–138; idem "Circumcision in the Ancient Near East," *JBL* 85 (1966), 473–476; idem, *The Military Establishment at Mari* (Rome, 1969); idem, "Yarim-Lim's War Declaration," *Miscellanea Babylonica Mélanges offerts a Maurice Birot* (Paris: Éditions Recherche sur les Civilisations, 1985), 237–255.

30. Sasson regularly offers a course in the modern Arabic novel.

31. See the convenient synthesis, J. Sasson, "Mari," in *Harper's Bible Dictionary*, 603–605.

32. See e.g. J. Sasson, 'On Relating 'Religious' Texts to the Old Testament," *MAARAV* 3 (1982), 217–229.

33. Baltimore: Johns Hopkins, 1979; See further idem, Ruth, in R. Alter and F. Kermode (eds.), *The Literary Guide to the Bible* (Cambridge: Belknap Press at Harvard, 1987), 320–328.

34. For another recent work on biblical and ancient Near Eastern narrative employing Propp's system see D. Irving, *Mytharion: The Comparison of Tales from the Old Testament and the Ancient Near East* (AOAT 32; Kevelaer: Butzon & Bercker, 1978).

35. Among other studies of interest to biblicists are J. Sasson, "The Worship of the Golden Calf," in H. Hoffner (ed.), *Orient and Occident Essays . . . Gordon* (Neukirchen-Vluyn, 1973), 151–159; idem, "On Choosing Models for Recreating Israelite Pre-Monarchic History," *Journal for the Study of the Old Testament* 21 (1981), 3–24; idem, "The Biographic mode in Hebrew Historiography," in W. Barrick (ed.), *In the Shelter of Elyon. . .Essays Ahlström* (Sheffield: JSOT Press, 1984), 305–312.

36. J. Sasson, *Jonah* (Garden City: 1991).

37. The thesis was published as C. Meyers, *The Tabernacle Menorah: A Synthetic Study of a Symbol from the Biblical Cult.* (Missoula, 1976); See further, conveniently, idem, "lampstand," in *Harper's Bible Dictionary* (New York; Harper and Row, 1985), 486.

38. See more recently, C. Meyers, E. Meyers and J. Strange, *Excavations at Ancient Meiron, Upper Galilee, Israel, 1971–72, 1974–75, 1977* (Cambridge, 1981).

39. See e.g. C. Meyers, "ark", "breastpiece", "cherub", "ephod" etc. in *Harper's Bible Dictionary*.

40. C. Meyers and E. Meyers, *Haggai, Zechariah 1–8* (Garden City: Doubleday, 1987). The continuation in the same series, *Zechariah 9–14 and Malachi*, is in preparation.

41. See e.g. C. Meyers, "Roots of Restriction: Women in Early Israel," *Biblical Archeologist* 41 (Sept., 1978), 91–103; idem, "Gender Roles and Genesis 3:16 Revisited," in C. Meyers and M. O'Connor (eds.), *The Word of the Lord Shall Go Forth. . .Essays D. N. Freedman* (Winona Lake: Eisenbrauns, 1983), 337–354; idem, *Discovering Eve Ancient Israelite Women in Context* (New York: 1988, Oxford).

42. (New York, 1988).

43. M. Fishbane, "Studies in Biblical Magic. Origins, Uses, and Transformations of Terminology and Literary Form," unpublished Ph.D. disserta-

tion, Brandeis, 1971.

44. See e.g. M. Fishbane, "The Qumran *pesher* and Traits of Ancient Hermeneutics," *Proceedings of the Sixth World Congress of Jewish Studies* I (Jerusalem, 1977), 97–114; idem, "The Teacher and the Hermeneutical Task: A Reinterpretation of Medieval Exegesis," *Journal of the American Academy of Religion* 43 (1975), 709–721.

45. See M. Fishbane, "Accusations of Adultery: A Study of Law and Scribal Practice in Numbers 5:11–31," *Hebrew Union College Annual* 45 (1974), 25–45.

46. See especially, N. Sarna, "Psalm 89: A Study in Inner Biblical Exegesis," in A. Altmann (ed.), *Biblical and Other Studies* (Cambridge: Harvard, 1963), 29–46.

47. See M. Fishbane, "Revelation and Tradition: Aspects of Inner-Biblical Exegesis," *JBL* 99 (1980), 343–361; idem, "Form and Reformation of the Priestly Blessing," *JAOS* 103 (1983), 115–121; idem, *Biblical Interpretation in Ancient Israel* (Oxford: Clarendon, 1985).

48. See e.g., M. Fishbane, "Biblical Origins of Exegesis: Roots of Midrash," *Brandeis Review* 3 (Winter, 1983), 13–14, 34–35.

49. See idem, "Biblical Prophecy as a Religious Phenomenon," in Green (ed.), *Jewish Spirituality,* 62–81.

50. See e.g. idem, *Text and Texture: Close Readings of Selected Biblical Texts* (New York: Schocken, 1979); Cf. J. Rosenberg, "Biblical Narrative," in B. Holtz (ed.), *Back to the Sources* (New York: Summit Books,), 77.

51. See P. Achtemeier (ed.), *Harper's Bible Dictionary* (New York: Harper and Row, 1985).

52. See F. Greenspahn, "Abraham ibn Ezra and the Origin of Some Medieval Grammatical Terms," *Jewish Quarterly Review* 76 (1986), 217–227; idem, "The Meaning of *'ein lo domeh* and Similar Phrases in Medieval Biblical Exegesis," *Association for Jewish Studies Review* 4 (1979), 59–77; idem, "Biblical Scholars, Medieval and Modern," in J. Neusner (ed.), *Judaic Perspectives on Ancient Israel* (Philadelphia: Fortress, 1987).

53. The thesis was revised and published as F. Greenspahn, *Hapaxlegomena in Biblical Hebrew* (Chico: Scholars, 1984). See especially, ibid, 31–46; Cf. idem, "The Number and Distribution of Hapax Legomena in Biblical Hebrew," *Vetus Testamentum* 30 (1980), 8–19.

54. ibid, 23.

55. *Hapax Legomena,* 29.

56. Following the Buber-Rosenzweig model, the renditions follow a Hebrew and ancient Near Eastern pattern of referring to literary collections by their opening phrases. Thus, E. Fox, *In the Beginning: A New English Rendition of the Book of Genesis, with Commentary and Notes* (New York: Schocken, 1983); idem, *Now These Are the Names: A New English Rendition of the Book of Exodus, with Commentary and Notes* (New York: Schocken, 1986).

57. See the preface to E. Fox, *In the Beginning.*

58. The Assyriologist Isaac Mendelsohn (1899 [or 1900?]–1965) who was Professor of Semitic Languages at Columbia from 1932–1965 had few students. Mendelsohn made important contributions to the study of ancient

Near Eastern institutions. Of interest to biblicists are I. Mendelsohn, "The Conditional Sale into Slavery of Free-Born Daughters in Nuzi and the Law of Ex. 21:7–11," *JAOS* 55 (1935), 190–195; idem, "Slavery in the OT," *IDBSup*, 383–391. For biographical information and an appreciation, see H. Orlinsky, "Professor Isaac Mendelsohn—In Memoriam," (in Hebrew), *Hadoar* 32 (July, 1965), 595.

59. The Teachers' Institute was established at JTS in 1909 by a contribution from Jacob Schiff. At that time Solomon Schechter entrusted the directorship of the Teachers' Institute to Mordecai Kaplan. It is noteworthy that despite Schechter's own opposition to biblical criticism, he protected Kaplan's right to have Bible taught there as Kaplan saw fit. See Hertzberg, "Introduction" to the 1981 reprint of Kaplan, *Judaism as a Civilization*, xxiv.

60. Another source of students was Union Theological Seminary. Altogether, Held sponsored twenty-two Ph.D. dissertations, including one at Dropsie, a large number for a Semiticist. Our survey excludes both Gentile scholars and those of Held's Jewish Ph.D. graduates whose scholarly work has not been in Bible proper.

61. Indirectly, one may include Held's primary teachers Albright and Landsberger as intellectual influences.

62. Alan Cooper, Richard Friedman, Tikva Frymer-Kensky, Jeffrey Tigay and to a lesser extent, Stephen Kaufman, should be included here.

63. For an appreciation of Bravmann see E. Greenstein, "M. M. Bravman—A Sketch," in *JANES* 11 (1979), 1–2.

64. D. Marcus, "Studies in Ugaritic Grammar in the Light of Comparative Semitic Grammar," (Columbia, 1970).

65. Among the noteworthy volumes that have appeared since 1968 are *The Gaster Festschrift* (1973) and the *Bravmann Memorial Volume* (1979).

66. See e.g. D. Marcus, "Studies in Ugaritic Grammar," *JANES* I/2 (1969), 55–61; For more recent grammatical work see, idem, *A Manual of Akkadian* (Washington, D.C.: University Press of America, 1978); idem; *A Manual of Babylonian Jewish Aramaic* (Washington, D.C.: University Press of America, 1981).

67. See e.g. D. Marcus, "The Verb 'To Live' in Ugaritic," *JSS* 17 (1972), 76–82; idem, "Ugaritic Evidence for 'The Almighty/The Grand'?" *Biblica* 55 (1974), 404–407.

68. See e.g. idem, "Civil Liberties under Israelite and Mesopotamian Kings," *JANES* 10 (1978), 53–60; idem, "Juvenile Delinquency in the Bible and the Ancient Near East," *JANES* 13 (1981), 31–52.

69. See most recently idem, *Jephthah and his Vow* (Lubbock: Texas Tech, 1986).

70. The revised dissertation appeared as the monograph, "The Phonology of Akkadian Syllable Structure," *Afroasiatic Linguistics* 9 (1984), 1–71.

71. *JANES* was founded at Columbia and is now located at Jewish Theological Seminary.

72. See the survey in A. Berlin, *The Dynamics of Biblical Parallelism* (Bloomington: Indiana University, 18–30).

73. See especially, E. Greenstein, "How Does Parallelism Mean?" in *A Sense of Text*, 41–70; idem, "Two Variations of Grammatical Parallelism in Canaanite Poetry and their Psycholinguistic Background," *JANES* 6 (1974), 87–105; idem, 'One More Step on the Staircase," *Ugarit-Forschungen* 9 (1977), 77–86.

74. See E. Greenstein and A. Preminger (eds.), *The Hebrew Bible in Literary Criticism* (New York: Unger, 1986); See further Greenstein, "Theory and Argument in Biblical Criticism," in *Hebrew Annual Review* 10 (1986), 77–93; idem, "literature, the Old Testament as," in *Harper's Bible Dictionary*, 567–571.

75. The thesis, written in 1975, was published in the SBL dissertation series, vol. 37 as, H. Cohen, *Biblical Hapax Legomena in the Light of Akkadian and Ugaritic*, (Missoula: Scholars, 1978).

76. See the criticism of Cohen's work in Greenspahn, *Hapax Legomena*, 13–15; Cohen reviewed Greenspahn's book somewhat unfavorably in *JBL* 105 (1986), 702–704; See further, E. Greenstein, *JAOS* 107 (1987), 538–539.

77. *Biblical Hapax Legomena*, 7.

78. Cf. the discussion of Held's method in the previous chapter.

79. See Cohen, *Biblical Hapax Legomena*, 33; See further his more recent, "The Semantic Range and Usage of the Terms ʾāmâ and šiphâ," *Shnaton* 5–6 (1983), xxv–liii.

80. See C. Cohen, "Neo-Assyrian Elements in the Speech of the Biblical Rab-Šaqê," *Israel Oriental Studies* 9 (1979), 32–48.

81. (Rome: Pontifical Biblical Institute, 1980) The book is a substantial revision of Gruber's 1977 Columbia dissertation.

82. See conveniently, M. Gruber, "Gestures" in P. Achtemeier (ed.), *Harper's Bible Dictionary* (San Francisco, 1985), 341–343. See further, idem, M. Gruber, "Akkadian *labān appi* in the Light of Art and Literature," *JANES* 7 (1975), 73–83; idem, "The Many Faces of Hebrew *nāśāʾ pānîm* 'Lift up the Face'," *ZAW* 95 (1983), 252–260.

83. *Revue biblique* 90 (1983).

84. *Beer-Sheva* 2 (1985); See also his "Women in the Cult according to the Priestly Code," in J. Neusner, B. Levine et al (eds.), *Judaic Perspectives on Ancient Israel* (Philadelphia: Fortress, 1987), 35–48.

85. See e.g. S. D. Sperling, "Genesis 41:40: A New Interpretation," *JANES* 10 (1978), 113–119, esp. 117, n. 36.

86. See e.g. S. D. Sperling, "Late Hebrew *ḥzr* and Akkadian *sahāru*," *JANES* 5 (1973), 397–404; See further, "Fragments of Tannaitic Letters Preserved in Rabbinic Literature," by Sperling in the collaboration with D. Pardee, *A Handbook of Ancient Hebrew Letters* (Chico: Scholars, 1982).

87. See recently S. D. Sperling, "Israel's Religion in the Ancient Near East," in Green (ed.), *Jewish Spirituality*, 5–31; idem, "God in the Hebrew Scriptures," in *Encyclopedia of Religion* 6, 1–8; idem, "Joshua 24: A Reexamination," *HUCA* 58 (1987), 119–136; idem, "Rethinking Covenant in Late Biblical Books," *Biblica* 70 (1989), 50–73.

88. See his forthcoming monograph *Rite and Writ in an Ugaritic Legend: Ritual and Literary Elements in the Curing of King Keret*.

89. Lichtenstein also acknowledges the influence of the writings of Parry

and Lord.

90. See e.g. M. Lichtenstein, "Psalm 68:7 Revisited," *JANES* 4 (1972), 97–112; idem, "Chiasm and Symmetry in Proverbs 31," *CBQ* 44 (1982), 292–211; idem, "Biblical Poetry," in Holtz (ed.), *Back to the Sources*, 105–127.

91. See M. Lichtenstein, "The Poetry of Poetic Justice: A Comparative Study in Biblical Imagery," *JANES* 5 (1973), 255–265.

92. J. Tigay, "Literary-Critical Studies in the Gilgamesh Epic: An Assyriological Contribution to Biblical Literary Criticism," (Yale dissertation, 1971); See also idem, "Was There an Integrated Gilgamesh Epic in the Old Babylonian Period?," in M. deJ. Ellis (ed.), *Ancient Near Eastern Studies in Memory of Jacob Joel Finkelstein* (Hamden, 1977), 215–218.

93. See further, J. Tigay (ed.), *Empirical Models for Biblical Criticism* (Philadelphia: University of Pennsylvania, 1985).

94. idem, *You Shall Have No Other Gods Israelite Religion in the Light of Hebrew Inscriptions* (Atlanta: Scholars, 1986).

95. *CBQ* 38 (1976), 455–482.

96. *JAOS* 103 (1983), 719–737.

97. ibid, 737.

98. The dissertation is entitled, "The Akkadian Influences on Aramaic and the development of the Aramaic Dialects." (Yale, 1970). With the aid and encouragement of E. Y. Kutscher, the dissertation was revised and published as *The Akkadian Influences on Aramaic* (= *Assyrological Studies* 19; Chicago, 1974)

99. See e.g. S. Kaufman, "An Assyro-Aramaic *egirtu ša šulmu,* in *Essays . . . J. J. Finklestein;* idem, "The Job Targum from Qumran," *JAOS* 93 (1973); idem, "Reflections on the Assyrian-Aramaic Bilingual from Tell Fakhariyeh," *MAARAV* 3 (1982); idem, "The Pitfalls of Typology: On the Early History of the Alphabet," *HUCA* 57 (1986); One can learn much Aramaic from a Kaufman review. See e.g. his critique of Hoftijzer and van der Kooij, *Aramaic Texts from Deir 'Allâ* (Leiden: Brill, 1976) in *BASOR* 239 (1980), 71–74; and of S. Segert, *Altaramäische Grammatik* (Leipzig, 1975) in *Bibliotheca Orientalis* 34 (1977).

100. e.g. S. Kaufman, "The Second Tablet of the Decalogue and the Implicit Categories of Ancient Near Eastern Law," in J. Marks and M. Good (eds.), *Love and Death in the Ancient Near East Essays in Honor of Marvin H. Pope* (Guilford: Four Quarters, 1987), 111–116; idem, "A Reconstruction of the Social Welfare Systems of Ancient Israel," in *In the Shelter of Elyon, Festschrift G. Ahlström*, 277–286.

101. See e.g. S. Kaufman, "The Structure of the Deuteronomic Law," *MAARAV* 1 (1978–79) 105–158; idem, "The Temple Scroll and Higher Criticism," *HUCA* 53 (1982), 29–43.

102. Cooper, who had taught previously at McMaster University in Ontario, Canada came to HUC-JIR to replace M. Tsevat, who had retired.

103. Pope directed Cooper's 1976 Yale dissertation, "Biblical Poetics: A Linguistic Approach."

104. See A. Cooper, "Psalm 24:7–10: Mythology and Exegesis," *JBL* 102 (1983), 37–60; idem, "MLK 'LM: 'Eternal King' or 'King of Eternity'?" *Essays Pope*, 1–7.

105. See A. Cooper, "On Reading the Bible Critically and Otherwise," in Friedman and Williamson (eds.), *Future*, 61–79; idem, "Myth, Midrash, and Meaning: The Case of Psalm 23," in *Proceedings of the Ninth World Congress of Jewish Studies* (Jerusalem, 1986), 107–114.
106. Cf. T. Frymer, "Ordeal, Judicial," in *IDBSup*, 638–640.
107. See e.g. idem, "Pollution, Purification and Purgation in Biblical Israel," in *Essays . . . Freedman*, 399–414.
108. See e.g. idem, "The Planting of Man: A Study in Biblical Imagery," in *Essays Pope*, 129–136.
109. See idem, "The Strange Case of the Suspected Sotah (Number 5:11–31)," *Vetus Testamentum* 34 (1984), 11–26.
110. See A. B. Lord, *The Singer of Tales* (New York: Atheneum, 1968). For his influence on Niditch see e.g. S. Niditch and R. Doran, "The Success story of the Wise Courtier: A Formal Approach," *JBL* 96 (1977), 179–193; Cf. S. Niditch, "Legends of Wise Heroes and Heroines," in Knight and Tucker (eds.), *Hebrew Bible*, 445–463.
111. S. Niditch, *The Symbolic Vision in Biblical Tradition* (Chico: Scholars, 1983). The book is a thorough revision of her Harvard dissertation written under Cross.
112. Niditch, *Symbolic Vision*, 12.
113. See F. Cross, *Canaanite Myth and Hebrew Epic* (Cambridge: Harvard, 1973), 343–344.
114. S. Niditch, *Chaos to Cosmos: Studies in Biblical Patterns of Creation* (Chico: Scholars, 1985).
115. ibid, 48.
116. See ibid especially, 30–43.
117. S. Niditch, *Chaos*, 11.
118. See ibid, 76–105; idem, "Father-Son Folktale Patterns and Tyrant Topologies in Josephus' Ant. 12:160–222," *Journal of Jewish Studies* 32 (1981), 47–55; idem, "The Cosmic Adam: Man as Mediator in Rabbinic Literature," ibid 34 (1983), 137–146.
119. See e.g. S. Geller, "Theory and Method in the Study of Biblical Poetry," *JQR* 73 (1982), 65–77.
120. See idem, "The Struggle at the Jabbok: the Uses of Enigma in a Biblical Narrative," *JANES* 14 (1982), 37–60.
121. Note his reference to the work of Viktor Shklovsky, in *JANES* 14, 60. Geller himself decries "narrow formalism".
122. See S. Geller, "Some Pitfalls in the 'Literary Approach' to Biblical Narrative," *Jewish Quarterly Review* 74 (1984), 406–415.
123. *Harvard Theological Review* 77, 413.
124. S. Geller, *Parallelism in Early Biblical Poetry* (Missoula: Scholars, 1979); Geller's work was published a year after T. Collins, *Line-Forms in Hebrew Poetry* (Rome: Biblical Institute Press, 1978); Following Geller however, were M. O'Connor, *Hebrew Verse Structure* (Winona Lake: Eisenbrauns, 1980); J. Kugel, *The Idea of Biblical Poetry. Parallelism and its History* (New Haven: Yale, 1981); A. Berlin, *The Dynamics of Biblical Parallelism* (Bloomington: Indiana University, 1985).
125. See also, S. Geller, "The Dynamics of Parallel Verse. A Poetic

Analysis of Deuteronomy 32:6–12," *Harvard Theological Review* 73 (1982), 65–77; idem, "A Poetic Analysis of Isaiah 40:1–2," ibid, 77 (1984), 413–420.

126. J. Levenson, "The Hebrew Bible, the Old Testament and Historical Criticism," in R. Friedman and H. Williamson (eds.), *The Future of Biblical Studies The Hebrew Scriptures* (Atlanta: Scholars, 1987), 47; See further, idem, "Why Jews are Not Interested in Biblical Theology," in Neusner (ed.) *Judaic Perspectives*, 281–307.

127. Harper and Row, San Francisco: 1985; See also J. Levenson, "The Jerusalem Temple in Devotional and Visionary Experience," in Green (ed), *Jewish Spirituality*, 32–61; idem, *Creation and the Persistence of Evil The Jewish Drama of Divine Omnipotence* (Harper and Row, San Francisco: 1988).

128. Friedman's thesis was published as R. Friedman, *The Impact of Exile on the Character of Biblical Narrative* (Chico: Scholars, 1980).

129. R. Friedman, "From Egypt to Egypt: Dtr[1] and Dtr[2]," in B. Halpern and J. Levenson (eds.), *Traditions in Transformation: Turning Points in Biblical Faith* (Winona Lake: Eisenbrauns, 1981), 167–192.

130. R. Friedman, "The Recession of Biblical Source Criticism," in Friedman and Williamson (eds.), *Future*, 81–101.

131. See idem, "Sacred History and Theology: The Redaction of Torah," in R. Friedman (ed.), *The Creation of Sacred Literature Composition and Redaction of the Biblical Text* (Los Angeles: University of California, 1981), 25–34.

132. See B. Halpern and R. Friedman, "Composition and Paranomasia in the Book of Jonah," *Hebrew Annual Review* 4 (1980), 79; See in general, E. D. Hirsch, *Validity in Interpretation* (New Haven: Yale, 1976). It may be observed that Hirsch's approach, in many respects a secularization of Aquinas' understanding of the relation of the OT to the NT, is itself ultimately grounded in biblical interpretation.

133. R. Friedman, *Who Wrote the Bible* (Englewood Cliffs: Prentice-Hall, 1987).

134. The revised thesis was published as B. Halpern, *The Constitution of the Monarchy in Israel* (Chico: Scholars, 1981).

135. B. Halpern, *The Emergence of Israel in Canaan* (Chico: Scholars, 1983); See also, B. Halpern, *The Constitution of the Monarchy in Israel* (Chico: Scholars, 1981).

136. *Emergence*, 16.

137. For the most extensive statement see N. Gottwald, *The Tribes of Yahweh: A Sociology of the Religion of Liberated Israel, 1250–1050 B.C.E.* (Maryknoll, N.Y.: Orbis, 1979).

138. G. Mendenhall, "The Hebrew Conquest of Palestine," E. Campbell and D. Freedman (eds.), *Biblical Archaeologist Reader 3* (Garden City: Doubleday, 1970), 107. For Mendenhall's subseqent statements and modifications see the bibliography in N. P. Lemche, *Early Israel* (= *VTSup* 37; Leiden: Brill, 1985) 461; Add G. Mendenhall, "Ancient Israel's Hyphenated History," in D. Freedman and D. Graf (eds.), *Palestine in Transition* (Sheffield: Almond, 1983), 91–103.

139. See M. Astour, "The Amarna Age Forerunners of Biblical Anti-

Royalism," in *For Max Weinreich on his Seventieth Birthday* (The Hague: Mouton, 1974), 13.
140. *Emergence*, 76.
141. See also B. Halpern, "The Resourceful Israelite Historian: The Song of Deborah and Israelite Historiography," *Harvard Theological Review* 76 (1983), 379–402.
142. San Francisco: Harper and Row, 1988.
143. ibid, 8.
144. ibid, 65.
145. ibid, 12.
146. The definition is not without problems. Suffice it at present to say that on Halpern's definition Ezekiel's chariot vision committed to writing by an author who believed what he or she wrote, should be considered historical.
147. The dissertation is entitled, "Studies in Biblical Poetry and Vocabulary in their Northwest Semitic Setting." (Berkeley, 1973).
148. See e.g. "The Khirbet el-Qôm Inscription Mentioning a Goddess," *Bulletin of the American Schools of Oriental Research* 255 (1984), 39–47. Zevit is also writing the article "Religion of Israel" for the forthcoming *Anchor Bible Dictionary*.
149. See e.g. Z. Zevit, "The use of ʿebed as a Diplomatic Term in Jeremiah," *JBL* 99 (1969), 74–77; idem, "A Misunderstanding at Bethel—Amos VII, 12–17," *Vetus Testamentum* 25 (1975), 783–790; idem, "A Phoenician Inscription and Biblical Covenant Theology," *Israel Exploration Journal* (1977), 110–118; idem, "Expressing Denial in Biblical and Mishnaic Hebrew and in Amos," *VT* 29 (1979), 505–509; idem, "Coverging Lines of Evidence Bearing on the Date of P," *Zeitschrift für die alttestamentliche Wissenschaft* 94 (1982), 481–511.
150. In this connection, note the author's dedication (vii): "To the memory of my grandfather, a student and a scholar, Ben-Zion, the son of Aharon Yosef Zwet, who would have understood that it too is *talmud Torah*."
151. Cambridge: American Schools of Oriental Research, 1980.
152. The dissertation appeared in published form as A. Berlin, *Enmerkar and Ensuhkešdanna, A Sumerian Narrative Poem* (Philadelphia: The University Museum, 1979).
153. See the chapter "Poetic Structure and Technique," in *Enmerkar*, 9–31; Cf. further, A. Berlin, "Shared Rhetorical Features in Biblical and Sumerian Literature," *JANES* 10 (1978), 35–42.
154. See e.g. A. Berlin, *Poetics and Interpretation of Biblical Narrative* (Sheffield: Almond, 1983); idem, "On the Bible as Literature," *Prooftexts* 2 (1982), 327–327; idem, "Motif and Creativity in Biblical Poetry," *Prooftexts* 3 (1983), 231–241.
155. See idem, "The Rhetoric of Psalm 145," in A. Kort and S. Morschauer (eds.), *Biblical and Related Studies Presented to Samuel Iwry* (Winona Lake: Eisenbrauns, 1985), 17–22.
156. See A. Berlin, "Grammatical Aspects of Biblical Parallelism," *HUCA* 50 (1977), 17–43; and especially, idem, *The Dynamics of Biblical Parallelism* (Bloomington: Indiana University, 1985).

157. See G. Rendsburg, "Late Biblical Hebrew and the Date of 'P'," *JANES* 12 (1980), 65–80; idem, *The Redaction of Genesis* (Winona Lake: Eisenbrauns, 1986), especially, 99–106.

158. J. Sasson, "The 'Tower of Babel' as a Clue to the Redactional Structuring of the Primeval History (Gen. 1–11:9)," in Rendsburg (ed.), *Bible World Essays Gordon*, 211–219.

159. Rendsburg, *Redaction of Genesis*, 3.

160. Ibid, 4, 107–120.

161. Note e.g. the camels in the Joseph story proper (Gen 37:25) as well as their prominence in Gen 24. For a recent survey of camel domestication in Palestine of the first millennium B.C. see P. Wapnish, "Camel Caravans and Camel Pastoralists at Tell Jemmeh," *JANES* 13 (1981), 101–121. On the linguistic and historical problems pointing to a far later date for the Joseph story, see D. Redford, *A Study of the Biblical Story of Joseph (Genesis 37–50)* (Leiden: Brill, 1970).

162. See e.g., M. Fox, "The Rhetoric of Ezekiel's Vision of the Valley of the Bones," *HUCA* 51 (1980), 1–15; idem, "Job 38 and God's Rhetoric," *Semeia* 19 (1981), 53–61; idem, "Ancient Egyptian Rhetoric," *Rhetorica* 1 (1983), 9–22.

163. J. Muilenberg, *JBL* 88 (1969), 1–18.

164. *HUCA* 51, 1; Cf. ibid, 4: "The audience hears only sequence and movement. It is more important for the critic to show the direction of the movement than to outline patterns discernible only in the completed and transcribed discourse."

165. See e.g. Deut 31:9–13 (Note the suasive motive given for the public reading ibid, 12–13); Neh 9:1–3.

166. See e.g. M. Fox, "The Cairo Love Songs," *JAOS* 100 (1980), 101–109; idem, "A Study of Antef," *Orientalia* 46 (1977), 393–423; idem, "The 'Entertainment Song' Genre in Egyptian Literature," *Scripta Hierosolymitana* 28 (1982), 268–316.

167. Madison: University of Wisconsin, 1985.

168. See e.g. J. Kugel and R. Greer, *Early Biblical Interpretation* (Philadelphia: Westminster, 1986).

169. J. Kugel, *The Idea of Biblical Poetry* (New Haven: Yale, 1981). There is a convenient summary by the author in *Harper's Bible Dictionary*, 804–805, s.v. "poetrty;" See further idem, "A Feeling of Déjà Lu," *Journal of Religion* 67 (1987), 66–79.

170. See Kugel, *Idea*, 31–32, 43.

171. See Kugel, *AJS Newsletter* 36, 22–24; Cf. our discussion in the "Introduction."

172. The dissertation is entitled, "Kingship vs. Kinship: Political Allegory in the Bible—a new reading of Gen. 1–3 and related Texts." (Santa Cruz, 1978).

173. J. Rosenberg, *King and Kin Political Allegory in the Hebrew Bible* (Bloomington: Indiana University, 1986), 5.

174. Rosenberg, *King and Kin*, 5.

175. See also J. Rosenberg, "The Garden Story Forward and Backward: the Non-Narrative Dimension of Gen. 2–3," *Prooftexts* 1 (1981), 1–27.

176. J. Rosenberg, "1 and 2 Samuel," in Alter and Kermode (eds.), *Literary Guide*, 132; For a similar reading of a biblical narrative as allegory see E. Greenstein, "The Riddle of Samson," *Prooftexts* 1 (1981), 237–260.

177. See R. Cohn, *The Shape of Sacred Space: Four Biblical Studies* (Chico: Scholars, 1981); See further Cohn's review of Niditch, *Chaos*, in *JBL* 106 (1987), 316.

178. See our chapter above on "The European background."

CHAPTER SIX
Translations, Collaborations and Compendia

Our account of Jewish biblical scholarship in North America turns now to a brief survey of Jewish Bible translations,[1] collaborations and compendia to which Jewish scholars have contributed. Because of its wide readership and accessibility, the most influential collaborative work on the Bible produced under North American Jewish auspices is: *TANAKH A New Translation of The Holy Scriptures According to the Traditional Hebrew Text*[2]. The reader will recall that under the editorship of Max Margolis, the Jewish Publication Society in 1917 had published its *Holy Scriptures*. That edition, which as a replacement for the Leeser Bible, had served the North American Jewish community as a Bible for synagogue and home, was itself but a modest revision of the Protestant Revised Version of 1885[3]. The primary differences between the JPS Bible of 1917 and the RV were liturgical and confessional. Accordingly, the JPS version adhered to the Masoretic Text, followed what had become the Jewish order of the biblical books, included a table of scriptural readings for the Jewish liturgical year and avoided christological renditions such as "virgin" in Isaiah 7:14 and "Kiss the Son" in Psalm 2:11. By the end of the Second World War the English of the *Holy Scriptures* with its "thee's thou's and thines," had become too archaic for Jewish anglophones of the mid-twentieth century.[4] Accordingly, the Jewish Publication Society undertook what was at first conceived of primarily as a modernization. Within a short period however, the Society abandoned its original project in favor of a much more ambitious goal; to produce a completely new English translation from the Hebrew original. The new translation into idiomatic English would reflect the enhanced understanding of classical Hebrew in light of modern discoveries in Semitics and archaeology.

The stated intention of those responsible for *TANAKH* was that it have a Jewish character. That goal would be realized by making "critical use of the early rabbinic and medieval Jewish commentators, grammarians and philologians." In addition, it was emphasized that the translators "would rely on the traditional Hebrew text, avoiding emendations."[5] This last point was highly significant for a Jewish audience. In contrast to the situation in Christianity, which for most of its history has transmitted both the OT and NT to the faithful in translation, the Jewish traditions have been unable to ignore the Hebrew text.[6] It must also be recalled that traditional Jewish liturgy is closely linked to the traditional forms of the biblical Hebrew text, so that to deviate from the text might undermine the liturgy.

As was the case with the 1917 JPS, *TANAKH* departed from translation traditions of a christological bent. RSV, for example, translates *ruʾah ʾelohim* (Gen 1:2) as "Spirit," thus enabling an allusion to a Person of the Trinity. *TANAKH* offers the neutral "a wind from God."[7] The case of Isa 7:14, a key verse in Christian interpretative tradition, is particularly illuminating. RSV translates: "Behold a young woman shall conceive and bear a son and shall call his name Immanuel." In its notes however, RSV offers the traditional Christian "virgin" as an alternative. In contrast, as an alternative to "shall conceive," of its text, RSV offers the grammatically preferable[8] "is with child and shall bear." While RSV thus does not completely support the interpretation given to Isa 7:14 in the New Testament (Matt 2:23), the translation leaves open the possibility of understanding the verse as a prediction of some future event and thus as a reference to the birth of Jesus. *TANAKH* however, eliminates all reference to future prediction by translating: "Look, the young woman is with child and about to give birth to a son. Let her name him Immanuel."[9]

The professional Bible scholars engaged by the Jewish Publication Society to produce the new translation were E. A. Speiser, H. L. Ginsberg, H. M. Orlinsky, Nahum Sarna, Jonas Greenfield and Moshe Greenberg. It was hoped that *TANAKH* would be broadly perceived by Jews as a quasi-official Jewish Bible for anglophones, along the lines of authorized Protestant and Catholic translations[10]. With this confessional end in mind, the Society augmented the panel of professional scholars with congregational rabbis of a scholarly bent.[11] In order to provide the broadest spectrum of denominational viewpoints, the rabbis were drawn from the Conservative, Orthodox and Reform groupings. To be sure, the presence of Orthodox representation, which had been lacking in the original JPS translation of 1917, did not shield this new Jewish version from the kinds of criticism that had attended the earlier work.[12] To borrow Yogi Berra's felicitous phrasing, it was "déjà vu all over again," when, within some orthodox circles, the Torah translation was condemned as "Apikursos" or "heresy."[13]

Name-calling notwithstanding, there can be no doubt that the committee was extremely successful in its undertaking. Although technically a translation, *TANAKH* turned out to be a highly original work of Jewish biblical scholarship. In their quest for intelligibility, the translators accurately reflected the sense of the Hebrew by attending closely to such devices as hendiadys and merism. Accordingly, a phrase like *me-ʾarṣeka u-mi-molodteka* (Gen 12:1) which in JPS of 1917 read "(Get thee) out thy country and from thy kindred," appears in *TANAKH* as "(Go forth) from your native land." Similarly, the full force of *ʾim mi-ḥûṭ wěʿad śerok naʿal* (Gen 14:23) is missed in JPS 1917 "I will not take a thread nor a shoe-latchet." The true sense is conveyed beautifully by *TANAKH*'s: "I will not take so much as a thread or a sandal strap."[14] Again to their credit, the translators emulated the great Jewish medieval translator and exegete Saadia in rendering the conjunction *waw* contextually, rather than mechanically as "and." It is no exaggeration to say, especially with regard to the translators of the Torah, Prophets and Five Megilloth that they provided ingenious new insights into the original Hebrew and the ancient realities behind the text, on every page. To cite just one example, in Exod 1:11 *siblôtām* was translated as "burdens" in JPS 1917. In contrast, *TANAKH*'s "forced labor" shows awareness that Hebrew *sebel* was an ancient technical term for corvée labor, attested as early as the Mari letters of the eighteenth century B. C.[15]

Yet despite its remarkable scholarly achievement, *TANAKH* demonstrates that serious critical study of the Bible continues to be a delicate matter within Judaism. One may put the matter as follows: On the one hand, Jewish Bible scholars employ uncompromising and critical standards in their researches. Indeed, as our historical survey of individual scholars has demonstrated, the research interests of Jewish biblicists and the teaching of Bible at non-Orthodox Jewish seminaries do not differ in substance from the research and teaching interests of Jewish and Gentile biblicists and semiticists at universities. At the same time, one still finds Jewish Bible scholars publicly insisting that they are "studying torah,"[16] that is, studying the sacred writings of Jewish tradition within that self-validating tradition, a pious activity hallowed within Judaism already in late biblical times.[17] Within *TANAKH* one may clearly see such scholarly equivocation. Thus, in contrast to the 1917 *Holy Scriptures,* which, absent some explanations of Hebrew wordplays, contains virtually no annotations, *TANAKH* often notes, at the bottom of the page, the meaning which would be yielded by emending a difficult text, prefacing such suggestions with the phrase "emendation yields." The circumlocution makes it possible to claim that an emendation "may be readily disregarded by those who reject it on either scholarly or religious grounds."[18] Inasmuch as "scholarly" and "religious" are not parallel criteria, it may be fairly said that *TANAKH* has revived the procedure employed decades earlier in the Bible articles of *Jewish Encyclopedia,* in which criticism was relegated to the final sections. On other occasions, emendations in *TANAKH* are simply not acknowledged.[19] To cite one example, *TANAKH* translates the difficult *šetŭm hāʿāyin* in Num 24:3c as: "whose eye is true," appending the note: "meaning of Heb. uncertain." Orlinsky[20] explains NJV's translation by reference to W. Albright's interpretation of the initial *shin* as a relative pronoun preceding the phrase "is true." The reader of *Notes* who chooses to check the reference to Albright however, finds that Albright's interpretation requires the emendation of both words in order to yield the proffered translation.[21] And this is not a unique example.[22] Nonetheless, the translators of *TANAKH* must be applauded for their boldness and courage in the enormously difficult effort to combine scholarly integrity with intelligibility, while at the same time bearing in mind the varied religious sentiments among the members of the English-speaking Jewish public.

The translators of the third section of *TANAKH* appear to have approached their task somewhat more conservatively. The following paragraph[23] is instructive:

"Divergences of the present translation from recent renderings reflect the committee's judgment that certain innovations, though interesting, are too speculative for adoption in the present state of knowledge. The as yet imperfect understanding of the language of the Bible, or what appears to be some disorder in the Hebrew text, makes sure translation of many passages impossible.[24] This uncertainty in *Kethuvim* is indicated in a note; and, where the Hebrew texts permits, alternative readings have been offered. However, emendations of the text of *Kethuvim*—except for the five Megilloth—[25] were not proposed, and notes were kept to a minimum."

Even before the completion of *TANAKH*, the Jewish Publication Society decided to accompany its Torah translation with a commentary in English, directed towards:

"the Jew who appreciates intellectual rigor matched by respect for the Jewish religious tradition, as well as for people of all faiths who wish to understand the first five books of the Bible in terms both of the Jewish tradition and the contributions of modern scholarship."[26]

The commentary is under the general editorship of Nahum Sarna, who has also authored the commentaries to Genesis and Exodus. An interesting innovation of the JPS project is the involvement of a best-selling novelist, Chaim Potok, as literary editor. It had been hoped to have all the volumes ready by the early 1980's[27]. As of this writing (1991), Sarna's *Genesis*, and *Exodus*, B. Levine's *Leviticus* and J. Milgrom's *Numbers* have appeared. *Deuteronomy* has been assigned to Jeffrey Tigay. Of interest to the historian of Jewish biblical scholarship is that Levine, Milgrom, Tigay and Potok are all rabbinic graduates of Jewish Theological Seminary, while Sarna taught at JTS until he left for Brandeis in 1965.

From the volumes that have appeared, it is apparent that the JPS commentary has its closest counterpart in Doubleday's *Anchor Bible* series (see below). As in AB, literary criticism, comparative Semitic philology and archaeological information are provided for a target audience envisioned as intelligent and educated, but not necessarily specialized in Bible and allied disciplines. None of the commentary authors argues for unity of authorship, but whereas Sarna stresses the unity of the finished product, Levine and Milgrom refer explicitly to the traditional "sources" of the Pentateuch. Curiously, Milgrom, despite his acceptance of source-criticism, makes what Alter has aptly termed "the astonishing theological claim that his commentary 'offers reliable support to those who believe that this book [Numbers] and the Torah at large were divinely revealed.' "[28]

The JPS commentary differs in substance from AB by adhering more closely to the masoretic texts; by consciously and purposefully utilizing the internal Jewish exegetical tradition; and especially by calling attention to the ways in which biblical institutions and laws were developed or transmuted in post-biblical Judaism, thus consciously linking Judaism to its roots in the Bible.

A particularly well-read compendium of scholarship under Jewish sponsorship is the *Encyclopaedia Judaica*,[29] a project that illustrates the close ties between Israeli academics and their colleagues in the

United States. The historian Cecil Roth (1899–1970) served as Editor in Chief of the entire *EncJud* project. In contrast to the earlier *Jewish Encyclopedia* in which most of the Bible articles had been written by Gentile scholars,[30] some forty Jewish scholars were responsible for the majority of articles on the Bible and the biblical period.[31] H. L. Ginsberg served as divisional editor for Bible. Shalom Paul, then a junior colleague of Ginsberg at Jewish Theological Seminary, was associate divisional editor for Bible as well as editor of the department of Ideas and Religion within the Bible division. Moshe Greenberg, who had recently left the University of Pennsylvania for the Hebrew University in Jerusalem, served as departmental editor for Biblical Society and Law. Nahum Sarna of Brandeis was editor of the department designated as: "Period of the Pentateuch, Desert, Joshua and Judges." It is of interest that although the critical approach was utilized by the contributors to all fields of Judaica covered by *EncJud*, the general editors found it necessary to comment only on its applicability to Bible articles:

"Special problems were posed in the Bible Division in view of the greatly varied and even radically opposing attitudes to the Bible and Bible scholarship. It was felt that an encyclopedia designed to reflect all aspects of knowledge relevant to Jewish culture must, in the sphere of Bible, bring to the reader all views—from the most traditional to the most critical. It was realized that the balance would be precarious and that, in view of the strong feelings held on either side, it would be difficult and probably impossible to satisfy all the readers all the time. All concerned agreed that both traditional and critical viewpoints should be fully represented."[32]

In keeping with this policy, *EncJud* does not relegate the critical view to the last section. To cite some examples, the article by Sarna on the book of *Genesis*[33] contains the critical view, including a source analysis in tabular form in the body of the article. The reader who wishes to learn of the traditional view is referred to another article, "Pentateuch," which concludes with a section headed "the traditional view," which outlines the contrasts between the unitary views of Pentateuch authorship and modern criticism."[34] Indeed, most of the Bible articles make little attempt to defend the pre-critical approach to the Bible.

Among compendia under non-Jewish sponsorship but with Jewish scholarly participation, special mention must be made of the *Anchor Bible* series, an ongoing project of Doubleday and Co., intended to cover both testaments and the apocrypha. The inaugural volume in the series was *Speiser's Genesis*. Other North American Jewish scholars whose *Anchor* volumes have appeared are M. Greenberg;[35] Carol Meyers and Eric Meyers[36] and Jack Sasson.[37] In addition, Leviticus has been assigned to J. Milgrom and Numbers to B. Levine.

A standard reference work since its publication has been the *Interpreter's Dictionary of the Bible*, a four volume encyclopedia first published by Abingdon in 1962, augmented by its *Supplementary Volume*, which appeared in 1976. Out of hundreds of contributors to the original edition, only 12 were Jewish biblicists. An additional 19 Jewish participants were in such allied fields as rabbinics and Jewish philosophy. In the 1976 *Supplementary Volume*, 54 out of 270 contributors, some 20%, were Jewish. Of these, approximately 18 were professional Bible scholars from North America, an increase of 33 percent.

The more recent *Harper's Bible Dictionary*,[38] published in cooperation with the Society of Biblical Literature, provides further evidence of increased Jewish participation in general biblical scholarship. *Harper's* has some twenty-five Jewish contributors, including an associate editor, out of a total of one hundred and seventy-nine participants. Twenty-three of these Jewish scholars are North Americans.[39]

Notes to Chapter Six

1. A new history of Jewish Bible translations from late antiquity to modern times, written by Professor Harry Orlinsky, is due to appear shortly.
2. (Philadelphia: Jewish Publication Society, 1985). The translation was initially published in parts, beginning with *Torah* in 1962, *The Prophets (Nevi'im)*, in 1978 and *The Writings (Kethubim)* in 1982. Note that in *TANAKH*, the spelling of the title of the third section was altered to *Kethuvim*.
3. See above, Chapter 2, n. 140.
4. For other good examples, see Orlinsky, *Essays*, 356–357. It may be observed that Christian anglophones who oppose modernization of "Bible English" can at least claim that are defending a liturgical traditon more than three centuries old. Orlinsky (ibid) found it "surprising" that some Jews were more tenacious than Christians in their loyalty to archaic English.
5. (*TANAKH*, xvii).
6. This is not to exaggerate Jewish literacy in biblical Hebrew. A contrary inference might be drawn from the history of Greek Septuagint, Aramaic Targums, Arabic Tafsir and various modern vernacular translations. Nonetheless, these translations never replaced the Hebrew. In contemporary Conservative and Reform synagogues the Torah scroll continues

to be read or chanted in Hebrew despite the fact that the overwhelming majority of congregants do not understand the language.

7. See Orlinsky, *Notes,* 52–55. Note that in Isa 44:3 RSV translates Heb *ruḥî* "my Spirit," with capital "S," while *TANAKH* offers lower case.

8. See the analysis of the passage in Ehrlich, *Mikrâ* III, 18; Cf. Peters apud Orlinsky, "Virgin," *IDBSup,* 940.

9. As such, the context of the verse becomes similar to that of Isa 8:3–4, which is to be expected. It is of interest that the new Revised English Bible (REB), which appeared in 1989, agrees with *TANAKH* in Gen 1:2; Isa 7:14 and 44:3.

10. The translation is often referred to as NJV, New Jewish Version, in obvious imitation of AV and RSV, although neither "Jewish" nor "version" appears on the title page of *TANAKH,* or of the sections issued previously. Note also Orlinsky's (*Essays,* 349) reference to his address to the annual meeting of the Jewish Publication Society on May 10, 1953 as having "the express purpose . . . to influence some reluctant members of the Society into agreeing to sponsor a new Jewish translation of the Bible." Of interest as well is the title of the published lecture (*Essays,* 349–362): "Wanted: A New English Translation of the Bible for the Jewish People."

11. Bernard Bamberger (1904–80) a Reform rabbi who served on the JPS committee which produced the translations of *Torah* and *Prophets,* subsequently prepared a serious popular commentary to Leviticus which appeared as Volume III of *The Torah a Modern Commentary* (New York: Union of American Hebrew Congregations, 1979). Dr. Orlinsky, who served as editor-in-chief of the *Torah* translation, informs us that the rabbinic members of the committee often made suggestions that won over the committee's professional scholars.

12. Not atypical in Orthodox circles was the characterization of the original JPS translation by one Rabbi Gerstenfeld, who felt that the translation contained innovations "sufficient to construct a new sect." See S. Hoening, "Notes on the New Translation of the Torah—A Preliminary Inquiry," *Tradition A Journal of Orthodox Jewish Thought* Vol 5 (No. 2 (Spring, 1963), 172–205, especially, 204.

13. See S. Hoenig, "Notes, p. 204." The term "apikursos," literally "Epicureanism," connotes in talmudic usage "skepticism" as well as "licentiousness." See Jastrow, *Dictionary,* 104. In rabbinic parlance, the term serves as a general invective with which to defame one's opponents, much like "judaizing" in classical Christian polemic. Dr. Orlinsky's personal files revealed a cartoon from a 1963 Yiddish-language newspaper in which a stereotypical paleo-Orthodox Jew is depicted pushing away the new Torah translation. The cartoon's caption reads: *Er iz nit meqabbel Orlinsky's toyra,* "he doesn't accept Orlinsky's Torah."

14. See Orlinsky, *Notes,* 36–37.

15. See M. Held. "The Root *ZBL/SBL* in Akkadian, Ugaritic and Biblical Hebrew," *Journal of the American Oriental Society* 88 (1968), 90–96; Cf. A. Rainey, "Compulsory Labour Gangs in Ancient Israel," *Israel Exploration Journal* 70 (1970), 191–202.

16. For roughly the past thousand years "studying torah" has usually

meant studying the Babylonian Talmud. See the discussion of the traditional Jewish curriculum in chapter 2.

17. See e.g. Ps 1, 119; Neh 8; 2 Chr 17:9.

18. *TANAKH*, xx.

19. To be sure, *TANAKH* has far fewer unacknowledged emendations than New English Bible.

20. *Notes*, 237. Orlinsky's book provides an account of the committee's work on the Torah and the reasoning behind many of its decisions. The book's indexes show which earlier scholars were most frequently consulted and followed. E. A. Speiser, a member of the original committee until his untimely death was especially influential in the Genesis translation which bears frequent and close resemblance to Speiser's commentary on *Genesis* in the Anchor Bible (cf. ibid 6). The notes to Speiser's *Genesis* shed additional light on some of the NJV Torah renderings.

21. See W. Albright, *"The Oracles of Balaam," JBL* 63 (1944), 216, nn. 36, 37.

22. For other examples of unacknowledged emendations see the review of *Nevi'im* by K. Carthcart, *Orientalia* 33 (1984), 152–153.

23. *TANAKH*, xx.

24. It may be objected that offering (acknowledged) conjectures at precisely such passages could be particularly beneficial to readers. Cf. H. L. Ginsberg, "Some Emendations in Psalms," *HUCA* 23 Part One (1950–51), 97.

25. The seeming inconsistency in proposing textual emendations only for those books which are read in the synagogue in their entirety but not for say, Job and Chronicles which are read in private, is due to the fact that the Megilloth were prepared by the members of the less conservative earlier committee. To encourage their use in synagogue liturgy, the Megilloth and Jonah were the first of the Writings to be translated.

26. From the publicity release of Spring, 1989.

27. Levine, "Decade of Jewish Bible Scholarship," 24–25.

28. See R. Alter, "Interpreting the Bible," *Commentary* 89, No. 3 (March, 1990), 55.

29. (Jerusalem: Keter, 1972): The introduction to *EncJud* (Vol 1, 1–16) contains a useful survey of previous Jewish encyclopedias.

30. See above, chapter 2.

31. Among the non-Jewish contributors to the Bible division in *EncJud* were D. Hillers, E. Lipinski and A. S. van der Woude.

32. Note the prominence of the passive voice in this passage.

33. "Genesis, Book of," *EncJud* 7, 386–398.

34. See "Pentateuch," *EncJud* 13, 232–264. The bulk of the article (ibid, 232–261) was written by the Israeli biblicist Moshe Weinfeld. The section on the traditional view (ibid, 261–264) was written by Louis Rabinowitz, who was Deputy Editor in Chief of *EncJud*. Authored by a scholar whose contributions have been outside biblical studies, the article is remarkable for its inversion of what has been traditional Jewish doctrine with regard to the Bible. Whereas Rabinowitz takes great pains to defend the inerrancy of the transmitted Hebrew text, he appears willing to discard the doctrine of

unitary composition of the Pentateuch. Indeed, he asserts (ibid, 264) that "the documentary theory, or at least the evidence that the Pentateuch is not a unitary document, has been so convincing to many Orthodox scholars."

35. M. Greenberg, *Ezekiel 1–20* (Garden City: Doubleday, 1983).

36. C. and E. Meyers, *Haggai, Zechariah 1–8* (Garden City: Doubleday, 1987).

37. *Jonah* (Garden City: Doubleday, 1991).

38. P. Achtemeier, (ed.), *Harper's Bible Dictionary* (San Francisco: Harper and Row, 1965).

39. To judge from the preliminary list of contributors to the *Anchor Bible Dictionary* now underway, that compendium will have significant Jewish scholarly participation.

CHAPTER SEVEN
On the Periphery: North American Orthodox Judaism and Contemporary Biblical Scholarship

B. Barry Levy

The previous chapters of this book describe the work of many American Jews who contributed to Biblical scholarship. Without prejudging any of the contributors themselves, it is clear that numerous kinds of Jews are included, among them religious, secular, nationalist, American and foreign-born. Many were ordained rabbis; others were not. Some were highly observant; others, minimally so or not at all. Initially, the majority taught in Jewish institutions; with time, the number who worked in secular universities increased. Many saw their efforts as Jewish contributions to knowledge; others defended, or would have defended, the non-sectarian nature of their work.

Normally, such observations would go unmentioned; they might even seem inappropriate, because one of the accepted (though far from universally correct) myths of the contemporary academy is that one's religious affiliations do not, or at least should not, influence one's scholarly work significantly. But when all is said and done, Orthodox Jews are conspicuously absent.

That very few Orthodox writers seem to have contributed to Biblical scholarship may startle some readers because, at first blush, Orthodoxy appears to maintain a strong commitment to the Bible, and is able to display proud lists of contributors to other areas of Judaic scholarship. One must wonder, therefore, if Orthodox scholars are actually discussed in these pages, even if they are not so identified; if the editorial selection has somehow prejudiced the case against Orthodox scholars; if Orthodoxy ranks Bible study below studying other aspects of the Jewish religious literature; if the term "Orthodox Bible scholar" is an oxymoron; or if other factors have prevented a large number of Orthodox Jews from sharing in the scholarly enterprise of Bible study. My colleagues have examined what exists; it is my task to explore what apparently does not, and to discuss this list of hypotheses (all of which I believe to be at least partly correct). And because it is my privilege to conclude our study, I have also taken the liberty of suggesting what perhaps could or should be.

PRE-ORTHODOX[1] JEWISH BIBLE INTERPRETATION

The modern period of Bible study began, in my estimation, when Napoleon sent scholars and surveyors to the Middle East with his military personnel in 1798 and thereby set in motion the ongoing quest to study Scripture against its Near Eastern cultural background.[2] To be sure, many earlier writers had recognized the need to reconstruct the historical contexts of Biblical passages in order to understand them properly;[3] as well, many had learned the value of using other languages to explain difficult or unusual Hebrew words.[4] Some had used in their exegetical endeavors questionably accurate but seemingly ancient data recovered from non-traditional sources about ancient life.[5] Several even discussed archaeological discoveries, if one may use that term for the accidental recovery of ancient buildings and objects.[6] Among these alert writers were some who noted the limitations imposed on their interpretative efforts by the dire shortage of information about ancient times, and a few who even discussed the implications of its potential contribution, should it ever become available.[7] But only in the nineteenth century was the search for this knowledge undertaken in a systematic way, and this watershed marks the beginning of modern Bible study.

Many other issues that seem to differentiate modern Bible study from its pre-modern antecedents including skepticism about God's role in the composition of the Bible, commitment to the application of literary-critical principles, awareness of contradictions between different Biblical passages, freedom of the individual reader to challenge the authority of, and to deviate from, traditional interpretation, and doubts about the accuracy of the transmitted text—have important analogues in ancient and medieval writings.[8] Contemporary interpretation often emphasizes them and ignores matters of faith and application, but archaeology and historical perspective, not rational thinking, are the primary differences between modern writers and many of their pre-modern counterparts.

By the time Napoleon's group embarked, Jewish Bible interpretation had undergone many metamorphoses. Ancient times had witnessed both the successful application of old Biblical laws to new situations and the reinterpretation of Biblical history for later times, as well as the writing and editing of the Bible itself. The hellenistic era had produced extensive efforts to rewrite and reinterpret the Bible in the light of Greek thought, and the talmudic period had left a new layer of Bible analysis done through rabbinic canons of interpretation. In medieval times, commentaries, philological works, philosophical tractates, halakhic codes, midrashim, kabbalistic works, and homiletical and poetic compositions that explained, amplified, and applied the Bible had been composed. And the Renaissance had offered a heritage of textual concern and broad-based interdisciplinary enquiry that derived from, advanced, and supplemented many earlier contributions.[9]

In the early nineteenth century, Jewish Bible interpreters were involved in the perpetual struggle to define precisely how they should carry out their chosen tasks and, while the potential role of archaeology was of some interest, it was not paramount. The development of printing in the late fifteenth and sixteenth centuries and its accompanying information explosion had provided commentators with virtually limitless Jewish resources. Midrashim, medieval and post-medieval commentaries, and works of philosophy, halakhah, kabbalah, and even philology were available in abundance and had contributed to a broad, eclectic approach to Bible interpretation, especially in Italy. But the unfolding of the eighteenth century was marked by a narrowing of interests and a visible focussing of exegetical activities on one of several key antecedent literatures. Gradually, Ashkenazic interpretation came to revolve around three orbits, though individual writers' precise locations in them varied.

The first orbit may be designated midrashic-kabbalistic. Midrashic interpretation was rarely practiced in isolation from the Talmud, so the latter should be understood as part of the definition; but the surge of kabbalistic thinking and influence in the sixteenth and subsequent centuries greatly increased the importance of the Zohar as an exegetical text, and fostered a revival of the midrashic mindset of earlier centuries.[10] Except for very radical individuals (some Sabbatians, for example), these writers were not anti-talmudic; they simply chose their interpretative materials and approaches from the midrashic and kabbalistic realms.[11] But their attitudes differed from those of two other learned groups, who sometimes criticized them and their positions.[12]

The second orbit was the locus of interpreters who based their work primarily on the Talmud and midrashim, and gradually allowed the Zohar and its speculative, other-worldly interpretative focus to dissipate. Non-zoharic rather than anti-zoharic, they preferred to base their Bible interpretations on the Talmud and its own interpretative literature: the medieval and post-medieval commentaries and codes. In effect, this position was a compromise that defended the unity of Scripture (especially the Torah) and the oldest rabbinic traditions, which became the almost exclusive key to interpreting it, while it challenged the time honored and now reemerging claim that the rabbinic traditions distorted the true meaning of the text. Simultaneously, it allowed the talmudist's literary world to dominate the biblicist's.

The third orbit contained the rational-scientific writers, who preferred philological accuracy and historical credibility to midrashic and zoharic alternatives. Often hostile to what they perceived as mystical distortion but sympathetic to some other forms of rabbinic interpretation (at least in the earlier days of the movement), these scholars tried to break new ground by adopting more open, intellectual approaches. Some even sought out and published unavailable or previously unknown medieval works that supported their beliefs, thereby contributing much to understanding the evolution of Jewish Bible interpretation, not only to their preferred position.

These three groups of writers, who are often counted respectively among the Hasidim, Mitnagdim and Maskilim in other contexts but are not identical to them in all respects, divided up the legacy of earlier Biblical interpretation into three complementary but not totally exclusive realms, and largely derived their exegetical sustenance and support from three different traditional literatures. In following the sixteenth century's fascination with mystical interpretation, the midrashic-kabbalistic writers continued the most recent of the traditional exegetical literatures. The enlighteners threw their lot in the older, medieval thinkers, and based much of their work on the writings of the philologists—authors largely committed to *peshat*—and the philosophers, especially Maimonides, who anticipated many modern interpretative attitudes and was credited with others.[13] The talmudic-midrashic orbit, on the other hand, was filled by strongly committed rabbinic writers, including some Hasidim (which is one reason these new designations are preferable in this context). In fact, it reformed traditional Bible interpretation by avoiding (in the case of its participating Hasidim, by downplaying) the kabbalistic literature—perceived as late or deviant by some writers and unapproachable by others—and even most of the medieval Bible interpreters, while it worked most closely with the talmudic and midrashic literatures, the oldest authoritative rabbinic texts.

To be sure, various orientations existed within these theoretical orbits, and every writer does not fit neatly into one of them; some were comfortable in several. But global considerations favour these classifications, even when they serve best as markers from which to measure relative distances.

The Vilna Gaon, who died in 1797, was perhaps the last important rabbinic commentator of this period who seriously valued the potential contributions of all three of these approaches. Questions about the authenticity of some of his writings and inadequately documented traditions attributed to him render it difficult to determine his precise thinking about all of their components, though his preferences seem to have lain with the first two.[14] While the crystallization of the three trends described above predated his demise, the following decades seem to have been characterized by most commentators' lack of interest in the broad range of exegetical works potentially available to them. In effect, the broad medieval model of PaRDeS (corresponding to the philological, philosophical-allegorical, midrashic, and mystical literatures of interpretation) was rejected, and special interests—possibly to be designated P, R, D, and S, though not identical to their medieval counterparts—reemerged and continued to develop.

Biblical scholarship, as practiced in the twentieth century, is not easily identified with any of the three traditional groups described above, though some aspects of it are definitely related. Indeed, several writers have cautioned that some of its underlying assumptions are more at home in Christian, specifically Protestant, theology than in Jewish or secular intellectualism.[15] Regardless of this generalization's accuracy—and it certainly is not completely false—the rational-scientific position that emerged during the Enlightenment and continued to evolve throughout the past two centuries undoubtedly assumed many critical values and postures, and diverged even further from what came to be perceived as the more traditional ones. In fact, one might question if or how the work of many modern

Jewish scholars differs from that of their non-Jewish colleagues; part of this book tries to answer this question.

Orthodoxy and The Bible

As a formal movement, Orthodoxy crystallized in the nineteenth century (the term seems to have been used first in 1795)[16] and then, in large measure, as a response to the perceived excesses of other Jewish groups. Even though it has identified itself as "normative" Judaism, Orthodoxy has given priority to certain aspects of the existing rabbinic tradition and neglected or rejected others. Defining itself amidst the melange of doctrines and practices of which the Judaisms of the previous several centuries were composed, but always with an eye to the more ancient sources on which they, in turn, drew, Orthodoxy did not present a static alternative to the dynamism of other groups. Nor could it possibly claim a monopoly on all aspects of authentic rabbinic tradition, though it continued to draw on more aspects of that tradition than its competitors. And the diverse groups that it comprised belied any monolithic consistency.

In other words, Orthodoxy—the plural, Orthodoxies, describes the reality more accurately but becomes a bit cumbersome—represented parts of the extant rabbinic traditions, which it developed and expressed in a variety of unique and creative ways; and its leaders tried, as best they could, to legitimate their stands from within the traditional rabbinic literature, which it supported and from which it drew its spiritual strength. In theory, it subsumed all of the tradition within its bounds, and the diverse and multi-faceted nature of that tradition coupled with a strong belief in the movement's independent legitimacy gave it strength and flexibility. Yet, the religio-political environments in which Orthodoxy grew forced it to respond negatively to potentially hostile and seemingly competitive intellectual trends and ideologies, sometimes at the expense of ideas that formerly held honored positions among rabbinic writers.

Orthodoxy's primary concerns have included the establishment and maintenance of rabbinic authority, the defense of rabbinic teachings, and the promulgation of halakhah according to the decisions of its acknowledged legal experts. Despite an enormous legacy of pre-Orthodox Bible interpretation—or, perhaps, because of its huge variety of attitudes—Orthodoxy's ideal role for the bible is less clear than its hermeneutical agenda, which, in large measure, moves in the talmudic-midrashic orbit of interpretation.

Whatever the ranking of Orthodoxy's political and educational priorities, they do not include serious devotion to Bible study (at least for males, though many observe the halakhic requirement to study the weekly Torah portion).[17] Surely Orthodoxy's tenets do not strive *a priori* to give the Bible a hearing that is independent of its accompanying rabbinic teachings. Orthodoxy is dedicated to halakhic living- defined as its adherants understand and practice halakhah- and the success of its movement. It is not Bible—centered, nor does it perceive itself as wholly Bible-based, though it does accept the sanctity of Scripture and would be repelled at the suggestion that its teachings violate, or even ignore, scriptural values and dictates. Orthodoxy does not reject the Bible nor, in most cases, does it negate its study. However, it is strongly supportive of the Talmud, dogmatic about the need to study and follow it, and jealous of early rabbinic control over Biblical interpretation, which often results in the Bible's being presented in ways that can seem far from its original intention.

In exegetical terms, Orthodoxy, especially in its most recently emerging American forms, generally has not resynthesized the three schools of interpretation that existed in pre-Orthodox times. Instead, it has favoured the talmudic-midrashic hermeneutical agenda and drawn secondarily from the midrashic-kabbalistic one, primarily through the perhaps unanticipated impact of Hasidisim. In short, it has favoured the mishnaic teaching *hafokh bah vehappekh bah, dekulah bah*[18] over the medieval application of the talmudic principle *'ein miqrâ' yotze' miyĕde peshuto.*[19] It has done so, in large measure, in imitation of earlier models that did likewise, and out of a compelling drive to use the Bible to encourage the observance of a proper Orthodox life style, regardless of the cost to literal and historically valid Bible interpretation.

By adopting this stance, American Orthodoxy has largely cut itself off from the rational-scientific school of the past several centuries. Simultaneously, it downgraded the significance and relevance of the established teachings of the medieval philologists and philosophers who were that school's revered models. Not only has the movement largely ignored this vast literature—in many ways the most Bible-centered of the pre-modern traditional exegetical efforts—some of its adherents, including many of the anthologizers and popularizers who select from the tradition what they want contemporary Jews to read and to believe, are actively purging it of rational-scientific thinking.

This selective process effectively isolates Orthodoxy from important Bible-related aspects of the pre-Orthodox rabbinic traditional literature and simultaneously destroys the paths that can link it with the scholarly approaches to Bible study that evolved from, or in conjunction with, the tradition. This avoidance of any serious synthesis of most Orthodox thinking and Biblical scholarship results from, among other things, the simple fact that few Orthodox rabbis and teachers value Biblical scholarship. Yet this need not be so, nor need it continue indefinitely, if a broader range of Orthodox leaders can learn to share the variety of interpretative approaches and the diversity of opinion offered by the rabbinic tradition. While this narrowing of interests has not been a unique contribution of American Orthodoxy, the intellectual openness encountered in the writings of many of its rabbinic predecessors does suggest the legitimacy of other options, some would say even the obligation to develop them. The movement might have chosen differently, and it still can, by following the leads of some modern and premodern writers and by exploiting the models created by some contemporary Israeli scholars.

The situation in Israel is beyond our immediate concern, but one finds there some institutionally backed Orthodox projects that reflect a very different attitude toward the Bible from that encountered in America. Of course, the Bible is Israel's national literature and a cultural focal point, not only a holy book, but the differences are still striking. Mossad HaRav Kook's new commentary, *Da'at Miqra'*, is a noteworthy step towards synthesizing modern and classical elements of Bible study.[20] In it, geography, archaeology, history and other modern contributions are blended with traditional interpretations, and the latter are even chosen with an eye to their potential harmony with the former. Also, this press's *Torat Hayyim*, a new Rabbinic Pentateuch (eventually to be a full Rabbinic Bible) contains only medieval commentaries that, for the most part, take the plain meaning of the Bible seriously. This project may be an even more significant statement than the first one, because it points traditionalists away from some of the later trends in homiletical interpretation and back to the more independent, Bible-based scriptural interpretation of medieval times.[21]

Rabbi Menahem Kasher's *magnum opus*, *Torah Shelemah*, hardly a typical project for a hasidic writer, wedded vast knowledge of early rabbinic Bible interpretation with an openness to exploring issues considered legitimate by many medieval writers but that were ignored or obscured by their successors.[22] Nehamah Leibowitz' presentations of the classical interpreters have helped to sensitize several generations of students and teachers to the exegetic finesse that flows through much of the traditional literature.[23] Essays by Mordecai Breuer and Yeshayahu Leibowitz, though occasionally the subject of great controversy, also have broken new ground in the synthesis of rabbinic tradition and modern thinking.[24] And *HaMiqra ' Va'Anahnu* contains a series of essays in which religious Israeli scholars discussed their approaches to the Bible.[25] These contributions have no real analogues in America and force one to acknowledge a real difference between New World Orthodoxy and at least one of the kinds thriving in Israel.

Examination of the contexts in which they evolved helps explain why many types of Orthodoxy preferred to derive their hermeneutic agenda from less open rabbinic predecessors. These reflect, in part, long-standing rabbinic resistance to certain types of Bible study (even if defended and taught by respected classical rabbinic writers) along with a positive commitment to rabbinic thinking.[26] But amplifying them was simultaneous contempt for, and fear of contamination by, Reform, enlightenment, and secularism, especially their seemingly related commitments to Biblical criticism and anti-halakhic rebellion. And some of these fears, as well as Orthodox freedom to overreact to them, may have been heightened by America's open society.[27] But whatever the reasons, the fact remains that the pre-Orthodox rabbinic tradition accepted the legitimacy of many options in Bible study that many Orthodox groups, including much of the American branch of the movement no longer recognize.

Rabbinic Hermeneutics and Orthodox Hermeneutics[28]

1. *The Religion of the Patriarchs and the Religion of the Jews.* Orthodoxy suggests that the Biblical patriarchs should serve as models of rabbinic-type piety and practice. In the synagogues of North America, thousands of sermons that portray the activities of Abraham, Isaac, and Jacob as models of proper Orthodox behavior are delivered annually during the weeks when the weekly Torah portions are read from Genesis—a pattern of preaching with long roots in the traditional literature. Rabbinic notions about marriage, honor due to parents, the origins of prayer and circumcision, laws of land acquisition, and virtually every other religiously significant theme are derived from the stories in Genesis.

The key phrase here is "derived from," because other rabbinic positions suggest that these laws should be associated with the stories, not derived from them. In other words, rabbinic Judaism recognizes the legitimacy of a position that accepts the independence of the patriarchs' religious practices from those of Mosaic and post-Mosaic times.[29] Important medieval interpreters suggested that some patriarchal practices followed the norms of the societies in which they lived,[30] but popular Orthodox teaching has, for the most part, overlooked this distinction in favor of one that redefines and portrays the lives of the characters in Genesis according to later rabbinic world views.[31]

2. *The Time of the Giving of the Torah.* Orthodoxy teaches that the entire Torah was given on Sinai. This is presented as part of the rationale offered for an observant Jewish life, is reflected in the popular preaching done in conjunction with the passages in the Torah that describe the events on Sinai, and plays an important role in the observance of the holiday of Shavuot, celebrated as *zeman mattan torateinu.* Few beliefs are assumed to be so essential to Orthodox doctrine by traditionalists and non-traditionalists, alike.

This position does reflect a popular rabbinic notion, but a key talmudic passage (BT Gittin 60a) suggests that the Torah was given either piece by piece, presumably throughout the forty years of wandering in the desert, or "sealed," at once. The latter alternative might suggest that the entire Torah was given on Sinai, but many medieval interpreters understand it to mean that it was given at the end of the forty years in the wilderness.[32] Notwithstanding the status of the Torah's many laws and the rabbinic "oral law"—traditionally taken to have been given to Moses on Sinai—rabbinic Judaism acknowledged the legitimacy of the notion that the full text of the Torah itself was not completely Sinaitic.

3. *Human Contributions to the Composition of the Torah.* Orthodoxy teaches that the Torah was composed by God and dictated to Moses. Indeed, some Orthodox spokesmen suggest that, were the Torah composed by Moses in the conventional sense, it would have no more value or authority than any other book, and that it could not serve as the legitimate source of religious directive it is.

In fact, a number of rabbinic writers suggested that Moses did have a personal impact on some aspects of the Torah. Most of those who considered this option assumed that God put his final approval on the text, and that, in its present form, it represents His version;

but the possible role of Moses is both acknowledged and used as a rationale for linguistic and orthographic irregularities.[33] A few traditionalists even suggested that writers other than Moses contributed to the production of the Torah, a notion discussed in the Talmud and throughout later centuries.[34] It was never popular in rabbinic Judaism, but its persistent appearance suggests both legitimacy and potential compatibility with other rabbinic teachings.

4. *The Authorship of the Other Biblical Books.* The authorship of the rest of the Bible is not a well developed area of Orthodox discussion; indeed, one of the hallmarks of Orthodoxy is the relatively little attention given to many of the non-Pentateuchal books (an attitude it shares with some medieval Ashkenazic predecessors). But when they are discussed, the talmudic and midrashic attributions of the books, particularly those listed in BT Baba Batra 14b–15a, are dominant. Many of the Biblical books associate all or part of their contents with specific writers, and rabbinic teachings augment and alter these suggestions. To the extent it deals with the issue, Orthodoxy accepts and often vigorously defends these early rabbinic attributions.

However, the contents of the famous list of authors presented in Baba Batra have been subjected to much critical scrutiny by later generations of rabbinic writers, who, following the lead of that same talmudic passage, offered their own suggestions and comments on the authorship of a number of books. In fact, virtually every attribution in the Talmud has been rejected by at least one highly respected rabbinic Bible interpreter, and the history of interpretation of this talmudic passage leaves one with the impression that it was taken as a midrashic source of no greater authority than many other midrashim that could be accepted or rejected more-or-less at will. In fact, the uses of the word *katav* in this text are so unclear (in different phrases it connotes wrote, compiled, edited, and copied) that in some places it is impossible to determine what it really claims about authorship. And regardless, many rabbinic authors accepted the notion that the Biblical books could have been composed in ways that differed from what this talmudic passage seems to state.

5. *The Accuracy of the Transmitted Text of the Torah.* Orthodoxy teaches that the Torah text has been transmitted in a letter-perfect manner, and countless presentations in sermons and classes are predicated on this assumption. In adopting this position, the movement follows a popular notion with antecedents in the Talmud

and surely reflects the ideal of the halakhic literature, which created an entire sub-category *(Hilkhot Sefer Torah)*, the almost exclusive purpose of which is to prevent errors from creeping into the sacred text. In recent years, this belief and accompanying arguments in favour of religious commitment have been supported through the "discovery" in the Torah's consonantal text of codes and late historical references that can be meaningful to only modern readers.[35]

However, the Talmud and the subsequent halakhic literature also acknowledge that the ideal of a letter-perfect Torah text has not been realized. Some rabbis conceded that it was virtually impossible to determine the precise manner in which many of the words in the Torah should be spelled. Rules requiring replacement of erroneous scrolls during public reading were compromised in many cases, because no one knew what was correct and, in some cases, the medieval presumption of a scroll's accuracy was replaced by the realization that, even if correct in one place, every scroll *would* contain (not only that it could contain) errors elsewhere. The justification for a scribe's not reciting a blessing when copying a Torah was sometimes based on the fact that no one really knew how to spell some of the words properly, a notion found in the Talmud itself. Some halakhic authorities admitted that it was altogether impossible to fulfill the commandment of writing a Torah Scroll, because the proper spelling of the text was no longer available.[36]

6. *The Binding Authority of Rabbinic Interpretation.* One of the issues in all treatment of the Bible by believers is the extent to which specific interpretations should control its official understanding and its applications to daily life. As might be expected of any group, Orthodoxy teaches that its interpretations are binding.[37] This is quite understandable and, particularly regarding legal exegesis, reflects the earlier rabbinic attitude.[38] But when one leaves the area of application—which, for most halakhists was controlled in theory and in practice by the Talmud and codes, not the Bible—the situation is quite different.

Rabbinic interpretation of the non-legal passages in the Bible is much more open than Orthodox spokesmen often acknowledge. In fact, the medieval and post-medieval positions on the authority of rabbinic midrash and aggadah—the repositories of much of these teachings and interpretations—were remarkably flexible. Although rabbinism did include staunch defenses of reading midrashim literally, it encompassed, as well, much more rational options. The geonim, many medieval Bible commentators, and most medieval philosophers recognized fully the need to control, rather than be controlled by, the midrashic literature. And their suggestions that much of this material was conjectural, private, and subject to both radical reinterpretation and open rejection were a recognized part of the rabbinic responses to it. Its value was not globally challenged by rabbinic writers (that task was undertaken by Karaites, Christians, and other opponents of rabbinic Judaism); but the presumption of its binding authority, especially when it posed problems for an interpreter, was not a major stumbling block. Dogmatic acceptance of its teachings was neither a necessity nor a universal priority.[39]

7. *The Role of Non-Traditional Sources in Bible Study.* To judge from the approach to Bible study put forth by many contemporary Orthodox leaders, non-traditional sources have no place in it.[40] This assumption extends to the potential contributions of Christians, secularists, non-Orthodox Jews, and scholars of the humanities—a list that would include many of the people whose works are described in this book and many of their teachers—and to any conclusions not preserved by the tradition and transmitted under its watchful eyes. The notion is not a new one, and many of the late responses to medieval philosophy reflect a similar exclusivity; but it is not the only option that rabbinic Judaism enjoys.

In fact, virtually all medieval philosophers and many Bible commentators actively supported the right, if not the obligation, to use non-traditional ideas as supplements (and even as replacements) for some of those preserved by the tradition. Linguistic, geographic, and historic explanations were frequently enriched by the contributions of non-traditional writers; and many whole literatures that had profound impacts on classical interpretative efforts—including philosophy, grammar, science, and lexicography—owe serious debts to non-Jewish trends and sources. Approaches to interpretation and modes of thinking, not only new information, could be borrowed from whatever source offered them, if they seemed useful. No *nihil obstat* was required.

Many similar examples of restraints adopted by Orthodoxy can be adduced: the requirement to read the narratives about Biblical miracles as history, the need to assume that all narratives relate precise historical information, the belief that rabbinic halakhot reflect the primary meanings of the Biblical texts from which they appear to be derived, etc. In each of these cases, the rabbinic tradition allows for a broad range of responses to specific intellectual issues related to Bible study, while Orthodoxy has generally chosen a position that is substantially narrower and not fully receptive to those traditional writers who prefer to give the Bible an independent hearing. It is no accident that many of these examples impinge on issues of religious authority. Of late, almost anything perceived as a potential impediment to accepting and following divinely ordained halakhic guidelines as taught by Orthodox leaders has been considered incompatible with Orthodoxy and rejected or ignored.

These choices were made for many reasons and not only because of the fears associated with rationalizing Bible study. Nor were they made in an intellectual vacuum. Perceiving the evolution of tradition as erosion and the influence of modernity as a threat, many Orthodox leaders have tried to exclude any doctrine that can lead toward religious compromise. Under these circumstances, is it any wonder that the movement has been no serious contribution to contemporary Biblical scholarship? One must ask, rather, if it has not consciously avoided the possibility.

Prospecting for Orthodox Bible Scholars

The Conservative and Reform movements have given much attention to the Bible; and their rabbinical seminaries, in contrast to virtually all yeshivot, consider it a central curricular text. While the former have produced and supported enough individual scholarly contributions to Bible study to subdivide them according to periods or approaches, as a group, the latter can barely support a claim of sustained curricular interest in the Bible at all. The American Orthodox treatment of the Bible is still in its infancy. One cannot discuss broad contributions of the movement, and, for reasons that will become clear, individual efforts of isolated rabbis and professors are not, for the most part, integrated into the fiber of modern Biblical scholarship.

Moreover, some Orthodox individuals who have made contributions during the period under discussion must be disqualified from consideration because they lived outside the American continent (*e.g.*, David Hoffman, Samuel David Luzzatto and Umberto Cassuto).[41] The same is true of Joseph H. Hertz,[42] Chief Rabbi of Britain and author-editor of the most popular English Torah commentary of the twentieth century. He, too, should be considered Orthodox, despite his having been educated at the Jewish Theological Seminary, but the commentary is not all his own, nor does it qualify as original scholarship. Many Orthodox Jews no longer recognize it as their own, but that is a different matter.

The one great American exception to the yeshivah's traditional avoidance of Bible study is Yeshiva University. During the past century, YU (including its predecessors and many constituent schools) has appointed numerous people to teach courses in Bible, and a brief examination of their efforts is very revealing.[43]

In its announcement of 5678 (1918), the department of Bible and Hebrew Philology of Yeshiva (at that time, still called the Rabbinical College of America) listed the following six courses: Psalms, with leading medieval and modern [!] Jewish commentaries; Joshua and Judges, with leading Jewish Commentaries and the geography of ancient Palestine; Samuel and Kings, with leading Jewish commentaries; Hebrew Grammar, history of Hebrew Grammar and comparative study of the language requiring knowledge of one other Semitic language [presumably Aramaic]; Biblical Aramaic; Babylonian and Palestinian Judeo-Aramaic.[44] The reasons for these particular choices are not clear, but omission of the Torah was probably due both to the student's greater familiarity with its contents and the desire to avoid issues associated with it.

The last three courses in this list were taught by Solomon Theodore Hurwitz; the others were the responsibility of Moses Seidel (1886–1971), an appointee of Bernard Revel. Seidel was educated at the Yeshiva of Telze and the University of Bern, where, through the suggestion of Rabbi Kook, he studied Semitic languages. Rabbi Kook knew Seidel well, admired him and his religious commitments, and devoted over twenty letters to answering his questions about religious intellectualism and matters of belief.[45] There is no evidence that Seidel's religiosity was ever in question, but he (and Solomon Zeitlin, who had also been appointed in 1917) was the subject of strong criticisms from some of YU's right-wing element.[46] Before long, he left New York for Baltimore and then moved to Palestine, where he directed a teacher's seminary and taught Bible.

Seidel's articles were collected into two volumes, *Hiqrei Miqra'* and *Hiqrei Lashon*,[47] devoted respectively to Biblical and Semitic studies. Much of the Bible volume deals with parallel passages in two Biblical books or what are perceived as citations of one book in another (e.g., Isaiah and Psalms, Isaiah and Proverbs, Hannah's Prayer and parallels). Seidel is best remembered for his work on

Biblical poetry, particularly on the chiastic form of many passages. half of *Hiqrei Lashon* deals with various grammatical and lexicographical problems in Biblical language, often through recourse to the standard texts and resources used in comparative Semitic linguistics. The remainder is devoted to studies in the language and poetry of Samuel HaNaggid. Seidel also contributed to the *Da'at Miqra'* commentary on *Micah.*[48]

Rabbi Chayim Heller (1878–1960), appointed to the YU faculty in 1929, was, for a time, a candidate for the position of Rosh Yeshiva, the senior talmudic scholar responsible for determining a candidate's academic readiness for rabbinic ordination. (The position ultimately went to the talmudist and theologian Rabbi J. B. Soloveitchik.) A contributor to both Biblical and rabbinic studies, his books include several volumes about Greek and Aramaic Bible translations, one about the Samaritan Torah text, an edition of Maimonides *Sefer HaMitzvot*, and an edition of the Peshitta of Genesis and Exodus in Hebrew script, prepared for those who could not read Syriac.[49] Heller's efforts were devoted largely to defending the integrity of the massoretic text against those who used the ancient versions to emend it. His knowledge of the Bible and his defense of the tradition are legendary in the North American Orthodox community, but most of his work was not well received by the critical world. He did, however, offer many insights into the dynamics of ancient interpretation, translation, and text transmission.

Joshua Finkel (1892–1983), ordained by the Jewish Theological Seminary, received his doctorate from Dropsie, and served as professor of Bible and Semitic Languages at Yeshiva University from the late 1930s until the 1970s. Primarily an Arabist, like many of Bible professors at other institutions, he also wrote several studies on the Bible.[50]

Prof. Michael Bernstein (1915–1980), a former *Rosh Yeshiva*, was, for many years, the leading Semiticist at Yeshiva, and it is reported that Yehezkel Kutscher once stated that Bernstein was the only person in North America who taught Aramaic properly. An outstanding linguist and master of both Bible and rabbinic literature, he was at home in Latin, Greek, and all of the Semitic languages. Bernstein personified many of the ideals of what Orthodox Bible scholarship can be, though he had little patience for much of the speculation that typifies the field. He devoted his life to teaching, not to publishing, and seems to have been lost to the history of the discipline, which is defined primarily through bibliographic, not educational, contributions. His impact has been very considerable. Dozens of his former students—including Abraham Zimmels, Moshe Sokolow, Moshe Bernstein, Isaac Gottleib, and Barry Levy—have held or continue to hold positions in the departments of Bible (and of other Judaic subjects) at Yeshiva, Stern (YU's school for women), Bar Ilan, and other Orthodox institutions, and it was far from unusual for graduate students in other local schools to join his classes.

Yeshiva University has also employed numerous other rabbis and professors as Bible teachers. Unlike most other yeshivot, almost all books of the Bible are taught in one or more of its many undergraduate programs (more rarely in the graduate ones). As an undergraduate in Yeshiva College and the Teachers Institute for Men (renamed Erna Michael College) from 1963–67, I enrolled in courses devoted to Pentateuchal Poetry, Biblical Holidays, Isaiah, Jeremiah, Ezekiel, the Twelve Minor Prophets, Psalms, Proverbs, Daniel and Ezra-Nehemiah (most were required); and these did not exhaust the available possibilities. Classes in some individual books of the Torah, in Job, and in other books of the Prophets and Hagiographa were also available for students in the other undergraduate schools, and subsequent years have seen the introduction of many other Bible courses.

Despite this impressive display, it was impossible to major in Biblical Studies at Yeshiva College (Jewish Studies and Hebrew Literature majors were allowed), though a very respectable undergraduate program could have been assembled from the above and Aaron Skaist's course in Ancient Near Eastern History, Manahem Brayer's course in Medieval Biblical Interpretation and, if desired, readily available graduate courses in Bible, Arabic, Ugaritic, Akkadian, Nahmanides' Torah Commentary, Onkelos, and several dialects of Aramaic. The Bible was studied, often quite seriously, but a Bible major was unthinkable because, at least at the undergraduate level, the Bible did not constitute an independent academic subject. While it was theoretically possible to complete a graduate degree in Bible, for many years there were so few courses that such a program could be considered only if it included a majority of courses in Semitic languages and/or rabbinics.

Each of the men who taught these Bible courses I attended possessed both rabbinic ordination and an academic doctorate (in many cases both were earned in Europe), though this was not true of all Bible classes. But none of their doctorates was in Bible.

In other words, as recently as several decades ago the teaching of

Bible at Yeshiva University was largely controlled by professors who were not Bible specialists. They were learned in many aspects of rabbinic and Judaic studies; as a group they taught almost every book in the Bible; they based much of their presentations on what they considered to be the best of the medieval commentators (depending on the passage, on Rashi, Rashbam, Ibn Ezra, Radak, Ramban, and/or Ralbag); they offered their students a modernized form of rabbinic Bible study; they were staunch Hebraists (all of these courses were taught in Hebrew); and many of them were active authors who contributed to a vast range of Jewish Studies. But they did not really present the Bible as an independent subject distinct from and unqualified by the rest of the vast world of rabbinic learning at their disposal. In fact, it seems that the qualifications for holding a position teaching Bible included (in addition to the confidence of the administration) rabbinic ordination and advanced training in some other area of Jewish Studies (often some aspect of post-Biblical history). Competence in the Bible was assumed, but no one was deemed ready to teach it unless he was also competent in at least one other area, as if to suggest that study of only the Bible could not prepare one to appreciate and teach it and its vast and quintessential interpretative literature.

Because at least dual competence was expected, and formal research was, more likely than not begun in that other area, the rabbinic or "other" interests dominated the professors' research. This is most clearly seen by a sample of the kinds of published studies a number of Yeshiva's former and present Bible professors have written during the past decades:

1. Meir Herskovics: A professor of Bible and Jewish History, he wrote a few articles on Biblical topics, usually dealing with the ways in which the Bible was understood in early rabbinic texts,[51] and on Aramaic Bible translations;[52] but many dealt with pure rabbinic issues.[53] The bulk of his work was devoted to the lives and writings of recent rabbinic figures,[54] especially to Jacob Reifman and Tzvi Hirsch Chajes (Hayyot).[55]

2. Moshe Carmilly-Weinberger: Primarily a professor of Jewish History, he also taught a number of Bible courses. He has written and edited a lengthy series of books and articles on the history and literature of the Jews in Transylvania and Hungary,[56] and many other pieces on the censorship of Jewish books.[57] To these are added articles on other subjects, but I am aware of none devoted solely to the Bible.[58]

3. Menahem M. Brayer: Being a psychologist as well as a Bible professor, most of his publications are devoted to psychological themes of Jewish interest.[59] A few deal with the Dead Sea Scrolls (here, too, treated from a psychological perspective) and Biblical themes, but these are not a major part of the whole.[60]

4. Sholom Carmy: An editor of *Tradition*, Carmy has published many of his articles there. They are divided between Biblical and general rabbinic studies.[61]

5. Sid Z. Leiman: Formally trained in rabbinics and ancient Near Eastern Studies, but also a recognized expert in many other areas, he served as a full-time professor at YU for a relatively short time, but has retained his affiliation. He has written a detailed book on the canonization of Scripture (his doctoral dissertation), and has edited a reprinted anthology of articles on canon and massorah.[62] His original articles deal with massoretic studies,[63] Jewish ethics,[64] and a wide range of rabbinic topics.[65] He is also an editor of *Tradition* and a regular contributor.

6. B. Barry Levy: Currently at McGill, he taught at Yeshiva in the late sixties and early seventies, but all of his publications appeared later. They include work in Aramaic targumim,[66] the history of Bible interpretation,[67] Jewish education,[68] and the relationship between Jewish intellectual history and science.[69]

7. Moshe Sokolow: A professor of both Bible and Biblical interpretation, his publications deal with Bible,[70] Judeo-Arabic Bible interpretation,[71] comparative studies of midrash and Arabic literature,[72] and medieval, Ashkenazic Bible interpretation.[73] He has also contributed a number of items in the area of Jewish education and in geniza studies.

8. Richard Steiner: Primarily a professor of Semitic languages, he has published in the area of Semitic linguistics, including Hebrew.[74] His most famous contribution is the recognition and decipherment of an Aramaic text in demotic script.[75]

9. Moshe Bernstein: Son of Michael Bernstein (see above) and trained originally in rabbinics and classics, he has taught Bible at YU for a number of years. His published work includes a number of studies on early Biblical interpretation and general rabbinic topics.[76]

This does not exhaust the list of men and women who have taught Bible at Yeshiva during the past several decades, nor does it attempt to deal with all of those who studied there and taught elsewhere, or with the many other professors in North America who might deserve consideration as Orthodox Bible scholars or who, though observant, might object to wearing the label.[77] But it does represent a reasonable sample of those whose Orthodoxy can be assumed, who have held full-time appointments of some duration at an Orthodox university, and who might be described as both Bible scholars and as authors of serious academic work.

While a detailed study of all appointments, publications, courses, and existing syllabi has not been attempted, these data suggest that the people who taught Bible at Yeshiva University were, generally speaking, active teachers and writers, but that they did not focus their research on the Bible. If, however, Semitic linguistics and the history of Bible interpretation are included, the percentage of attention to Bible study rises significantly, which suggests that their omission is unfair to the Orthodox Bible professor's vision of his profession.

As a group, their earlier publications tended not to appear in the most prominent professional journals, neither those devoted to Biblical nor general Judaic themes. Instead, we see repeated contributions to Festschriften, to the Yeshiva University annual *Gesher,* to *Tradition,* and to a series of other independent publications, many of which allow the contributors to avoid normal channels of peer review by non-Orthodox scholars, though this is clearly changing. Place of publication need not reflect negatively on the quality of the research, but it does remove a certain amount of discomfort that might be associated with publication elsewhere, and it contributes to the isolation of the writers and their work.

Also noteworthy is the very high percentage of articles written in Hebrew, though this is also changing. Constant use of Hebrew suggests that many of the older, European-born scholars lacked substantial integration into the American scholarly milieu. In all cases it indicates a strong and conscious commitment to Hebraism. Perhaps it also suggests a previously unnoticed religious, intellectual, and emotional affinity with Israel and the type of Orthodox Israeli scholarship described above.

Of course there is nothing inappropriate in any of these choices of what to teach, what to study and where or in what language to publish. Collectively, these men have fought against the isolation of the Bible from the rest of the Jewish religious tradition, they have kept alive in the yeshiva world the commitment to *peshat* (however it be understood), and they have supported the integration of Biblical and post-Biblical research. But when the personal preferences of those writers who avoid writing about many of the central issues of Biblical scholarship are coupled with the editorial decision to ignore some of those who worked in areas perceived as peripheral to Biblical studies or who are generally unknown in scholarly circles, the combined effect helps widen the perceived gap between Bible scholarship as it is practiced and Orthodox Bible study.[78]

RESTRICTIONS ON ORTHODOX BIBLE STUDY

Orthodox academics may have some reservations about Bible scholarship, but other factors complicate the situation. Until recently, virtually all Jews who considered careers in any aspect of classical Jewish scholarship were encouraged to make rabbinic training a part of their studies.[79] For American Orthodox scholars, this is still an expectation, though one being changed by the availability of very fine Jewish Studies departments in many secular universities. Years of intense study of Talmud, talmudic exegesis, and halakhic codes long stood as a major prerequisite for entry into a scholarly career in history, philosophy or Bible. If their training in another field—and, at this point, we are interested only in the Bible—was to be completed under Orthodox auspices, it required that one first satisfy the rigourous intellectual and religious requirements of Orthodox rabbinic education, which inevitably led to shaping one's Bible studies around it. Non-Orthodox scholars frequently completed formal rabbinic training as well, but their programs were radically different in their relative emphases on the study of rabbinics and Bible, and in the manner in which they were taught.

The Orthodox Bible student who chose to continue his education in a non-Jewish institution (or, even worse, from the popular perspective, in a non-Orthodox Jewish one) risked being disenfranchised and isolated from his community—which remains a serious threat. And even if he completed his studies without leaving the fold, the risk of *de facto* excommunication was ever present, because, in the final analysis, the assumptions of Bible scholarship are perceived by the Orthodox community to be foreign and hostile to its interests.

As an observant Jew in his private life, the Orthodox Bible scholar (or the candidate for this designation) would seek to be part of an active, observant community, to worship in synagogues that welcome him, and to educate his children in schools that satisfy his religious and intellectual needs. But the North American Orthodox community and most of its constituent institutions have not favoured—more accurately, they often openly opposed—the involvement of anyone who shares the academic interests of the Bible scholar. All too frequently he is libeled privately and insulted publicly by his clerical rabbinic colleagues (armed with ordination from the same institutions that ordained him and far less general education), because, like many of his non-Jewish colleagues, he, too, is assumed to be a non-believer.

The Orthodox Bible scholar's upbringing, education, and social well being are heavily influenced by popular Orthodox values that may be somewhat remote from his thinking about the Bible, but unlike other Orthodox professionals, the proximity of his work to the axis of religious life often renders it very difficult for him to remain neutral or merely to ignore these differences. If his religious commitments preclude leaving the community, he is often forced to remain a lone voice in the crowd or silent; and if he deviates, however slightly, from accepted norms, his actions are merely taken to confirm the insincerity the sly observer always anticipated. Is it any wonder that few Orthodox Jews have sought careers as Bible scholars; that those who have done so also have chosen to affiliate with the safer areas of Jewish Studies; that they remain somewhat distant from the mainstream of Biblical scholarship; that they have made contributions to other, more "legitimate" areas of Jewish Studies; and that they have avoided publishing scholarly works about the Bible?

Despite the difficulties, Orthodox Jews have completed doctorates in Bible and pursued professional careers in this area; their thinking may, indeed, differ from that of some other Orthodox Jews. Sometimes they offer private admissions that their religious beliefs do not correspond fully with their religious behaviors. While accepting the legitimacy of critical attempts to explain the Bible, they refrain from applying their implications to their religious lives, thereby compartmentalizing the two spheres. They give each full rein in its designated area but do not allow them to interact. This position resembles somewhat the interrelationship of professional and religious life that one might expect of Orthodox plumbers or mailmen. Some argue that the sanctity and applicability of the Bible are really functions of only rabbinic belief. Therefore, in any halakhic discussion, the rabbinic understanding of the Bible's origins and essence are paramount. Critical judgements, however contrary to rabbinic teachings, are legitimate everywhere except in halakhic discussions, where they are irrevelant.[80]

Some suggest that belief should be defined only through action—living an halakhic life is all that really matters. Many are unwilling to take stands on certain issues; they merely suspend judgment on a few critical matters and attempt to live in peace, hoping that natural and inevitable changes in scholarly trends will produce more sympathetic answers to certain gnawing questions. Others have tried to synthesize the tradition and scholarship by choosing carefully from the available critical positions and orienting them with similar ideas, or the projected trajectories of similar ideas, found in classical sources. Many have exploited the specialization that renders some critical issues almost irrelevant to much scholarly work. These attitudes may be accepted by some Orthodox Bible professors, but in all likelihood, they are not impressed upon the many hundreds of Bible students that meet annually; nor do they appear in print. Sharing them widely would be considered by many to be irresponsible at best and possibly heretical; in any case, they would not be a part of contemporary Bible scholarship.

The Orthodox scholar may differ, as well, from his non-Orthodox or non-Jewish colleagues, and this too deserves a few words. Ultimately, the Orthodox scholar is linked very closely to the Bible text. Regardless of his area of research or creative speculations, the text talks to him, and he takes a personal, not only a professional, interest in it. The Bible suggests that God spoke to the ancients and responded to individual personal needs, a value often challenged by modern scholars; it also makes, and wishes the reader to take seriously, many other statements that are equally troubling. Because the Orthodox scholar identifies with the text, he must begin his reading by taking all of it, including these difficult statements, seriously. This can help him appreciate the text better than some readers who are further removed from it. Similarly, by virtue of his talmudic education and halakhic lifestyle, implications and applications of many Biblical statements that no longer affect western society may remain meaningful to him. Moreover, because his early education may have included study of Bible interpretations written in vastly differing societies and cultures, his perspectives on modern theories are likely to be more critical—and hence possibly more creative—than those of scholars educated only through them.

Many modern scholars are innocent of the history of Biblical interpretation, but the Orthodox scholar cannot afford this lack. This should cultivate in him a healthy self-awareness that keeps alive the questions of earlier commentators, while it helps avoid both outdated responses to them and faddish adherence to new and unsubstantiated theories. Being raised from childhood on Hebrew and, to a lesser extent, on Aramaic, he is very comfortable with them and the accessibility of comparative Semitic studies. If he served as a public reader of the Torah or Megillot, he may well have memorized the Hebrew text of ten Biblical books, in addition to many chapters of Psalms and other books that appear in the liturgy.

To be sure, not all of these qualities are limited to Orthodox Jews. The non-Orthodox can share many of them, and some of these experiences and commitments can backfire, by creating barriers to independent reading of texts, as is sometimes encountered in Christian Bible interpretation. But there is no *a priori* reason why that should be the case; and these skills are potentially useful to the scholar who can exploit them properly.

Is Synthesis Possible?

Despite the theoretical possibility of synthesis and even certain advantages that a traditional education can offer the potential Bible scholar, it should be clear that popular American Orthodoxy does not encourage people to choose careers in this field. To ask, nonetheless, that Orthodoxy or a repesentative sample of its scholars share in the enterprise of modern Bible study is to confront it with the challenge to absorb and assimilate—or at least to encounter creatively—a host of seemingly foreign and hostile ideas, some originally Christian attitudes, and a system of thought that derives, in large measure, from the Enlightenment. Before Orthodoxy can consider the possibility, it must attempt to understand what Biblical scholarship is and to assess whatever potential value lies in it. And as a prerequisite, it must develop enough self-awareness to examine its own role within the existing forms of Bible-related rabbinic expression.

To spell this out in greater detail: Orthodoxy must examine its own hermeneutical agenda and compare it with the ever-changing concerns of modern writers. But it must also define and reevaluate its positions in the midrashic-kabbalistic and talmudic-midrashic exegetical orbits; it must examine candidly the extent to which it should accept, reject, or modify them, and it must then integrate them with the assumptions and precedures of the traditionally based rational-scientific exegesis that was developed by some of the early enlighteners and that can claim a legitimate share in the religious literature of Bible interpretation. It must do these things, even though the founders or modern practitioners of Orthodoxy did not. Having acknowledged and reassimilated the hermeneutical assumptions (not merely the exegetical conclusions) of the more enlightened medieval thinkers—many of whom really took the Bible seriously—and begin to redefine itself and its approach to the Bible. Then, and only then, can it confidently open itself to the continually growing and evolving literature of Biblical scholarship.

But even if Orthodoxy reaches this distant goal and retraces its steps to the crossroads at which those fateful, pre-modern decisions were made, and even if it then chooses to head down another road, centuries of discussion, analysis, and debate will separate it from modern scholarship. To return to the examples above, even if Orthodox writers grow comfortable about the legitimacy of positions that attribute Biblical books to authors not acknowledged by the early rabbis; that date parts of the Torah to post-Mosaic times; that concede, however hesitantly, the fallible transmission of the Bible text; and that reopen the doors of rabbinic interpretation to non-rabbinic contributions, much distance will remain between them and their modern colleagues. The seven examples listed above are simply not significant issues for Bible scholars, however crucial they may appear to Orthodox laymen.

It may be impossible for most Orthodox educational institutions and communities to concern themselves with this synthesis, because it is too complex and ranks too low among their religious and political priorities. One might hope that institutions of higher learning would identify with it and would impress its importance on a good share of their students. But as things stand, when the task is accomplished at all, it is only through the efforts of isolated individuals.

Twenty-five years ago, it appeared that Modern Orthodoxy, in its American form, would assume the responsibility for this undertaking. Recent decades, however, have witnessed major, unanticipated shifts in the Orthodox community that make these self-examinations less likely in the foreseeable future. Indeed, Modern Orthodoxy has been found wanting by many of its adherents, not only its opponents, and it may be incapable of considering the steps I have outlined, at least for now.[81]

Perhaps new designations are needed in place of the customary geographic, political or cultural labels that identify Orthodox Jews as Lithuanian, Polish, Sephardic, Hungarian; Hasidic, modern, sectarian, ultra-Orthodox; centrist and rightist (I know no one who calls himself a leftist these days); or as members of Agudah or Mizrachi. "Intellectual Orthodoxy"—a designation that can accommodate all cultural groups and recognizes no geographic or political boundaries—should be capable of the type of self-evaluation and change of which I speak. Enough appropriately sympathetic Orthodox rabbis, scholars, and laymen exist in North America to warrant the designation of such a sub-group within the movement, and the contribution to the religious community that would derive from its formal recognition is badly needed. Should it ever emerge, it will not solve the social problems of the Orthodox scholar, but it would enhance the legitimacy of his work on the Bible.

On the other hand, "Popular Orthodoxy," the larger division in my theoretical reorganization, must, so it seems, give higher priority to other, perhaps more practical, religious goals. It therefore seems unable, at least for the present, to undertake the intellectual self-evaluation of which I speak. Indeed, the Orthodox success at developing a strong, committed, practicing laity is one of its greatest achievements, as leaders of other movements have noted. Attracting, inspiring, educating, and fostering the commitments of this laity may have necessitated certain intellectual compromises and contributed to the pervasive folksy qualities—the Orthodox myth, one might say—noticed to be spreading. The limited, temporary legitimacy of these compromises does not justify their being treated as permanent ideals, and perhaps this new nomenclature—which reflects a two-tiered approach to religious knowledge that existed in medieval times—can help place things in proper perspective. At the very least, by highlighting the contributions of previous generations of intellectually open traditionalists, the movement might help its followers establish more sophisticated, but no less legitimate, religious ideals and models; might help people establish priorities for the use of the classical sources on which they can rely; and might eliminate some of the less essential notions that have been popularized during the hasty reestablishment of Orthodoxy in the post-holocaust era and amidst the wave of eager returnees to religious ideals and practices.

In the meantime, if one seeks those who really know and think about the literature of rabbinic Judaism; those who still enjoy debating the fine points of interpretation that appear in classical rabbinic texts; those who are ready to assume—and therefore to suspend concern for—commitment to the halakhic system and who are willing to discuss the issues; those who have the fortitude to base their beliefs and actions on the interpretation of rabbinic texts; those who remain most open to pre-Orthodox rabbinic teachings; those who by virtue of their commitment to all of Jewish religious literature also care about what all rabbis said about the Bible, one looks in yeshivot, not in synagogues.

The true Talmud scholar of the classical mold *(talmid hakham)*, especially the Lithuanian type—who, in the process of mastering the vast rabbinic literature has considered its different responses to Bible-related issues and has the confidence to decide what actually constitutes a legitimate answer to a serious question—is the closest potential ally in the exploration of old or new religiously acceptable answers to questions that derive from, or touch on, rabbinic interpretation of Scripture. Of course, few yeshiva leaders are eager to be involved in issues related to Biblical scholarship, and it is the rare yeshiva that offers any formal training in Biblical hermeneutics. Yet many of these institutions, first and foremost Yeshiva University, provide more hospitable environments for the potential synthesis of rabbinic learning and Biblical scholarship than do most other educational institutions or synagogues, which are more strongly influenced by popular needs, beliefs, and fears.

UNITING ORTHODOXY AND BIBLICAL SCHOLARSHIP

Essentially, contemporary Bible study can be divided into four concerns: Text, Texture, Context and Pretext. Theoretically, Orthodox scholars can share in all four, though some areas are more troublesome than others.

"Text" deals with the physical text, what it is and what it says. Lower criticism, still an important element in all textual work, may cause ideological concern, but surely less than several generations ago, when scholarship was almost synonymous with rewriting the Bible. The ancient versions, the Dead Sea Scrolls, and other pre-talmudic and talmudic witnesses to divergent Biblical texts are actually one of the more popular areas among the few visible Orthodox Bible scholars (especially in Israel), and the search for *peshat*, regardless of popular prejudices against it, is an honored part of the tradition. Philological work should offer no serious obstacles; indeed, the contemporary models for comparative Semitic philology derive from medieval Jewish writers (*e.g.,* Ibn Kuraish, Ibn Ezra and Ibn Janah), whose works exerted strong influences on certain aspects of classical Bible interpretation. In fact, Semitic linguistics is one of the preferred areas of Orthodox Bible study.

"Texture" concerns the Bible's literary qualities. Earlier this century, reading the Bible as literature was synonymous with atheism, but anyone familiar with the midrashic literature, or with the commentaries of Rashi, Rashbam, Ibn Ezra, Radak, Rambam, Abarbanel, and many other writers, realizes that literary concerns have been an essential part of classical interpretation throughout the past two millennia. Literary criticism is the label under which the Bible has sometimes been dissected, shredded beyond recognition, and attributed to wide-ranging authors, glossators and editors, in some cases far removed from their traditional settings. While such assumptions remain important in much Bible study, the newer attempts at literary criticism tend to respect the integrity of the books as they are preserved. They serve as counters to some of the earlier critical excesses and pose no certain problem or threat. Indeed, once the historical issues are bypassed, one finds many similarities between the classical interpretations and much contemporary literary analysis. Modern writers would benefit from much more careful examination of their rabbinic predecessors' works and should consult them before claiming originality for their observations.

"Context" centers on the recovery of the original historical, geographic, and cultural settings in which the Biblical texts were composed. Reconstructing the backgrounds of Biblical passages is one of the most important and subjective areas of contemporary research. While archaeology often confirms the Bible's general claims, new discoveries coupled with literary criticism and historical reconstructions sometimes challenge cherished beliefs. And yet, despite the potential problems, how can anyone who thinks that the Bible actually relates to historical events ignore the potential contributions of archaeology, the single most significant modern contribution to Bible study and the one that confirms scientifically the reality of the Biblical world?

"Pretext" includes the use and misuse of the Bible by later generations of readers who shaped it for their own purposes or sought guidance and new levels of relevance to their personal situations in it. Many of the interpretations of the Bible offered over the centuries qualify as manipulation, at least to the extent that they do not attempt to recover the original or simple meaning of the text. But once this has been clarified, the study of this use and misuse of the Bible—often called *derash* in other contexts and inclusive of much that would identify itself as scholarship—presents no serious religious problem. Indeed, by virtue of their exposure to many diverse methods of looking at the Bible, Orthodox scholars are in an almost unique position to contribute to this area, which is a part of the growing field of the history of Jewish Bible interpretation—Jewish intellectual history mirrored against the Bible.

Real conflicts between rabbinic teachings and Biblical scholarship do exist, but perhaps fewer than often assumed. Since many of the techniques of textual study used by scholars are shared (and even encouraged) by the tradition, most of the serious conflicts center upon ancillary beliefs, a problematic subject at best (as many Christian scholars will admit) and one that demands constant reconsideration, but usually remains negotiable.

Even if a person can be both a Bible scholar and Orthodox, one must still ask if ultimately it is in one's interest to pursue this type of career, or in the interest of the Orthodox community to support or even to tolerate this type of work. If the answer to this question is positive, and I believe it is, much benefit would be derived from more *public* attention to the contributions of Biblical scholarship by the Orthodox intellegentsia, many of whom are familiar with it but choose to ignore it out of disinterest, fear, or concern for more pressing needs. Independent scholarly research can serve as an antidote to certain radical positions. Allowed to run its own course, rabbinic thinking is capable of unnecessary excesses; and it sometimes needs an external anchor to help guide and control it. Scholarship also helps stimulate new thinking about old issues and prevents religion from stagnating. It can demonstrate the intellectual fortitude of religion, can enhance Orthodoxy's political and religious goals by making it more attractive to those Jews for whom intellectualism is a valued priority, and can contribute some measure of truth about the Bible. It can also provide a common language of discourse through which otherwise divided positions on religious matters can be united. Last, and by no means least, it also can claim to be a legitimate part of the traditional quest to interpret and to find meaning in the Bible.

Orthodoxy has found new strength in recent years, and this means that it has little to fear from the openness required to accomplish what I suggest; it also means that it has less reason to consider the proposal. Only if its respected leaders choose to emphasize this effort can it succeed. Potential risks will always remain, as will skepticism about its ultimate benefits. And what is to be gained if the effort succeeds? Few people really believe that many Jews will become more committed, observant, or religious—Orthodox, in a word—because Orthodoxy formally embraces Biblical scholarship; but the opposite is a real and constant fear. Even the overriding argument for intellectual honesty has lost much of its force in our relativistic society. How, one might ask, has Biblical scholarship helped the other Jewish movements enhance their positions in the Jewish world?

A New Model

Many of those who teach the Bible in Orthodox institutions often act as if tethered to a large block (rabbinic tradition) with a rubber band. The band can be stretched; it can be thinned and made more elastic; it can be twisted in many directions. But in the last analysis, the teacher is forced either to cut the band and separate himself from the block or to allow the tether to limit his movement and to snap him back to his starting point (or even further backwards), if he forces it too far. One who is restrained in this way has another alternative, namely to move the block closer to the desired location, which is what previous generations of religious interpreters of scripture—mystics, philosophers, philologists, hellenists, and rabbis—did. But that has proved impossible of late, because it can be accomplished only by creating whole systems of religious thought that effectively reorganize, reprioritize, and redistribute essential rabbinic teachings; and thus far Orthodoxy has failed to accept modern scholarship (or any other intellectual system) as a moving religious force to exploit for this purpose.

However, this model is incompatible with academic freedom and cannot be accommodated to it. Perhaps more can be accomplished by considering the various schools of Bible interpretation to be analogous to the electron rings circling the nucleus of an atom. Orthodoxy would probably prefer to identify the talmudic-midrashic orbit of interpretation (the exegete's D[erash]) as the first ring (the chemist's S orbit), closest to the nucleus and least apt to be removed from it through normal chemical reaction. At the present time, the midrashic-kabbalistic interpretations—a less essential but still very popular orbit (the chemist's P ring, the exegete's S[od])—would probably be placed second, and the rational-scientific orbity (the chemist's D, the exegete's P[eshat]) would be the outer ring.

Chemical reactions normally take place in the outermost orbit, where electrons are shared by more than one atom and exchanged with those offered by other donor atoms—from related systems of interpretation. Proper stimulus might also induce electrons to change orbits (to influence issues outside their regular interpretative frame of reference), to break free, and even to roam briefly as independent particles.

Some would suggest that Orthodox atoms be joined only with other Orthodox atoms to produce a pure substance, but this is not the possible model, and surely not that advocated by many of the religious writers who dominated Jewish thinking over the centuries. Others might have Orthodox Bible interpretation complete its outermost ring of electrons by grasping hold of several loose hermeneutical principles or disciplines now present in other systems—perhaps comparative philology, literary criticism, or archaeology—and link them permanently to the still independent Orthodox atom. This is, to some extent, what was done in earlier times when Aristotelian philosophy, for example, was synthesized with the tradition, or more recently when Orthodox writers assimilated elements of William F. Albright's now somewhat outdated but very appealing archaeological research into their work.[82] This possibility is enhanced by the highly specialized and somewhat fragmented nature of contemporary Biblical scholarship, which allows some parts of it to be accepted or rejected without others.

Other possibilities also suggest themselves, including the creation of a compound in which the Orthodox atom and one or more others are all joined and share some of their electrons. In this case, each remains the distinctive element it was, but also shares in, and contributes to, the qualities of the new compound. The identities of those new atoms might change over time, especially if the compound is not stable or is subjected to external stimuli; but for the present, it would help Orthodoxy to share its rich heritage with non-Orthodox Bible study (which tends to focus only on the scholarly contributions of recent decades) and simultaneously learn to appreciate the potential contributions of these other approaches. The traditional and modern resources for Bible study are so great, so poorly shared, so potentially valuable, and so readily accessible, that one wonders why more progress has not been forthcoming.

Should Orthodox thinkers actively enter the world of Biblical scholarship, its continuous evolution will insure that their evaluations of it cannot remain stagnant. Both Bible study and religious thinking continually evolve, focusing their attention on new and sometimes unanticipated issues and forcing interested followers to grow in the unending quest for the proper understanding of the text. What seems acceptable or problematic today may appear very different in a generation or two, and the danger of hasty assimilation to ephemeral notions is ever present. Yet, for many centuries, honest, creative rabbinic Bible commentators were open to new ideas and receptive of what they could learn from the educated world around them. They gave their readers and students their best efforts, and left the posthumous critiques and eulogies to those who could or could not improve on them.

Some sixteenth century kabbalists suggested that failure to study the Bible according to the full potentiality of the system of PaRDeS would require returning to earth in future lives to continue the task until it was completed properly.[83] In their estimation, full and proper appreciation of the Bible could take more than a single lifetime (a notion with which most of us can sympathize). A real synthesis of American Orthodox thinking and contemporary Bible scholarship—whether or not they qualify as PaRDeS—is not likely to occur in our lifetimes, when there is so much to reconsider and so few people involved with it. If it happens at all—whether as an adjunct of *peshat* and *derash* or of Text and Context—future generations will have much to contribute to the debate. But if those who speak for the tradition continue as they are—which has never been true for very long—Jewish Bible study could be eternally embarrassed. The common error of ignoring the potential contributions of many pre-Orthodox rabbinic Bible interpreters will be compounded by the folly that results from Orthodox and non-Orthodox moderns treating each other as if *they* do not exist.

Notes to Chapter Seven

1. The term "pre-Orthodox" is used to help periodize the evolution of rabbinic Judaism, not to deny Orthodoxy's claim to be its primary modern manifestation. Just as it is historically improper to identify Abraham as Israelite, Moses as Jewish, Isaiah as Pharisaic, and Ezra as Rabbinic, one can not properly consider Maimonides or the Maharal of Prague to be Orthodox.

2. The new interest in the Biblical world that emerged at the close of the eighteenth century has been described, in part, by Yehoshua Ben-Arieh in *The Rediscovery of the Holy Land in the Nineteenth Century* (Jerusalem: Magnes, 1979, 1983) and by Neil Asher Silberman, *Digging for God and Country: Exploration, Archeology, and the Secret Struggle for the Holy Land, 1799–1917* (New York: A. A. Knopf, 1982), but interest in Biblical antiquities is a good deal older than Napoleon. Already in the first century, Josephus confirmed the historicity of some questionable Biblical stories by citing the existence of ancient relics (*e.g.*, the ark in *Antiquities* I:93–95 and the salt pillar that was believed to be Lot's wife, *ibid.*, 203). Traditions regarding the burial of sacred objects from ancient times were preserved in the apocryphal literature (cf., 2 Maccabees 2:4–8, 4 Baruch 1–3, and the discussion in L. Ginzberg, *Legends of the Jews* [Philadelphia: Jewish Publication Society, 1928] Vol. 6, p. 410). These, in turn, encouraged searches for other equally old artifacts, which were also augmented by periodic accidental discoveries of ancient texts (note the survey by G. R. Driver in *The Judaean Scrolls* [New York: Schocken, 1965], pp. 7–15).

I am aware of no ancient Jewish parallel to the Christian search for holy relics that escalated during the fourth century under the patronage of Constantine and Helena, though BT Berakhot 54a–b contains a theoretical discussion of which blessing is to be recited upon seeing some of them. While this search for relics had a significant impact on the evolution of Christianity and is an important precursor to formal archaeology, it is probable that unsubstantiated and often false claims associated with many relics contributed to the frequent denials of authenticity that accompanied the announcement of many authentic discoveries (e.g., the Mesha Inscription and many of the Dead Sea Scrolls).

The records of medieval Jewish travellers in the Middle East regularly deal with the locations of Biblical sites and buildings, especially the graves of Biblical characters, but they generally demonstrate relatively little concern for relics. Over the centuries many observers claimed to have seen remnants of the ark (cf. the summary of accounts Tim La Haye and John Morris have assembled in *The Ark on Ararat* [Nashville: Thomas Nelson, 1976], especially pp. 14–27). Josephus' quotation from Berosus has influenced the evolution of the entire matter, but later Jewish writers often took a different approach. Benjamin of Tudela (twelfth century) recounted that the ark had been removed from the mountain and made into a mosque by Omar ben al-Khatab (J. D. Eisenstein *Otzar Massa 'oth* [reprint: Tel Aviv: 1969] p. 39, translation in *The Itinerary of Benjamin of Tudela*, [n.p.: Joseph Simon, 1983?]). And Petahyah of Ratisbon, who visited Mesopotamia toward the end of the twelfth century, said specifically that the ark could no longer be seen "because it rotted" (Eisenstein, p. 54). On the other hand, Zusimus (Zosimy), a fifteenth century Russian priest, noted the presence of Noah's axe (and the rock from which Moses made water flow) in Constantinople (cf. Joel Raba, *Eretz Yisra'el BeTei'urei Nose'im Rusiim* [Jerusalem: Yad Ben Zvi, 1986], p. 95). None of these searches or reports of discoveries qualifies as archaeology. Nor does even the more systematic work, *Kaftor VaFereh* by Ishtor HaParhi, written in the early fourteenth century (see, further, its treatment in Joshua Prawer, *The History of the Jews in the Latin Kingdom of Jerusalem* [Oxford: Oxford University Press, 1988] pp. 128–250), which is concerned primarily with halakhic and geographic issues, though these and similar works paved the way for it. Some contemporary archaeological and historical investigations are motivated by forces not unlike those that moved early Christian figures, though they are more nationalistic than religious. See the initial paragraphs of H. Ben Sasson's *A History of the Jewish People* (Cambridge: Harvard University Press, 1976) or the changing titles of M. Avi-Yonah's *BiYemei Romah uVizantiyon,* which has been translated and reissued as *The Jews of Palestine: A Political History from the Bar Kokhba War to the Arab Conquest* (New York: Schocken, 1976), *Geschichte der Juden im Zeitalter des Talmud* (Berlin: De Gruyter, 1969), and *The Jews Under Roman and Byzantine Rule: A Political History from the Bar Kokhba War to the Arab Conquest* (Jerusalem: Magnes, 1984).

3. Historical reconstruction is so essential to the midrashic process that Heinemann has described the midrashic literature as a mixture of creative historiography and creative philology (*Darkhei HaAggadah,* third edition [Jerusalem: Magnes, 1970] pp. 15–95). Note, also, the routine steps taken by medieval interpreters to resolve contradictions and inconsistencies between parallel or related passages, including: reading two differing accounts of the same event as two different events, prioritizing one description over another, harmonizing two descriptions into one, and suggesting the addition of previously unknown facts that facilitate resolution of the conflict. All of these processes change the perception of individual passages in the hope of reconstructing what actually happened.

4. Ibn Ezra relied on foreign languages (including Aramaic, Arabic, and Persian) to explain Biblical Hebrew (a list of examples is found in E. Z. Melammed, *Mefarshei HaMiqra'* [Jerusalem: Magnes, 1975] Vol. 2, pp. 617–623). Note his use of Egyptian traditions translated into Arabic to identify the "correct" name of Moses (Ex. 2:10), and similar comparative steps that even entered Kurdistani presentations of midrashim about Moses (Shabbetai ben Meir Alfayyah, *Midrash Moshe* [Jerusalem: 1987, p. 64]). Compare, also, the observation of Rabbi Naphtali Tzvi Yehudah Berlin in *HaAmeq Davar* (reprint, Jerusalem: Lewin-Epstein, 1967) Exodus 2:10; etc. Despite the displeasure with comparative philology voiced in some pious circles (cf. Ibn Aknin, *Hitgalut HaSodot VeHofaʿat Ha Me'ora'ot* [Commentary on the Song of Songs], [Jerusalem: Mekize Nirdamim, 1964] pp. 494–5 ff), Ibn Ezra was far from the only medieval writer to employ it in his work. The most extensive treatment of this issue is Aharon Maman, *Hashvaʿat*

Otzar HaMilim Shel Ha'Ivrit LeAravit uLeAramit LeMin RaSaG ve'ad Ibn Baron (Jerusalem: Hebrew University Doctorate, 1985).

5. The use of non-Jewish sources for non-linguistic purposes is documented in Yossipon, who borrowed the Apocryphal Additions to Esther from the Vulgate. Nahmanides referred to *Sefer Hokhmeta deShelomo* (the Wisdom of Solomon) in the introduction to his commentary on the Torah, and it is also cited in *Livnat HaSapir,* the Torah commentary attributed to David ben Judah HeHasid (introduced by Solomon Wertheimer [Jerusalem: 1913, reprint, Jeruselem: n.d.]). Maimonides made extensive use of non-Jewish sources in reconstructing the religious life of ancient times which he understood to be opposed by many of the mitzvot, *e.g., Guide For the Perplexed* III, 50, and *Sefer HaMitzvot,* Negative Commandments #42; see, also, Z. H. Chajes *Mavo HaTalmud,* in *Kol Kitvei HaMaHaRaZ Hayyot,* Vol. 1 (Jerusalem: 1958), chapter 18; English translation, *Students Guide Through the Talmud* (New York: Feldheim, 1960) pp. 152–153. Abarbanel's uses of Christian interpretations were collected and discussed by M. Segal in *Massoret uBiqqoret* (Jerusalem: Qiryat Sefer, 1957) pp. 255–257. Cf. also the extensive use of non-Jewish writers in Menasseh Ben Israel's *Conciliator,* Azariah De Rossi's *Me'or Einayyim,* Hertz's commentary on the Pentateuch, etc..

6. The discussion about the coin from the late first century held in Akko, which is found at the very end of Nahmanides' Torah commentary, highlights both the unusual nature of the find and the author's eagerness to use it in his halakhic deliberations (*Peirush HaRamban Al HaTorah,* ed. C. Chavel, Vol. 2 [Jerusalem: Mossad HaRav Kook, 1965] pp. 507–508). Compare the even greater availability noted in responsum #74 of Moses Alashqar (1466–1542), *She'eilot uTeshuvot Maharam Alashqar* (Jerusalem: 1988) pp. 229–231. See further chapter 56 of Azariah De Rossi's *Me'or Einayyim* [1866, reprint Jerusalem: Makor, 1970], where Nahmanides' recording of *sheqel hasheqalim* on the coins is challenged and the matter is discussed in detail. Note, also, the sources cited in M. M. Kasher, *Torah Shelemah,* addenda to Vol. 22 (Jerusalem: Makhon Torah Shelemah, 1967) pp. 125–169, and Vol. 29 (Jerusalem: Beit Torah Shelemah, 1979) as well as the reproduction in B.B. Levy, *Planets, Potions and Parchments: Scientifica Hebraica from the Dead Sea Scrolls to the Eighteenth Century* (Montreal: McGill-Queens, 1990) pp. 62–63.

7. Melammed lists examples from Ibn Ezra's comments to Gen. 49:19, Num. 21:14, Is. 40:12, Zech. 12:10, and Hag. 2:22 in *Mefarshei HaMiqra',* Vol. 2, p. 633. As well, Maimonides discusses the matter his *Guide for the Perplexed,* III, 50.

8. For discussion of the early history of Biblical criticism, see Menahem Soloveitchik and Zalman Rubasheff, *Toldot Biqqoret HaMiqra'* (Berlin: Devir Miqra', 1925); Judah Rosenthal, *Hiwi AlBalkhi* (Philadelphia: Dropsie College, 1949); Isaiah Sonne, "Biblical Criticism in the Middle Ages," in *Freedom and Reason: Studies in Philosophy and Jewish Culture in Memory of Morris Raphael Cohen* (Glencoe, Ill.: The Free Press, 1951) pp. 438–446; the statements of various ancient writers who attacked oral or

written accounts of Biblical events and beliefs, conveniently collected (with other texts) in Menahem Stern's *Greek and Latin Authors on Jews and Judaism*, Vol. 1–3 (Jerusalem: Israel Academy of Sciences and Humanities, 1976–84); and some of the gnostic passages discussed in Alan F. Segal's *Two Powers in Heaven* (Leiden: E.J. Brill, 1977).

9. The most useful, pocket-size history of Jewish Biblical interpretation is M. Greenberg (ed.) *Parshanut MaMiqra' HaYehudit* (Jerusalem: Mossad Bialik, 1983).

10. See G. Scholem, *On The Kabbalah and Its Symbolism* (New York: Schocken, 1965), Chapter 3, "Kabbalah and Myth."

11. The treatments of Exodus 21–23 in some Hasidic works on the Torah highlight this. Those writers who drew their exegetical sources extensively from the Talmud and midrashim treated these Biblical laws in more-or-less the traditional rabbinic way. Writers who normally drew their exegetical inspiration from the Zohar and other mystical works that do not enter into the type of legal analysis found in the earlier rabbinic texts, had a different exegetical agenda that followed the more theological and mythological concerns of kabbalistic thought.

12. For example, Samuel Dresner's *The Zaddik: The Doctrine of the Zaddik According to the Writings of Rabbi Yakov Yosef of Polnoy* (New York: Shocken, 1960, 1974), which analyzes the polemical thrust of the Biblical interpretation in *Toldot Ya'aqov Yosef*. This polemic extended to the Zohar, as well. While contemporary religious writers exploited it fully, scholars like Heinrich Graetz were highly critical of its innovations and interpretations; see, for example, his *History of the Jews*, Vol. 4 (Philadelphia: Jewish Publication Society, 1984, 1956) chapter 1.

13. James H. Lehman, "Maimonides, Mendelssohn, and the Me'asfim," *Leo Baeck Institute Yearbook* 20 (1975) pp. 87–108, and Jay Harris, "The Image of Maimonides in Nineteenth Century Jewish Historiography," PAAJR 54 (1987) pp. 117–140. S. D. Luzzatto is somewhat unusual in this respect, as he was an ardent critic of both Ibn Ezra and Maimonides; see further, M. B. Margolies, *Samuel David Luzzatto: Traditionalist Scholar* (New York: Ktav, 1979).

14. Detailed evaluation of the various historians' treatments of the Vilna Gaon's attitudes toward enlightenment is found in Emanuel Etkes, *"HaGra' VeHaHaskalah: Tadmit uMetsi'ut,"* in idem. and Y. Salmon (ed.), *Peraqim BeToldot HaHevrah HaYehudit BiYemei HaBeinayyim uBaEt HaHadashah Muqdashim LeProfessor Ya'aqov Katz...* (Jerusalem: Magnes, 1980) pp. 192–217. For examples of the widely divergent exegetical approaches to the Vilna Gaon, compare his comment on resolving the discrepancy between the different lengths reported for the Egyptian enslavement (*Qol Eliyahu* to Ex. 1:14 [reprinted in Israel, n.d.]) with the open admission that most of what the rabbis wrote about the laws in Exodus and other places was derash (*Aderet Eliyahu* to Ex. 21:3, reprinted in *Otzar Peirushim al HaTorah* [New York: Shulsinger, 1950]).

15. This position was presented by Y. Kaufmann in his *Toldot HaEmunah HaYisra'elit* and developed by James Kugel. See the introduction to this volume.

16. *Encyclopaedia Judaica,* s.v., "Orthodoxy."

17. It is truly fascinating to see how centuries of rabbinic interpreters have deflected the talmudic teaching that one should devote one's years of study equally to Bible, Mishnah, and Gemara (BT Qidushin 30a).

18. Mishnah Avot, 5:22. ("Turn it and keep turning it in all directions, for it contains all.")

19. BT Shabbat 63a ("No scriptural verse may be permitted to escape its plain sense.")

20. Having completed the commentary on the later books of the Bible, the series is now beginning to publish the long awaited commentary on the Torah. But several differences, not the least of which is the inclusion of Rashi's commentary, show that this aspect of the project differs from the other.

21. *Torat Hayyim,* which began to appear in 1986, offers some rather sriking suggestions about what a rabbinic Bible should and should not contain. In addition to the Bible text and Onkelos' translation, this new edition contains the commentaries of ten medieval interpreters, the bulk of whose efforts were directed to *peshat* and generally high quality rabbinic interpretation: Rashi, Rashbam, Ibn Ezra, Radak (Genesis), Ramban, Hizquni, Seforno, Maharam Rotenberg, Saadiah, and Rabbeinu Hananel. It omits the Massorah, a feature found in virtually every other Rabbinic Bible; all super-commentaries; and all commentaries written after the sixteenth century, including *OrHaHayyim, Keli Yaqar,* the commentaries of the Vilna Gaon, and the entire hasidic literature. See, further, B. Barry Levy, "Rabbinic Bibles, *Mikra'ot Gedolot,* and Other Great Books," *Tradition* 25 (1991), 65–81.

22. A sketch of Kasher's activities is found in Aaron Greenbaum, "Architect and Builder: The Life of Harav Menaham M. Kasher," in Leo Jung (ed.), *Sages and Saints* (Hoboken: Ktav, 1987) pp. 231–272.

23. See, in particular, her *Limmud Parshanei HaTorah uDerakhim LeHora'atam: Bereishit* (Jerusalem: World Zionist Organization, 1975).

24. See, for example, M. Breuer's essay *Emunah uMadaʿ BeFarshanut HaMiqra'*, *De 'ot,* No. 11 (1960) pp. 18–25, No. 12 (1960) pp. 12–27, and No. 13 (1960) pp. 14–24, as well as the introduction to his *Pirqei Mo'adot* (Jerusalem: Horev, 1986); also Y. Leibowitz' *Yahadut im Yehudei Medinat Yisrael* (Jerusalem: Shocken, 1975) pp. 346 ff.

25. Uriel Simon (ed.), *HaMiqra' VaAnahnu* (Tel Aviv: Devir, 1979).

26. These begin, it would seem, with statements in BT Berakhot 28b and BT Baba Metzi'a 33a, and include a vast range of their interpretations and applications.

27. Moses Stern, *She'eilot uTeshuvot Be'ere Moshe,* Volume 8 (Brooklyn: Simhah Graphic, 1987) pp. 9–12 #3 prohibits use of religious books written by the rabbis of Yeshiva University and even editions of the works of great medieval and modern rabbis edited by them. Several decades ago one sometimes heard such attitudes being expressed toward the use of works like Saul Lieberman's *Tosefta KiFeshutah* or his edition of *Hasdei David;* obviously it has spread.

28. The first part of each of the next seven numbered sections is based

primarily on my observations of Orthodox rabbis and teachers—in classes, sermons and private conversations—and on popular, contemporary, Orthodox publications; accordingly, I have not attempted to document the sources for the reader. One might question the extent to which either of these types of sources should be taken as a policy statement of contemporary Orthodoxy, especially since many English publications disclaim any such authority (cf. B. Barry Levy, "The Orthodox Publication Explosion," in *Jewish Book Annual,* Vol. 44 [1986–87] pp. 6–17). Even so, I believe that the sources accurately reflect the reality that exists.

Most of the positions in question are also taught in the Artscroll Bible Commentaries, and their virtually universal support among Orthodox groups in North America allows one to assume that they reflect contemporary Orthodox attitudes quite well. Note, for example, the approbations accompanying the volumes, the formal endorsements of important Orthodox organizations and institutions, and the groundswell of general support from Orthodox laymen. (See, further, B. Barry Levy, "Our Torah, Your Torah and Their Torah: An Evaluation of the Artscroll Phenomenon," in H. Joseph, *et al.* [ed.], *Truth and Compassion: Essays on Judaism and Religion in Memory of Rabbi Dr. Solomon Frank* [Waterloo, Ontario: Wilfred Laurier University Press, 1983] pp. 137–190; "Judge Not A Book By Its Cover," *Tradition* 19 [1981] pp. 89–95; and "Artscroll: An Overview," in M. L. Raphael [ed.] *Approaches to Modern Judaism* [Chico, Cal.: Scholar's Press, 1983] pp. 111–140, 157–162. Note, also the letters to the editor of *Tradition* that appeared in many issues after publication of my article there.) Few contemporary projects have garnered as much broad-based Orthodox support as this one, which, regardless of its faults, must be taken to represent accurately the dominant, contemporary, American Orthodox approach to the Bible.

29. The issue centers upon the interpretation of Gen. 26:5 in the Talmud and later commentators, as well as a series of other passages, in which the patriarchs seemed to be in violation of what later became normative expectations. See, for example, the treatments of Gen 26:5 in the commentaries of Rashbam, Ibn Ezra, Radak, and Ramban, in contrast to the more popular and more influential presentation of Rashi.

A good example of how rabbinic ideas have been projected onto the three patriarchs is found in the talmudic teaching that each of them instituted one of the three daily prayer services. Initially, BT Berakhot 26b records two opinions: the patriarchs themselves instituted the services, or the rabbis instituted them on analogy to the system of temple sacrifices. The corresponding passage in the Palestinian Talmud presents the first position as *the rabbis* instituted the services to make them correspond to the prayers of the patriarchs; the second is similar to that of the Babylonian Talmud. The historical validity of the Palestinian Talmud's version of the former opinion is obvious, but it has yet to emerge as the preferred one.

30. Rashbam, Gen. 26:6, etc.

31. See further, Arthur Green, *Devotion and Commandment: The Faith of Abraham in the Hasidic Imagination* (Cincinnati: Hebrew Union College Press, 1989).

32. See, for example, the many sources cited in *"Kuntres Seder Ketivat HaTorah,"* the lengthy appendix to volume 19 of M. Kasher, *Torah Shelemah* (New York: American Biblical Encyclopedia Society, 1960) pp. 328–379.

33. See, for example, Jacob ben Asher, *Baʿal HaTurim* to Lev. 1:1, Hayyim ibn Atar, *Or HaHayyim,* to Num. 33:2, and *Torah Shelemah, ibid.,* pp. 369 ff.

34. Cf. the sources cited in *Torah Shelemah, ibid.,* pp. 328–379, as well as the passages in I. Lange (ed.), *Peirushei HaTorah LeR[abbi] Yehudah HeHasid* (Jerusalem: 1975) that were censored (with recommendations that they be burnt) by Rabbi Moses Feinstein, *Igrot Moshe,* Vol. 4 (New York: 1981) pp. 358–361. Fortunately, he cited the questionable passage in the course of his discussion, so they are readily available for all who are forced to use the later, expurgated edition of the commentary.

35. The fullest explanation of this new fad is found in Doron Weiztom, *HaMeimad HaNosaf* (Jerusalem: 1989). Norman Lamm has rejected the approach: "No amount of intellectual legerdemain or midrashic pyrotechnics—or even sophisticated but capricious computer analysis of sacred texts—can convince us that the Torah somehow possesses within itself the secrets of quantum mechanics, the synthesis of DNA, and the like." *Torah Umadda* (Northvale, N.J., Jason Aronson, 1990) p. 47.

36. See, for example, BT Qidushin 30a, and the commentary of Menahem Meiri, *Beit HaBehirah,* edited by A. Sofer, third edition (Jerusalem: 1963); *idem, Qiryat Sefer,* edited by M. Herschler (Jerusalem: 1957); Jacob Barukh ben Judah Landau, *Sefer HaAgur HaShalem,* edited by M. Hershler (Jerusalem: 1960) pp. 42 ff; Moses Isserles, glosses to *Shulhan Arukh, Orah Hayyim,* chapter 143; Judah Leib Saraval, note at the end of Moses HaLevi Abulafia's *Massoret Seyyag LaTorah* (Florence: 1750); Aryeh Leib Gunzberg, *Sha'agat Aryeh,* Hilkhot Sefer Torah (Warsaw: 1879, reprint, n.d.) #36; Moses Sofer, *She'eilot uTeshuvot HaHatam Sofer, Orah Hayyim* (Vienna: 1895, reprint, Jerusalem: Makor, 1970) #52; Maharam Schick, *She'eilot uTeshuvot HaMaharam Schick, Yoreh Deʿah* (reprint, Jerusalem: n.d.) #254; Ovadiah Yosef, *Yehaveh Daʿat,* Vol. 6 (Jerusalem: 1984) #56. Compare the presumption of accuracy attributed to Torah scrolls in the responsa of Solomon ben Adret, *She'eilot uTeshuvot HaRashba HaMeyuhasot LeHaRamban* (Warsaw: 1883) #232 and *Teshuvot HaRashba,* edited by H. Z. Dimitrovsky (Jerusalem: Mossad HaRav Kook, 1990 #14, and by David ben Solomon ibn Zimra, *She'eilot uTeshuvot HaRadbaz,* Vol. 2, part 4 (reprint, New York: Goldman-Otzar Sefarim, 1967) #1172 (101), with the lack thereof in the responsum of Yehezkel Landau, *Nodaʿ BiYehudah, Yoreh De'ah,* Second Series (reprint, New York: Otzar Sefarim, 1973) #178.

37. Cf. Aaron Kotler, *How to Teach Torah* (Lakewood, N.J.: 1972), also available in Hebrew as *"HaHavanah HaAmitit Shel Sippurei HaTorah"* in *Osef Hidot HaGra Kotler* (Jerusalem: 1983) pp. 402–411, and as *"BeDarkhei Hora'at Torah SheBiKhtav"* in *Mishnat Rabbi Aharon* (Lakewood, N.J.: Makhon Mishnat Rabbi Aharon, 1988), Vol. 3, pp. 177–187.

38. Indeed, two central passages in the Mishnah that list people who

have no share in the world to come (Sanhedrin 10:1 and Avot 3:11) are essentially rejections of those who did not accept fully the normative rabbinic Bible interpretation and other closely related matters. Excluded thereby were Christians, gnostics, Saducees, and members of other Jewish sects. *Sanhedrin:* one who denies the belief in resurrection of the dead (or that this belief is found in the Torah); one who says the Torah is not from Heaven; an *epikuros;* one who reads non-canonical books (presumably for religious purposes as an alternative to the Torah); one who whispers a Biblical verse over an injury; one who pronounces the tetragrammaton as it is spelled. *Avot:* one who violates holy things; one who desecrates the holidays; one who embarrasses his fellow man; one who violates the covenant of Abraham (circumcision); and one who explains the Torah improperly.

The precise meanings of these passages are debated by the commentators, but only the case of one who embarrasses his fellow does not revolve around a methodological issue of sectarian significance in Biblical interpretation (though the Vilna Gaon and some other commentators tried to find Biblical roots for it). It is interesting to note that this phrase is not found in most manuscripts of the Mishnah or in most early witnesses to the text, and is probably a late addition. It does offer a poignant comment on the zeal that sometimes accompanies doctrinal debates about the Bible and the proper way to discuss it.

39. See, for example, the sources and discussion in the first chapter of Marc Saperstein, *Decoding the Rabbis: A Thirteenth-Century Commentary on the Aggadah* (Cambridge: Harvard University Press, 1980).

40. See, for example, Mordecai Gifter, *"Torah BaGoyyim, Al Ta'amin,"* in his *Pirqei Emunah,* (Jerusalem: Feldheim, 1969) pp. 141 ff.

41. Alexander Marx's biography and recollections of his father-in-law, David Hoffman, appear in his *Essays in Jewish Biography* (Philadelphia: Jewish Publication Society, 1947) pp. 185–222. See also, Morris B. Margolies, *Samuel David Luzzatto: Traditionalist Scholar* (New York: Ktav, 1979). Cassuto's publications have been listed in H. Beinart (ed.), *Mehqarim BaMiqra' Yotse'im BiMele'ot Meah Shannah LeHoladeto Shel M. D. Cassuto* (Jerusalem: Magnes, 1987) pp. 9–38.

42. Cf. the doctoral dissertation of Harvey Warren Meirovich, *Judaism on Trial: An Analysis of the Hertz Pentateuch* (Jewish Theological Seminary, New York: 1986).

43. The history of Yeshiva University has been described in detail by Gilbert Klaperman, *The Story of Yeshiva University: The First Jewish University in America* (Toronto: Macmillan, 1969) and by Jeffrey S. Gurock, *The Men and Women of Yeshiva: Higher Education, Orthodoxy and American Judaism* (New York: Columbia University Press, 1988). Much additional information can be culled from Aaron Rothkoff, *Bernard Revel: Builder of Amerian Jewish Orthodoxy* (Philadelphia: Jewish Publication Society, 1972); Aaron Ben-Zion Shorin, *Bein Yehudei Artzot HaBerit* (Jerusalem: Mossad HaRav Kook, 1981) pp. 189–284; Hyman Grinstein, *Toldot Beit HaMidrash LeMorim shel Yeshiva University MiShenat 1917 ve'ad 1955,"* in M. Carmilly and H. Leaf (ed.), *Sefer Zikkaron LeShemuel Belkin* (New York: Yeshiva University, 1981) pp. 256–274; and N. Lamm, *Torah uMadda*.

With the exception of Dr. Lamm's book, all of these other presentations focus on the political and economic history of the institution, not its intellectual history, and Lamm has not devoted a significant amount of attention to Bible study. A full history of the teaching of Bible at YU is still a desideratum, which I am unable to provide because of distance from the university archives.

44. Klaperman, pp. 260–261; see Gurock, pp. 48–49.

45. Y. Kil, introduction to *Hiqrei Miqra* (Jerusalem: Mossad HaRav Kook, 1978) p. 8; *Igrot HaRAYa* (Jerusalem: Mossad HaRav Kook, 1965) letter #101. Three of the letters have been translated in Tzvi Feldman, *Rav A. Y. Kook: Selected Letters* (Ma'alei Adumim, Ma'aliot, 1986).

46. Rothkoff, p. 60; Gurock., p. 57. This situation, which is mentioned by both Rothkoff and Gurock but is described by neither, is typical for the profession, as many colleagues have reported to me in private conversation.

47. *Hiqrei Lashon* (Jerusalem: Mossad HaRav Kook, 1986)

48. Cf. *Trei Asar*, Vol. 2 (Jerusalem: Mossad HaRav Kook, 1966) p. 3, first note. A bibliography of Seidel's publications is found in E. Eliner, *Sefer Seidel* (Israel: HaHevrah LeHeqer HaMiqra', 1962).

49. Heller's many publications include: *"LeHeqer HaMiqra',"* [on Mandelkern's Concordance], *Bitzaron* 1 (1939), pp. 78–81, 521–526, 5, pp. 186–193; *Maimonides' Sefer Ha-Mizwoth, Kritische Ausgabe der Ibn Tibbon'schen Uebersetzung unter Berücksichtigung des arabischen Originals und der Uebertragung Ibn Ajjub's Hrsg* . . . (Petrikau: M. Cederbaum, 1914, reprint, Jerusalem: Mossad HaRav Kook, 1980); *Al HaTargum Ha-Yerushalmi LaTorah* (New York: Alpha Press, 1921); *HaNusah HaShomroni shel HaTorah* (Berlin: 1924); *Untersuchungen zur Septuaginta* (Berlin: 1932); *Untersuchungen ueber die Peschitta zur gesamten hebraeischen Bibel* . . . (Berlin: 1911). On his candidacy for the position of Rosh Yeshiva, see Gurock, pp. 139 ff.

50. A bibliography of Finkel's publications appears in S. Hoenig and L. Stitskin (ed.), *Joshua Finkel Festschrift* (New York: Yeshiva University Press, 1974) pp. 177–186. Of some 30 items (#31 is not numbered), most deal with Arabic and Judeo-Arabic texts; some study aspects of classical Bible interpretation, and only two or three are devoted to Bible proper. Note also, "A Criticism of Higher Criticism," *Horeb* (New York: 1944) pp. 28–48. To the published list one may add: *"HaAggadah al Tehiyyat HaPegarim Ba-Verit Bein HaBetarim," Sefer HaYovel LeKhevod Shalom Baron*, Hebrew Volume (Jerusalem: American Academy for Jewish Research, 1975) pp. 269–28; *"BeDamayyikh Hayyi," Sefer Zikkaron LeShemuel Belkin*, pp. 45–54, and possibly others.

As further evidence of Finkel's distance from Biblical studies, one may note that of the eleven Hebrew and fourteen English submissions to the volume, only one (of less than two pages in length, by Cyrus Gordon) deals with Bible. Jonas Greenfield's article is about Talmudic Aramaic lexicography and Moshe Goshen-Gottstein's deals with Ibn Kuraish. No other "Bible people" participated.

51. "Megillat Esther Ne'emrah Liqrot VeLo' Ne'emrah Likhtov," *Or HaMizrah* 23 (1974) pp. 116–130; "Hotamo Shel HaKohen HaGadol, *Or HaMizrah* 19 (1970) pp. 137–149; "Zeihuto Shel Haman VeHitmodeduto

Neged Yehudah ViYerushalim," Or *HaMizrah* (1973) pp. 233-241; *"Hahodashim BeYisrael: Mashma'ut Shemoteihem uMisparam,"* Or *HaMizrah* 20 (1971) pp. 133-146; *"Mashma'ut HaShem Ivri BaTanakh uViMeqorot Talmudiim,"* Or *HaMizrah* 21 (1972) pp. 25-33, (1973) pp. 29-38.

52. *"Yahas HaZaL LeTargum Onkelos Al HaTorah,"* Finkel Volume, pp. 169-176; *"LeMi No'ad Targum Onkelos?,"* Peraqim 4 (1966) pp. 93-7; *"LeMi No'ad Targum Onkelos?,"* HaDarom 32 (1971) pp. 155-70, 36 (1973) pp. 212-226.

53. *"HaTanna'im SheNilhamu Neged HaNatzrut,"* Or *HaMizrah* 26 (1978) pp. 229-246; 28 (1980) 332-349, 376; 29 (1981) pp. 404-414, (1982) pp. 75-89; *"Hinukh HaBanot,"* Or *HaMizrah* 17 (1968) pp. 40-52, 124-132.

54. *"Mikhtav Me'et HaRav Mordecai Shemuel Gerondi,"* HaDarom 25 (1967) pp. 205-210; *"HaReqa HaHistori LeTeshuvah Ahat Shel HaGaon Rabbeinu Shelomo Kluger,"* Belkin Memorial Volume (1981) pp. 162-180. *"Rabbi Eliezer HaLevi Ish Horowitz,"* Areshet 5 (1972) pp. 215-253; *"Shenei Mikhtavim MeHaGaon Rav Hayyim Berlin LeRabbi Eliezer Lippman Prinz,"* Or *HaMizrah* 35 (1987) pp. 40-47.

55. On Reifman: *"Milu'im LeTiten Emet LeYa'aqov,"* Darom 22 (1966) pp. 142-146; *"VeHaKesharim LeYa'aqov,"* Darom 23 (1966) pp. 126-150; *"He'arot R. Y. Reifmann BeFeirush HaRa'Va',"* Sinai 66 (1970) pp. 253-262; *"VaYaqom Edut BeYa'aqov,"* Talpiot 9 (1970) pp. 785-811; *"He 'arot al 'Megillat Esther' ve 'al 'Targumei Esther' LeHaHakham R. Ya'aqov Reifman,"* HaDarom 25 (1967) pp. 195-204; on Chajes: *"Sho'alei uMeshivei Rabbi Tzvi Hirsh Hayyot,"* Or *HaMizrah* 18 (1969) pp. 262-273; *"Ha-Yehasim Bein HaGeonim R. Shaul Natanson VeHaMaHaRaTz Hayyot,"* Or *HaMizrah* (1971) pp. 63-73; and *MaHaRaTz Hayyot* (Jerusalem: Mosad HaRav Kook, 1972).

56. *"Ahavat Tziyon uSefatah BaShirah HaIvrit BeHungaria,"* Bitzaron 53 (1966) pp. 119-128; "Statistics Concerning the Mixed Marriages in Transylvania and Banat," "Hebrew Culture in Transylvania," "Jewish Education in Transylvania in the Days of the Holocaust," "The Tragedy of Transylvanian Jewry," in *Memorial Volume for the Jews of Cluj-Kolozsvar"* (1970); *"Sharat Yahadut Hungariah Ba 'Havatzelet',"* Talpiot 9 (1970) pp. 853-872; *"Hitpathut HaShirah HaIvrit BeHungariah,"* Areshet 5 (1932) pp. 254-265; *"Helqah Nishkahat,"* [on Jewish writers in Hungary] *HaDoar* 46 (1967) pp. 293-4; "Hebrew Poetry in Hungary," in R. L. Braham (ed.), *Hungarian Jewish Studies* (New York: 1966) pp. 295-342; *"Romantism BaShirah HaIvrit BeHungariah,"* Proceedings of the World Congress of Jewish Studies (1978) pp. 229-240; *"Beit HaMidrash LeRabanim BeVudapest Ben Me'ah Shanah,"* HaDoar 56 (1977) pp. 295-296; *"Pidyon Shevuyim Yehudiim BaMe' ah Ha17 Behungariah,"* World Congress of Jewish Studies 8 (1982) pp. 77-83; *The Rabbinical Seminary of Budapest 1877-1977* (New York: Sepher-Hermon, 1986) he edited the volume and contributed articles entitled "One Hundred years of the Seminary in Retrospect," "The Students," "Hebrew Language and Literature," Jewish Historiography of Transylvania, Banat and Croatia," "The Seminary and its Achievements"; *Irgun LaHatzalat Yehudim BeTransylvania BiYemei HaSho'ah,"* Preceedings of

the *World Congress of Jewish Studies* 9 (1986) pp. 211-216; "Jewish Education in Transylvania in the Days of the Holocaust," *Yad VaShem Bulletin* 21 (1967) pp. 21-27.

57. *"Soferim Yehudim uMosad HaTzenzura BeMa'arav Eiropa," HaGut Ivrit BeAmerica*, pp. 120-130; *"Sefarim [She] Mehabrim Yehudim] Muharim [al yedei Yehudim] BeMeshekh HaDorot, Peraqim*, Vol. 4 (1966), pp. 223-241; "External and Internal Censorship of Hebrew Books," JBA 2 (1970) pp. 9-16; *"Peirush Tehilim Metzunsar Shel R. Shelomo ben Atya,"* in M. Carmilly and H. Leaf (ed.), Belkin Memorial Volume, pp. 55-62; *"Sefer, Sefer VeGoralo: Sefaraim ShHushmedu BeYedei Mehabreiheim," HaDoar* 47 (1968) pp. 49-51; *Sefer VeSayif* (New York: 1966); *Censorship and Freedom of Expression in Jewish History* (New York: Sepher-Hermon Press, 1977); Introduction to the reprinted edition of William Popper, *The Censorship of Hebrew Books* (New York: Ktav, 1969), pp. v-xxvii.

58. "The Life of Spanish Jews in the Balkans," *ACIEB* 3 (1969) pp. 781-783; *"Haggadah Me'uteret BeBulgaria," HaDoar* 48 (1969) pp. 342-343; *"Yitzhaq Yehudah Goldzhier: Derashat HaBarMitzvah,"* Finkel Festschrift, pp. 185-200; *"Shelomo Levinsohn KeHistorion, Bitzaron* 67 (1976) pp. 20-27; "The Magic Bird," in Victor D. Sanua (ed.), *Fields of Offerings: Studies in Honor of Raphael Patai* (Rutherford: Fairleigh Dickinson University Press, 1983) pp. 129-141.

59. "The Psychology of Bereavement: A Jewish Psychological Perspective on Hilchot Semachot," *Gesher* 3 (1966) pp. 56-71; "Psychomatics, Hermetic Medicine, and Dream Interpretation in the Qumran Literature," *JQR* I 60 (1969) pp. 112-127, 213-230; "LSD: A Jewish View," *Tradition* 10 (1968) pp. 31-41; *"HaSamim HaPsikhodelim LeOr HaYahudat, Bitzaron*, 61 (1970) pp. 211-221, 263-273; *"HaYahadut BeOr HaPsikhologiah," Peraqim*, 4 (1966) pp. 365-86 *'HaRefu'ah HaGenuzah uPitron Halomot BeMegillot Midbar Yehudah uBaSefarim HaHitzonim," Hagut Ivrit BeAmerica*, pp. 174-185; "Jewish and Psychological Factors in the Teaching of the Holocaust," *Political Psychology*, 4 (1984) pp. 99-102.

60. "On the Psalmodic Musical Superscriptions," *Journal of Jewish Music and Liturgy"* 6 (1983-4) pp. 20-23, 9 (1986-7) pp. 31-35; *"Midreshei Aggadot uBei'urim Temuhim Ve'Alumei Maqor BeTargum haTorah HaMeyuhas LeYonatan ben Uziel,"* Belkin Memorial Volume, pp. 63-83.

61. "The Sphinx as Learner: A Reading of Judges 13-16," *Tradition* 14 (1974) pp. 66-79; "Psalm 24 as the Key to the Problem of HaShem S-Vaot," *Gesher*, Vol. 5 (1976) pp. 164-85; "The Courage to Suffer: Isaiah 53 and Its Context," *Gesher* 7 (1979) pp. 102-124; "Rav Kuk's Theory of Knowledge," *Tradition* 15 (1975) pp. 193-203; "Halakha and Philosophical Approaches to Abortion," *Tradition* 16 (1977) pp. 126-57; "Rav Yitzhak Hutner's Lecture to a Teaching Conference," *Tradition* 19 (1981) p. 218.

62. *The Canonization of Hebrew Scripture* (Hamden, Connecticut, 1976); *The Canon and Masorah of the Hebrew Bible: An Introductory Reader* (New York: Ktav, 1974).

63. "The Inverted Nuns at Num. 10:35-36 and the Book of Eldad and Medad," *JBL* 93 (1974) pp. 348-355; "Inspiration and Canonicity: Reflections on the Formation of the Biblical Canon," in E. P. Sanders (ed.), *Jewish*

and *Christian Self-Definition, Vol. 2: Aspects of Judaism in the Graeco-Roman Period* (Philadelphia, Fortress, 1981), pp. 56–63.

64. "Jewish Ethical Teaching and Technological Advance," in F. E. Greenspahn (ed.) *Contemporary Ethical Issues in the Jewish and Christian Traditions* (Hoboken: Ktav, 1986) pp. 9–29.

65. "Abarbanel and the Censor," *Journal of Jewish Studies* 19 (1968) pp. 49–61; "R. Israel Lipshutz and the Portrait of Moses Controversy," in I. Twersky (ed.) *Danzig, Between East and West: Aspects of Modern Jewish History* (Cambridge, Harvard University Press, 1985) pp. 51–63; "Torah Scholarship Since the Holocaust," *JBA* 43 (1985) pp. 45–55; *"Peirush HaGaon Rabbi Yonathan Eibshitz ZaTzaL LeQetzat Aggadot BeMasakhet Berakhot," Or HaMizrah* 29 (1981) pp. 418–428; "The Scroll of Fasts: The Ninth of Tebeth," *JQR* 74 (1983) pp. 174–195; *"Temunato Shel Rabbi Shaul HaLevi Morteira, Alei Sefer* 11 (1982) pp. 153–155.

66. *The Neophyti Targum: A Textual Study*, (Lanham, Maryland: University Press of America, 1986–1987); "Why *Bar-Nash* Cannot Mean "I," *Memorial Volume for Professor Frank Talmage* (Haifa University Press, In Press).

67. In addition to those mentioned in notes 21 and 28, "Rashi's Commentary on the Torah: A Survey of Recent Publications," *Tradition* (1988).

68. *Planets, Potions and Parchments: Educational Kit* (Montreal: Jewish Public Library, 1990); "Teaching the Bible in High School," *The Canadian Jewish Educator*, Fall, 1984; "Who Will Teach Our Grandchildren?: Some Thoughts on the Training of Judaica Teachers in Canada," *The Canadian Jewish Educator*, Summer, 1986; "The Bible Laboratory," *Ten Da'at*, Fall, 1989.

69. Above, note 6.

70. *"uMah Qol HaTzon HaZe BeOznai?: LeVa'ayat HaShallal VeTohar HaTakhlit," Ma'ayanot* 11 (1986) pp. 194–211.

71. *"Shelilat Zekhutam Shel HaMuslamim LeSWhelitah BeEretz Yisrael BeShnei Peirushim Qara'iyim Min HaMe'ah HaAsirit," Shalem* 3 (1981) pp. 309–318; *"HaOmnam Heqif Peirush R. Shemuel Ben Hofni et Kol HaTorah?" Alei Sefer*, 8 (1980) pp. 137–139: "The Book of Judges in Medieval Muslim Historiography," *JANES* 11 (1979) pp. 113–130; "Kidnapping in Karaite Law According to the Commentary of Sahl ben Masliah," *JQR* 73 (1982) pp. 176–188; "Saadiah Gaon's Prolegomenon to Psalms," *PAAJR* 51 (1984) pp. 131–174.

72. *"Goliat VeOg BaMidrash uVaHadith," Sefunot* 16 (1980) pp. 49–58; *"Aggadot Muslamiyot BeNose' Gan Eden VeGeihinom VeYahasan LeTalmud VeMidrash," Belkin Memorial Volume*, pp. 181–186.

73. "Rashi's Commentary on Job: Some Preliminary Observations Towards the Preparation of a Critical Edition," *Gesher* 7 (1979) pp. 125–134; "The Commentary of Rashi on the Book of Job," Proceedings of the World Congress of Jewish Studies 8 (1982) pp. 139–144; *"HaPeshatot HaMithadshim: Qeta'im Hadashim MiPeirush HaTorah LaRashbam," Alei Sefer* 11 (1984) pp. 72–80; "On Moshe Max Ahrend, *Le Commentarire sur Job de Rabbi Yoseph Qara'*, *JQR* 72 (1981) pp. 153–155.

74. "From Proto-Hebrew to Mishnaic Hebrew: The History of *-akh* and

-*ahh,*" *Hebrew Annual Review* 3 (1979) pp. 157-174; "*Lulav* versus **lu*/law: A Note on the Conditioning of **aw>u* in Hebrew and Aramaic," *JAOS* 107 (1987) pp. 121-122.

75. "A Paganized Version of Psalm 20:2-6 from the Aramaic Text in Demotic Script," *JAOS* 103 (1983) pp. 261-274; "Ashurbanipal and Shamash-shum-ukin: A Tale of Two Brothers from the Aramaic Text in Demotic Script," *RB* 92 (1985) pp. 60-81.

76. "Midrash Halakhah at Qumran? 11 Q Temple 64, 6-13 and Deut. 21:22-23," *Gesher* 7 (1979) pp. 145-166; "*Ki Qilelat Elohim Talui* (Deut. 21:23): A Study in Early Jewish Exegesis," *JQR* 74 (1983) pp. 21-45; A New Manuscript of *Tosefta Targum* [Gen. 45:4; from Columbia University] *World Congress of Jewish Studies* 9 (1986) pp. 151-7.

77. Isaac Nordheimer (1809-1842), educated at Pressberg during the time of the Hatam Sofer, received his doctorate from Munich in 1834 and later taught at the University of the City of New York (now New York University) and Union Theological Seminary. His work is described briefly in H. Orlinsky, "Jewish Biblical Scholarship in America," *JQR* 45 (1955) pp. 378-9.

Zolomon Zeitlin taught non-Biblical subjects at Yeshiva prior to the death of Bernard Revel; his modest impact on Biblical scholarship has been summarized by Robert Gordis in S. B. Hoenig, *Solomon Zeitlin: Scholar Laureate* (New York: Bitzaron, 1971), pp. 49-50.

Other relatively unknown figures are listed by Hyman Grinstein in his survey of the history of YU's Teacher's Institute (see above, note 43), and many more could be added.

But the really intriguing question is how many of the people whose contributions are discussed could be included as Orthodox, and it is one I must decline to answer. If Orthodox upbringing were a criterion, many would qualify, as would be the case if observance of basic halakhah were the criterion; but that would not be fair to the observant non-Orthodox. Several of the scholars who had extensive advanced level educations under Orthodox auspices (and seem to congregate in Israel and Boston) may require a second look, but my goal has been to examine the visibly Orthodox involvement with Biblical scholarship, not to check into the personal lives of my colleagues. The fact that many of these people are observant suggests that important developments in Jewish religious thinking about the Bible loom barely beneath the surface of the contemporary scene. Because of their numbers and location in the universities of North America (and the presence there of many like-minded colleagues), these seemingly secular and detached institutions now possess one of the most important untapped resources for the religious development of American Judaism.

78. Isaac Gottlieb and Aaron Skaist, two men ordained by Yeshiva University who earned doctorates in Bible and ancient Near Eastern studies and teach at Bar Ilan have also escaped notice, as has Barry Eichler, who is an Assyriologist.

79. Obviously this does not apply to Orthodox women. My description has assumed a primary role for males, which has been the normative Orthodox position throughout much of the period covered in this volume.

But due to both negative and positive factors (the lack of interest in the Bible in most yeshivot and the greater attention it receives in schools for women), in some circles women are actually provided with superior educations in Bible and have assumed a leading role in teaching it. Unfortunately, this is often taken as a sign that the inferior subject should be taught to the inferior students (Talmud, the premier text, being reserved for males). But it also means that one may find more sophisticated appreciation of the Bible among Orthodox women, though this may have less than an optimal impact. It is generally agreed that Nehamah Leibowitz is the leading Orthodox Bible teacher in Israel, yet rightists have sometimes challenged her right to teach (male) yeshiva students, even after she received the consent of the chief rabbi (personal conversation with Dr. N. Leibowitz). Despite these problems, her impact on several generations of Israeli teachers has been quite noticeable, but given the social and religious dynamics of the Orthodox community, males still dominate most educational and religious institutions and also lack Bible-centered educational experiences.

80. For instance, Y. Leibowitz, *op. cit.*

81. The recent development of various initiatives to advance the cause of Torah *uMadda*ᶜ ("Torah and secular learning") must also be extended to Bible study, or the desired impact cannot be felt. There is hope that attitudes toward Bible study can change, if the materials presented by Lamm in *Torah uMadda*ᶜ have a serious impact on the direction of American Orthodoxy. Among the interesting examples of synthesis that differ substantially from the present norms and can be explored further are Rabbi Kook, many of whose writings are still in manuscript, Aaron Marcus' *Qadmoniot,* Second edition (Tel Aviv: Sinai, 1973), and A. Kaplan, *The Living Torah* (New York: Moznaim, 1981).

82. For example, Max Kapustin, "Biblical Criticism: A Traditionalist View," *Tradition* 3, reissued in Aryeh Carmell and Cyril Domb (ed.) *Challenge* (New York: Feldheim, 1976); and Emanuel Feldman's essays from *Tradition* 7 and 8, "Changing Patterns in Biblical Criticism," *ibid.*, pp. 432–444, also issued as "The Traditional Jew and Biblical Criticism" in Feldman, *The Biblical Echo: Reflections on Bible, Jews and Judaism* (Hoboken, N.J.: Ktav, 1986) pp. 93–103.

83. Hayyim Vital, *Sefer HaGilgulim,* introduction #7.

CONCLUDING EXTREMELY UNSCIENTIFIC POSTSCRIPT

We have attempted to trace the history of Jewish biblical scholarship in North America from its tentative beginnings to the present day. Jewish Bible scholarship has come a long way in the century and one-half since Isaac Leeser. Our chapter on "The Current Scene" illustrated the uncompromising professionalism and the diversity of approaches among contemporary Jewish biblicists. If the past two decades are any indication, more and more Jews will pursue the academic study of the Bible. Because the non-Orthodox Jewish seminaries do not appear to be in period of growth[1], more and more Jewish biblicists will tend to work in the institutional framework of the university.[2] We have seen that the scholars of the "Second Wave" had all shared a seminary background in some fashion, something no longer true of their successors and even less so of the students of their successors. Whereas the seminary background restricted inquiry to areas defined by the *Wissenschaft* movement of the nineteenth century, specifically philology and political history, scholars without seminary background tended more easily to study Bible in the light of general linguistics, sociology, anthropology, literary criticism, field archaeology, quantitative history, minority history, and history of religion; in short, in light of many disciplines undreamed of in *Wissenschaft des Judentums* but within the curriculum of the contemporary university. Employment opportunities in that setting will be tied to the general economy and to the place of America and Canada in the world. Given that general uncertainty, we may hazard some guesses about coming intellectual trends.

First, we expect to see a greatly enhanced role for the computer. Textual criticism, philology, and studies of biblical grammar and syntax should become increasingly rigorous as the time required for the collection of data and access to its analysis decreases precipitously.[3] Such rigor, in turn, will bring more precision to source-criticism and to decisions about unity and diversity of authorship.[4] With a little luck we might no longer have to take J, E, D, P and their relative dates on faith. Practitioners of the literary approach should likewise be better equipped to decide whether the pericopes they examine are artful or fortuitous.

Second, the above should faciliate a return to interest in comparatism. One will not necessarily have to be a thoroughly trained Assyriologist for example, in order to make responsible use of the data supplied by that area of study.

Third, we may expect greater concentration on the realia of ancient Israel, thanks to refinements in archaeological technique. These should make it easier to approach the ideal situation in which archaeological and biblical data are assessed apart from each other and only then brought into comparison.[5]

Fourth, increased precision in the social sciences will enable biblicists to suggest answers to such questions as, how big was a prophet's constituency; how did a prophet make a living; how does one distinguish a "Canaanite" from an Israelite; what did it mean to be a slave, a woman or a resident alien?

Fifth, absent some changes yet unforeseen in North American Jewish Orthodoxy, which continues to move intellectually to the right, we should expect its scholarly contributions to biblical studies to be indirect. From the Orthodox sector we will continue to receive reliable editions of texts of classical and medieval rabbinics, which are potential sources of important biblical textual variants, as well as treasures of exegesis and its history.

The reader will not fail to note that our predictions do not provide for a distinctive role of Jewish Bible scholarship in contrast to Gentile. In his day, Isaac Leeser was sure that his approach to the Bible was specifically Jewish and significantly different from the work of Christians whose understanding of the Hebrew Bible, sincere as it might be, undermined Israel's hope and faith. Whereas Lesser was an amateur, contemporary Jewish biblical scholarship has moved into the mainstream so that it is now practiced by women and men who are trained professionals but whose work usually does not distinctively identify them as Jews.

Indeed, the relocation of Jewish Bible study to the university and the simultaneous diminution of the role of seminaries in the formative Bible training of Jewish scholars has increased the chances that future Jewish biblical scholarship will be no different from any other. There are two reasons why this is likely to happen. First, to study Bible at JTS or HUC meant to study almost exclusively with other Jewish students who had similar theological views and similar commitments to Jewish ritual. The specifically Jewish character of Bible study in these seminaries was supplied more by the setting than by the instructors' approach. The same professor who in class might challenge the historical existence of the biblical Patriarchs could be heard in chapel praising "the God of Abraham, Isaac and Jacob." There was no need to seek a specifically Jewish approach to the Bible because it appeared to be self-evident. Bible study was part of a complex of Jewish activities that included celebrations of holidays and participation in communal affairs. That was no longer true when one studied the same subject in the same way at a university where the instructor might be Jewish but the religious traditions of the students might include Judaism, Christianity, Islam or secularism.

Secondly, in seminaries outside of Bible classes proper, students examined the ways in which Jews had read and misread the Bible in classic texts such as Babylonian Talmud, Midrash and medieval commentaries. Those seminary graduates who went on to become biblicists, even those who rarely referred to the classical Jewish sources in their professional work, gained access to what the Bible has meant in Jewish tradition. They were conscious that Jews and Gentiles read the Bible in different ways, even when confessional issues were not at stake. Biblicists without seminary training are less likely to acquire a background in classical Jewish sources unless they are willing to take significant time away from their precious professional time, an unlikely prospect, especially in their probationary (read: pre-tenure) years. Will the coming generations of Jewish biblicists be willing to make the investment? Will they continue to seek to approach the Bible from a perspective that is critical, academically respectable and distinctively Jewish as well? The answer must be left to future chroniclers.

Notes to Concluding . . . Postscript

1. As of this writing, Jewish Theological, Hebrew Union and Reconstructionist Rabbinical are all having financial difficulties, and are trimming programs.

2. Cf. J. Neusner, "American Study of Judaism the Academic Setting," in idem, *Major Trends in Formative Judaism* (Chico: Scholars, 1984), 123–49. Although the above is not devoted to biblical studies, we are indebted to Neusner's work for inspiring some of the comments that follow.

3. For two highly successful examples in related fields see M. Sokoloff, *A Dictionary of Jewish Palestinian Aramaic* (Bar-Ilan: Ramat-Gan, 1990) (On the method see ibid, 5.) and S. Parpola, *The Correspondence of Sargon II, Part I* (Helsinki: Helsinki University, 1987). The volume is part of State Archives of Assyria, an ongoing publication of the Neo-Assyrian Text Corpus Project of the Academy of Finland in cooperation with Deutsche Orient-Gesellschaft. Four volumes have appeared thus far.

4. See the pioneering study by F. Andersen and A. D. Forbes, *Spelling in the Hebrew Bible* (Rome: Biblical Institute, 1986).

5. See e.g. W. Dever, "The Contribution of Archaeology to the Study of Canaanite and Early Israelite Religion," in P. Miller et al, *Ancient Israelite Religion Essays . . . Cross* (Philadelphia: Fortress, 1987), 209–47; J. Holladay, Jr., "Religion in Israel and Judah Under the Monarchy: An Explicitly Archaeological Approach," ibid, 249–99.

GENERAL INDEX

This index was prepared by Ms. Alice R. Goldfinger. A subvention provided by the Hebrew Union College—Jewish Institute of Religion is gratefully acknowledged.

Abrahams, I., 54, 56, 57
Abulafia, Moses HaLevi, 197
Achtemeier, P., 139, 141, 158
Ackerman, James, 133
Adler, Cyrus, 42, 44, 50, 62, 75, 85
Adler, R., 84
Agnon, S. Y., 113
Ahrend, Moshe M., 203
Ahroni, R., 85
Alashqar, Moses, 193
Albright, William F., 72, 74, 78, 80, 87, 95, 102, 103, 124, 127, 140, 152, 157, 189
Alpert, R., 135
Alt, 84
Alter, Robert, 104, 105, 113, 131, 133, 136, 137, 147, 157
Altmann, A., 16, 29, 30, 110
Andersen, F., 208
Anderson, B., 136
Annenberg, Walter, 66
Arfa, M., 84
Aronson, Evelyn, 49
Assaf, I., 57
Astour, M., 144
Atkin, M., 55
Avi-Yonah, M., 192

Baltzer, Klaus, 129
Bamberger, Bernard, 67, 108, 156
Barnett, R., 110
Barrick, W., 138
Barth, J., 2
Barton, George, 54, 70
Bat-Adam, 136
Baumgardt, D., 30

Beinart, H., 198
ben Adret, Solomon, 197
Ben-Arieh, Yehoshua, 191
ben Asher, Jacob, 197
Ben Israel, Menasseh, 193
ben Judah Landau, Jacob
Ben-Sasson, H., 192
ben Yehudah, Eliezer, 69
Bentwich, N., 60
Berger, D., 137
Berlin, Adele, 131, 135, 140, 145
Berlin, Naphtali Zevi Judah, 21, 192
Bernstein, Michael, 174, 175, 177
Bernstein, Moshe, 177
Bezold, Carl, 52, 61
Blank, Sheldon, 54, 59, 66, 67, 74, 85
Bloch, J., 63
Boadt, L., 54
Boyarin, D., 109
Braham, R. L., 200
Bravmann, Meir, 123, 140
Brayer, Manahem, 175, 177
Breuer, Mordechai, 167, 195
Brichto, Herbert C., 96, 105, 109, 110
Brickman, W., 57
Briggs, C. A., 38, 43
Brown, J., 58
Buber, Martin, 89, 107, 118, 120, 121, 122, 136, 139
Budde, K., 54
Buhl, F., 54
Buttenwieser, Moses, 53, 67, 70, 74

Campbell, E., 144
Caquot, A., 112

Carmell, Aryeh, 204
Carmilly-Weinberger, Moshe, 176, 199, 201
Carmy, Shalom, 177
Carthcart, K., 157
Cassian, John, 6
Cassuto, Umberto, 3, 20, 102, 103, 118, 131, 136, 137, 172, 198
Cederbaum, M., 199
Chajes, H. P., 66
Chavel, C., 193
Chazan, R., 32
Cheyne, T. K., 18, 30, 32
Childs, Brevard, 125, 126
Clay, A. T., 85
Cohen, C., 103, 112, 141 (see also Cohen, Hayim.)
Cohen, Hayim, 124, 134, 141
Cohn, Robert, 134, 135, 135, 147
Collins, A. Yarbro, 135, 143
Conybeare, A., 54
Cook, S. A., 32
Cooper, Alan, 126, 127, 134, 140, 142, 143
Crenshaw, J., 137
Cross, Frank, 126, 127, 128, 129, 130, 143
Culley, R., 137

Dannenbaum, Suzanne Gimbel, 71
Davies, W. D., 111
Davis, M., 55, 58, 59, 60, 63, 66, 86
De Rossi, Azariah, 193
De Sola Mendes, Frederick, 65
De Sola Pool, 63
Delitzsch, Franz, 45, 63
Delitzsch, Friedrich, 43, 52
Derenbourg, H., 51
Dever, W., 208
Dimitrovsky, H. Z., 197
Domb, Cyril, 204
Doran, R., 143
Dresner, Samuel, 194
Driver, S. R., 18, 191
Dropsie College for Hebrew and Cognate Learning, 50, 64, 65, 66, 70, 71, 73, 75, 78, 81, 82, 83, 84, 86, 89, 96, 97, 102, 120, 123, 128, 137, 140, 174
Dropsie, Moses, 50, 66

Eagleton, T., 136
Ehrlich, Arnold, 2, 44, 45, 46, 47, 62, 63, 64, 70, 80, 156
Eichhorn, Johann Gottfried, 16, 30
Eichler, Barry, 204
Eisenstein, J. D., 191, 192
Eitan, Israel, 2, 69, 70, 71, 82, 83
Eliade, Mircea, 134
Eliner, E., 199
Elior, R., 60
Ellis, M. de J., 142
Encyclopaedia Judaica, 4, 54, 55, 66, 71, 76, 85, 86, 88, 96, 107, 110, 135, 153, 154, 157, 195
Enslin, Morton, 65
Etkes, Emanuel, 194
Euting, J., 51
Ewald, H., 45

Feigin, S., 82, 83
Feinstein, Moses, 197
Feldman, Emanuel, 204
Feldman, Tzvi, 199
Finkel, Joshua, 174, 199, 200
Finkelstein, Jacob, 71, 83, 84, 85, 125, 126, 127, 142
Finkelstein, Louis, 62, 111
Fiorenza, A. Schüssler, 135
Fischel, W., 66
Fishbane, Michael, 121, 131, 133, 134, 136, 137, 138, 139
Fitzmyer, Joseph, 126
Forbes, A. D., 208
Fox, Everett, 122, 139
Fox, Michael, 132, 146
Frank, H., 87
Frank, Solomon, 196
Frankel, Zacharias, 42, 45, 60, 61
Frazer, Sir James, 81, 88
Freedman, D. N., 110, 127, 138, 144
Frerichs, E., 110
Friedlaender, Israel, 62, 66, 70, 75

INDEX / 211

Friedman, Richard, 129, 134, 140, 143, 144
Frymer-Kensky, Tikva, 127, 135, 140, 143
Fürst, J., 36

Gaster, Moses, 81, 125, 135
Gaster, Theodor, 80, 81, 87, 88
Geiger, Abraham, 2, 23, 24, 25, 26, 27, 28, 29, 31, 32, 134
Gelb, Ignacz, 91, 92
Geller, Stephen, 128, 137, 143
Gerstenberger, E., 137
Gerstenfeld, 156
Gensenius, Wilhelm, 57
Gevirtz, Stanley, 92, 106, 106, 108
Gifter, Mordecai, 198
Gimbel, Charles, 71
Ginsberg, H. L., 47, 75, 76, 77, 80, 82, 86, 88, 95, 96, 98, 102, 103, 123, 125, 127, 150, 154, 157
Ginzberg, E., 57, 60, 63
Ginzberg, Louis, 42, 43, 46, 57, 61, 67, 85, 86, 191
Glatzer, Nahum, 120
Glueck, Nelson, 73, 74, 85
Goetze, A., 87
Goldenberg, D., 66
Goldziher, Ignaz, 43
Good, Edward, 134
Good, M., 142
Gordis, Robert, 64, 66, 73, 77, 78, 86, 88
Gordon, Cyrus H., 64, 65, 73, 74, 83, 84, 85, 96, 97, 98, 99, 102, 120, 131, 199
Gorelick, L., 108
Goshen-Gottstein, Moshe, 2, 200
Gottheil, Gustav, 44, 46, 63, 64, 87, 135
Gottheil, Richard, 44, 48, 49, 63, 67, 69, 70, 78, 135
Gottleib, Isaac, 175, 204
Gottschalk, A., 85, 86
Gottwald, N., 111, 130, 144
Graetz, Heinrich, 2, 20, 30, 31, 45, 194

Graf, D., 144
Green, Arthur, 60, 110, 139, 141, 196
Greenbaum, Aaron, 195
Greenberg, Moshe, 2, 3, 62, 72, 83, 86, 92, 93, 101, 105, 108, 109, 127, 131, 137, 150, 154, 155, 158, 194
Greenfield, J. C., 94, 100, 101, 106, 111, 112, 130, 150, 199
Greengus, S., 84
Greenspahn, Frederick, 121, 122, 124, 139, 141, 202
Greenspoon, L., 64, 65, 87
Greenstein, Edward, 112, 123, 124, 133, 135, 136, 140, 141, 147
Grinstein, Hyman, 199, 203
Greer, R., 146
Gressmann, H., 74
Gruber, Meyer, 124, 125, 135, 141
Gunkel, Hermann, 133
Gunsberg, Aryeh Leib, 197
Gurock, J., 60, 62, 198, 199

Habermann, A., 61
Halkin, A. S., 86
Hallo, Rudolf, 91, 107
Hallo, William, 91, 106, 107, 108, 125, 126, 127, 137
Halpern, Baruch, 129, 130, 144, 145
Haran, Menachem, 132
Harrelson, W., 87, 136
Harris, Jay, 194
Haskalah, 28
Haupt, Paul, 44
Hayyuj, Judah, 48
Hebert, E., 31
Hebrew Union College, 39, 40, 48, 49, 52, 53, 55, 58, 59, 60, 63, 65, 70, 74, 75, 79, 83, 85, 86, 87, 89, 91, 92, 96, 105, 122, 125, 126, 132, 133, 205, 206
Heinemann, J., 192
Held, Moshe, 76, 86, 95, 101, 102, 103, 106, 112, 123, 124, 127, 135, 140, 141, 156
Heller, Chayim, 174, 199

Herder, Johann G., 16, 17, 30, 38, 57
Herschler, M., 197
Herskovics, Meir, 176
Hertz, Joseph H., 172, 193
Hertzberg, A., 54, 55, 57, 59, 60, 62, 140
Hillers, Delbert, 126, 157
Hilprecht, H., 85
Hirsch, E. D., 129, 144
Hirsch, Samson Raphael, 22, 23, 31
Hitzig, F., 45
Hoenig, Sidney, 4, 5, 156, 199
Hoffman, David Zevi, 20, 23, 30, 43, 172
Hoffner, H., 138
Hoftijzer, J., 142
Holladay, J. Jr., 208
Holtz, B., 139, 142
Horowitz, Y., 31
Hoschander, Jacob, 70, 75, 85
Hrushovsky, Benjamin, 104
Huffmon, H., 110
Hurwitz, Solomon T., 173

Ibn Gabirol, Solomon, 87
Ibn Kuraish, J., 200
Ibn Zimra, Bavid ben Solomon, 197
Ihde, Don, 136
Irving, D., 138

Jackson, Solomon, 56
Jacob, Benno, 3, 59, 118, 133, 136
Jacobsen, Thorkild, 112
Jaquett, Joseph, 56
Jastrow, Marcus, 40, 44, 49, 62, 64, 65, 87, 135
Jastrow, Morris, 47, 48, 64, 70
Jellinek, Adolph, 87
Jewish Encyclopedia, 4, 48, 53, 61, 67, 152, 154
Jewish Institute of Religion, 70, 71, 74, 79, 80, 86, 87, 91, 96, 105
Jewish Publication Society, 4, 29, 30, 31, 35, 37, 47, 48, 49, 56, 57, 50, 55, 60, 61, 64, 65, 66, 70, 71, 76, 80, 86, 94, 97, 98, 101, 110, 149, 150, 151, 153, 155, 156, 172, 173, 191, 194, 198
Jewish Quarterly Review, 18, 19, 30, 50, 61, 62, 66, 75, 85, 88, 112, 137, 139, 143, 201, 203
Jewish Theological Seminary, 40, 41, 50, 60, 61, 65, 66, 70, 75, 76, 77, 78, 82, 85, 86, 88, 92, 97, 102, 103, 104, 105, 116, 120, 122, 123, 124, 125, 128, 135, 140, 153, 154, 174, 206, 207
Joseph, H., 196
Joseph, Jacob, 62
Jüdisch-Theologisches Seminar, 42, 45, 55, 61, 89, 105
Jung, Leo, 195

Kabakoff, J., 63
Kaddari, M., 31
Kahana, A., 50, 66
Kant, Immanuel, 1, 107
Kaplan, A., 204
Kaplan, Israel, 62
Kaplan, Mordechai, 32, 60, 62, 135, 140
Kaplan, Z., 31
Kapustin, Max, 204
Karff, S., 54, 58, 59, 60, 63, 64, 65, 83, 85, 86, 87
Karp, Abraham, 54, 55, 56, 57, 59, 60, 61, 62
Karp, Deborah, 62
Kasher, Menehem, 166, 193, 195, 197
Kass, A., 60
Katsh, A., 66
Katz, J., 55, 57
Kaufman, Stephen, 126, 134, 135, 140, 142
Kaufmann, Yehezkel, 77, 86, 93, 104, 108, 109, 125, 128, 134, 194
Kermode, Frank, 136, 138, 147
Kevelaer, 138
Kil, Y., 18, 199
Kitchen, K., 84
Klaperman, Gilbert, 198, 199

Klausner, I., 31
Klenicki, L., 54
Knight, D., 137
Kohler, Kaufmann, 49, 52, 59, 64, 65
Kohut, Alexander, 40, 59, 86
Kook, A. Y., 173, 199, 204
Korn, Bertram, 35, 56, 58
Kort, A., 145
Kotler, Aaron, 197
Kraemer, J., 107
Kramer, Samuel Noah, 131, 135
Kraus, Samuel, 66
Kuenen, Abraham, 27, 48
Kugel, James, 5, 6, 133, 134, 136, 143, 146, 194
Kutscher, E. Y., 142, 174

La Haye, Tim, 191
Lambdin, T., 129
Lamm, Norman, 197, 199, 204
Landau, Yehezkel, 197
Landsberger, Benno, 95, 102, 103, 124, 140
Lange, I., 197
Lauterbach, Jacob, 58
Leaf, H., 199, 201
Leavis, F. R., 136
Leavis, Q. D., 136
Leeser, Isaac, 1, 33, 34, 35, 36, 37, 44, 49, 50, 55, 56, 59, 80, 107, 205, 206
Legasse, S., 112
Lehman, James H., 194
Leibowitz, Nehamah, 167, 204
Leibowitz, Yeshayahu, 167, 195, 204
Leibush, Meir, 22
Leiman, Sid Z., 177
Levenson, E., 30
Levenson, Jon, 128, 129, 135, 136, 144
Levi-Strauss, C., 127, 128
Levine, Baruch, 30, 54, 73, 97, 105, 110, 111, 115, 121, 141, 153, 155, 157
Levy, Barry, 175, 177, 193, 195, 196
Lewis, B., 66

Lewy, Hildegarde, 75, 85, 135
Lewy, Julius, 74, 75, 85, 89, 107
Lichtenstein, Murray, 125, 134, 141, 142
Lieberman, S., 112, 125, 195
Lipinski, E., 157
Lipman, V. D., 113
Lillienthal, Max, 55
Loewe, B., 110
Lord, Albert, 127, 142, 143
Lowth, Robert, 16, 29
Luther, Martin, 7
Luzzatto, S. D., 2, 19, 20, 30, 47, 70, 172, 194, 198

Machinist, Peter, 126, 135
Maimonides, 162, 174, 191, 193
Maimonides College, 35, 37, 44, 56, 58
Malamat, Abraham, 101
Malbim, 22, 31, 47, 70
Malter, Henry, 65
Mamam, Aharon, 192
Marcus, Aaron, 204
Marcus, David, 87, 112, 123, 140
Marcus, Jacob Rader, 58
Margolies, M. B., 194, 198
Margolis, Max, 2, 48, 49, 50, 51, 52, 64, 65, 66, 69, 70, 71, 72, 78, 80, 84, 87, 149
Marks, J., 142
Marsh, James, 30
Marshall, Louis, 41, 60
Marx, Alexander, 51, 66, 198
May, Herbert G., 87
McHardy, W. D., 85
Meek, Theophile, 78
Meiri, Menahem, 197
Meirovich, Harvey, W., 198
Meissner, Bruno, 52
Meklenburg, Jacob Zevi, 21, 22
Melammed, E. Z., 192, 193
Mendelsohn, Issac, 102, 128, 139, 140
Mendelssohn, Moses, 16, 17, 19, 20, 21, 28, 29, 30, 36, 194
Mendenhall, G., 129, 130, 144
Meshi-Zahav, M. M., 197

Meyer, Michael, 23, 25, 30, 31, 58, 59, 60, 63, 64, 65, 74, 83, 85, 86, 87
Meyers, Carol, 110, 121, 138, 155, 158
Meyers, Eric, 121, 138, 155, 158
Milgrom, Jacob, 103, 104, 105, 112, 115, 153, 155
Miller, P., 87
Montefiore, Claude, 18, 30, 41, 61
Montgomery, James, 70, 71, 73
Morgenstern, Julian, 52, 53, 66, 70, 74, 89, 135
Morais, Sabato, 40, 58, 59
Morris, John, 191
Morschauer, S., 145
Mossad HaRav Kook, 166, 193, 199
Muelhausen, Yom Tov Lippman, 197
Muffs, Yochanan, 94, 95, 105, 109, 123, 127, 137
Muilenberg, James, 3, 27, 132, 136, 146
Murray, Gilbert, 81

Nemoy, L., 66
Neusner, J., 55, 109, 110, 139, 141, 144, 207
Neumann, A., 65
Newman, M., 88
Niditch, Susan, 127, 135, 143, 147
Nöldeke, Theodor, 43, 51, 61
Nordheimer, Isaac, 203
Noth, M., 84, 129

O'Connor, M., 110, 138, 143
Obermann, Julian, 71
Oppenheim, A. L., 84
Origen, 6
Orlinsky, Harry, 32, 47, 54, 57, 61, 62, 63, 64, 65, 71, 78, 79, 80, 83, 85, 86, 87, 140, 150, 152, 154, 156, 157, 203

Parry, 141
Parzen, H., 66
Paul, S., 95, 105, 106, 109, 154
Pereira, H., 40

Perles, Felix, 66, 70
Perles, Joseph, 30
Petuchowski, Jacob, 31, 32
Plaut, W. G., 108
Polish, D., 59, 65, 67
Pope, Marvin, 126, 142
Popper, William, 51, 52, 66, 201
Porten, B., 111
Posnanski, Samuel, 43
Potok, Chaim, 153
Pratico, G., 85
Pratt, I., 63
Prawer, Joshua, 192
Preminger, A., 141
Preschel, T., 31
Propp, Vladimir, 120, 138

Raba, Joel, 192
Rabbi Isaac Elhanan Theological Seminary, 62
Rabinowitz, L. I., 30, 55, 56, 157
Rainey, Anson, 2, 98, 99, 100, 106, 111, 156
Ramsey, P., 54
Raphael, M., 32, 196
Redford, D., 146
Reed, W., 87
Reider, J., 64, 66, 83
Reifman, Va'aqov, 200
Rendsburg, G., 84, 131, 134, 146
Reuchlin, J., 46
Revel, Bernard, 173, 198
Rice, Abraham, 55
Rogerson, J., 30, 57, 58
Rosenthal, Judah, 193
Roth, Cecil, 154
Rothkoff, Aaron, 198, 199
Rosenberg, Joel, 133, 134, 139, 146, 147
Rosenthal, Franz, 126
Rosenzweig, F., 91, 107, 118, 120, 121, 122, 136, 139
Rubasheff, Zalman, 193

Sachar, A. L., 137
Salmon, Y., 194
Sanders, E. P., 202
Sanders, J., 85

Sandmel, S., 58, 137
Saperstein, Marc, 198
Saraval, Judah Leib, 197
Sarna, Nahum, 23, 24, 31, 65, 84, 94, 96, 97, 101, 105, 110, 115, 121, 122, 131, 139, 150, 153, 154
Sasson, Jack, 120, 121, 131, 135, 137, 146, 155
Saunders, E. W., 58, 86
Schechter, Solomon, 19, 30, 40, 42, 43, 44, 50, 60, 61, 62, 140
Schick, Maharam, 197
Schiff, Jacob, 41, 60, 140
Schloessinger, Max, 65
Scholem, G., 194
Schorsch, Ismar, 61
Segal, Alan F., 194
Segal, M. H., 66, 118, 136, 193
Segert, S., 84, 142
Seidel, Moses, 173, 199
Selzer, M., 57
Sharfman, I. H., 55
Shargel, B., 44, 61, 62, 66
Shklovsky, Viktor, 136, 143
Shorin, Aaron, Ben-Zion, 198
Silberman, L., 57, 58, 136
Silberman, Neil A., 191
Silberschlag, E., 55, 57
Simon, Joseph, 191
Simpson, William Kelly, 91, 108
Skaist, Aaron, 175, 204
Smith, Henry Preserved, 38
Smith, Morton, 65
Smith, W. Robertson, 18, 26, 27, 28, 32
Society of Biblical Literature, 44, 48, 51, 52, 63, 78, 132, 135, 136, 141
Society of Biblical Literature and Exegesis, 44
Sofer, A., 197
Sofer, Moses, 197
Sokoloff, M., 208
Sokolow, Moshe, 175, 177
Solis-Cohen, Solomon, 42
Soloveitchik, J. B., 174
Soloveitchik, Menahem, 193

Speiser, Ephraim A., 1, 71, 72, 73, 83, 84, 92, 93, 94, 95, 96, 125, 126, 131, 150, 155, 156
Sperber, Alexander, 75
Sperling, S. David, 54, 57, 83, 125, 135, 141
Spina, F., 110
Spinoza, Benedict, 17
Staerk, W., 74
Stein, S., 110
Steiner, Richard, 177
Stern, Menahem, 194, 195
Stitskin, L., 199
Strange, J., 138
Stuart, Moses, 30
Sulzberger, Mayer, 42
Sussman, L., 55, 56, 57
Sutro, Abraham, 33
Szold, Benjamin, 2, 40, 44, 45, 46, 47, 59, 63
Szold, Henrietta, 45

Tadmor, Hayim, 86, 96, 108, 126, 129
Talmon, Shmaryahu, 134
Tardieu, M., 112
Thoma, C., 137
Thomas, Winton, 85
Thompson, T., 84
Tigay, J., 86, 125, 126, 134, 140, 142, 153
Tobias, A., 30
Torrey, C. C., 54, 82
Toy, Crawford H., 67
Tsevat, Mattitiahu, 56, 57, 89, 142, 90, 101, 105, 106, 107
Tucker, G., 137
Turner, Victor, 128, 134
Tur-Sinai, N. H., 47
Twersky, I., 202

University of Pennsylvania, 1, 48, 62, 70, 71, 72, 73, 78, 92, 94, 96, 126, 142, 154

van der Kooij, 142
van der Woude, A. S., 157
van Dijk, J., 108

van Gennep, Arnold, 128
van Seters, John, 64, 84
Vogel, E. K., 85
von Rad, G., 3, 136
Voss, C., 86

Wapnish, P., 146
Warburg, Felix, 41
Waxman, M., 60, 61
Weinfeld, Moshe, 157
Weippert, Manfred, 129
Weiss, I. H., 60
Weiztom, Doron, 197
Wellhausen, Julius, 4, 27, 38, 44,
   48, 51, 52, 53, 57, 58, 61, 62,
   69, 77
Wertheimer, Solomon, 193
Wessely, N., 36
Williams-Forte, E., 108
Williamson, 143, 144
Winter, N., 84

Wise, Aaron, 86
Wise, Issac Mayer, 38, 39, 40, 42,
   48, 52, 53, 58, 59, 79, 134
Wise, Stephen S., 79, 80, 86
Wissenschaft des Judentums, 1, 15,
   19, 20, 21, 23, 24, 26, 28, 29,
   42, 46, 205
Wolf, Immanuel, 29
Wright, G. E., 87
Wyschogrod, M., 137

Yellin, David, 69, 89
Yeshiva University, 62

Zalman, Elijah ben Solmon, 21
Zeitlin, S., 65, 173, 203
Zeitschrift für die Wissenschaft des
   Judentums, 15, 38
Zelson, 124
Zevit, Ziony, 130, 135, 145
Zimmels, Abraham, 175

www.ingramcontent.com/pod-product-compliance
Lightning Source LLC
Chambersburg PA
CBHW020755160426
43192CB00006B/337